A FEMINIST HISTORY SOCIETY BOOK

D1359677

The Unconventional

NANCY RUTH

RAMONA LUMPKIN

Second Story Press

Library and Archives Canada Cataloguing in Publication

Title: The unconventional Nancy Ruth / Ramona Lumpkin.
Names: Lumpkin, Ramona, author.
Description: Series statement: A Feminist History Society book | Includes bibliographical
    references and index.
Identifiers: Canadiana (print) 20200332872 | Canadiana (ebook) 20200333070 | ISBN
    9781772601688 (softcover) | ISBN 9781772601695 (EPUB)
Subjects: LCSH: Nancy Ruth, 1942- | LCSH: Women legislators—Canada—Biography.
    | LCSH: Legislators—Canada—Biography. | LCSH: Feminists—Canada—Biography.
    | LCSH: Women political activists—Canada—Biography. | LCSH: Political activists—
    Canada—Biography. | LCGFT: Biographies. Classification: LCC FC651.N36 L86 2021 |
    DDC 971.07/3092—dc23

Copyright © 2021 by Ramona Lumpkin

www.FeministHistories.ca

Edited by Andrea Knight

Every effort has been made to secure permission and provide appropriate
credit for photographic material. The publisher deeply regrets any omission
and pledges to correct errors called to its attention in subsequent editions.

Printed and bound in Canada

*Second Story Press gratefully acknowledges the support of the Ontario Arts Council
and the Canada Council for the Arts for our publishing program. We acknowledge the
financial support of the Government of Canada through the Canada Book Fund.*

Published by
Second Story Press
20 Maud Street, Suite 401
Toronto, ON M5V 2M5
www.secondstorypress.ca

In memory of my mother,
Willie Mae Braswell Lumpkin (1925–2019),
and my father, William Hayward Lumpkin (1918–2003).
Their lives have shown me how to love.

CONTENTS

A NOTE ON FOOTNOTES

The footnotes supporting the author's extensive research
can be accessed online at: http://secondstorypress.ca/resources

INTRODUCTION

*To say that Nancy Ruth is unique would
be an understatement. To say that she is
incomparable would be more accurate.*
                    —The Honourable James Cowan[1]

NANCY RUTH, born a Jackman, has been a Canadian
voice for social reform for much of her life. Her mother,
Mary Coyne Rowell Jackman, came from a prominent
Methodist family in Toronto and was herself a quiet
crusader for social justice. Her father, Henry Rutherford
(Harry) Jackman, served as a member of parliament and
made a fortune in the financial industry, establishing himself as a business leader within the Toronto community.
Nancy Ruth's childhood was one of affluence and privilege,
although her advantages did not protect her from family
tensions and pressures. She was a misfit both at home and
at school; rebelling against authority, failing academically,
and struggling to find a useful purpose for her life. Yet
her energy, creativity, and capacity for love and joy were
equally apparent from an early age.

Nancy Ruth's encounter with feminism in 1968 flipped a switch in her worldview, introducing her to the concept of systemic discrimination against women in all of society's institutions. Just over a decade later, her entry into Toronto's feminist community opened the door to a profound sense of belonging. She engaged wholeheartedly in the fight to entrench equality for women in Canada's new Charter of Rights and Freedoms, heading up the Charter of Rights Coalition and working to establish the Women's Legal Education and Action Fund (LEAF). She also tried to integrate feminist values within the established church; commissioned as a diaconal minister in The United Church of Canada, she served as associate minister in Toronto's Metropolitan United Church in the 1980s but ultimately left the church when she could not create the change she passionately sought.

After her father's death in 1979 and her decision to convert her inheritance into cash that she could control, Nancy Ruth began to shape her role as an influencer through feminist philanthropy—done, as always, in her own way. In addition to providing major financial support for LEAF, she helped found the Canadian Women's Foundation, and she and her mother were its first major donors. She was instrumental in establishing The Linden School, a Toronto girls' school incorporating feminist principles into its curriculum and pedagogy. CoolWomen.ca, a women's history website, grew from her belief that women's stories should be preserved and made accessible so that girls and young women would have the chance to be empowered through them. Over the past forty years, she has directed the resources of Nancy's Very Own Foundation to projects that advanced economic and social justice for women and girls, as well as to other central concerns, such as environmental and peace activism. She has also been a patron of the arts—a love shared with and nourished from childhood by her mother.

A firm believer in the importance of political action on behalf of social change, Nancy Ruth ran unsuccessfully for a federal nomination in 1988, and then ran twice for a seat in Ontario's legislature (1990 and 1993) but was defeated both times. Over a decade later—and to her great surprise— she was appointed to Canada's Senate by Prime Minister Paul Martin. She devoted her twelve years in the Senate to unrelenting advocacy on behalf of social justice issues, particularly those that affected women and girls. When she reached mandatory retirement age at seventy-five, she was lauded by her fellow senators as a woman of steely determination, a crusader, and fearless advocate on behalf of the causes she championed. By that time, her work in the public sphere and her contributions to social change had been recognized by numerous honours, including the Order of Canada, the Governor General's Award in Commemoration of the Persons Case, and four honorary doctorates, from Mount Saint Vincent, York, Trent, and Laurentian universities.

I first met Nancy Ruth in 1994, when I was on the Women's Studies Steering Committee at the University of Windsor and she accepted an invitation to visit our campus. We, of course, hoped that she would make a donation to our women's studies program, but we also hoped to be inspired by an outspoken feminist who shared with us a common cause. We got the inspiration but not the donation. A few years earlier she had endowed the Nancy's Chair in Women's Studies at Mount Saint Vincent University in Halifax, and her loyalties remained with that program.

As fate would have it, my own career path led me in time to Mount Saint Vincent, where I became president and vice-chancellor in 2010 and, soon after, renewed my acquaintance with Nancy Ruth. She came to our campus in 2011 to celebrate twenty-five successful years of the Nancy's Chair, and we met from time to time in Ottawa where she was now a senator. Acquaintance deepened into friendship as I learned more of her life, her struggles, her remarkable achievements. When our retirement dates converged in 2017, we agreed that I would write her biography. I believed hers was a story that should be told, and Nancy Ruth knew from hard-won experience growing up in a patriarchal household the importance of bearing witness to the truth that *women's lives matter*.

In preparation for writing the biography, I have been given full access to all of Nancy Ruth's records. My first visit to her basement archives taught me that, even as a child, she must have cherished a hope that one day her life would be worthy of attention. The materials I found there are extraordinary: diaries from the age of twelve; love letters; decades of newspaper clippings and of correspondence from others, as well as copies of her own correspondence; speeches; copies of articles she has written; photographs; legal documents; family papers; political campaign brochures and buttons. I soon found myself tracing the arc of a life lived with emotional intensity, one in which self-examination and reflection were daily habits. Her archives also reveal a complex web of social connections; she is an extrovert who has a wide network of friends and has devoted countless hours to nurturing her friendships.

Over the years, Nancy Ruth has been written about regularly in the print media, and many of these articles and sketches depict her as larger-than-life. News clips and television programs such as CBC's *Man Alive* and *National Treasures* have sometimes homed in on her more outrageous moments—or presented these moments in an outrageous way. It is true that she often chooses to be blunt rather than subtle, and many of us have relished her outspoken voice as we hear it speak truth to power. Yet hers is a voice equally capable of careful argument and nuanced reasoning reflected in the myriad speeches and addresses on women's equality and human rights that she has delivered across Canada throughout her career. If she is a crusader, she is also a woman whose life has been woven on the loom of Methodism and feminism, with its warp and woof of social gospel, women's rights, spiritual questing, and justice activism. Her life has been spent in search of both communion and community—a transcendent connection with a larger purpose and common cause with other activists who share her passion.

In the chapters that follow, along with chronicling what I have learned from my research into her public and private affairs, I aim to share Nancy Ruth's own voice with readers. I quote extensively from her diaries, speeches, and letters, letting her words help shape the portrait of who she is and what she stands for. And although she has read my drafts, she has chosen not to censor them. We both believe that this account of her life should come as close as possible to the honest bone.

Footnotes for this chapter can be found online at:
http://secondstorypress.ca/resources

Chapter 1

A CLUBHOUSE OF ONE'S OWN

HEADING EAST from Mount Pleasant Road along Roxborough Drive, strolling through Toronto's exclusive north Rosedale enclave, in about a kilometre you'll come upon a massive granite boulder on your left, just outside the gates of a city park. Affixed to the boulder, a plaque proclaims in bold type that "**Nancy Ruth (née Jackman)—feminist, social and political activist, and philanthropist—lived at 184 Roxborough Drive, the house just east of this entrance to Chorley Park, from 1980 to 1996.**"[1]

If you wonder briefly how the house and its former owner have earned their commemoration, the plaque's lengthy citation will leave you in no doubt. From this house, you are told "women influenced the history of the city and the nation"—and the list of examples that follows is persuasive:

> Women of the Ad Hoc Committee of Canadian
> Women on the Constitution organized at this house
> their successful campaign to entrench equality

Nancy Ruth and colleagues at the unveiling of
the Heritage Toronto plaque commemorating
the feminist work done at 184 Roxborough
Drive, Toronto, between 1980 and 1996, on
October 16, 1999.

guarantees for women in the Constitution of Canada when it was patriated in 1982. The Ad Hoc Committee continued its work here during the campaigns against the Meech Lake and Charlottetown Accords in 1987–1990 and 1992.

Women of the Charter of Rights Coalition here planned to influence how governments set out equality guarantees in law and to educate people on the Canadian Charter of Rights and Freedoms.

Women gathered here to form LEAF—the Women's Legal Education and Action Fund—to support women who assert their equality rights in the courts.

Women came here to found the Canadian Women's Foundation to promote the economic development of women and girls.

Women worked here under the constitutional lawyer Mary Eberts to support the court challenge by the Native Women's Association of Canada to the Charlottetown Accord.

Women met here to go on-line, across time, by creating the *CoolWomen* Internet website to highlight and celebrate the contributions of women to the history and future of Canada.

Nancy Ruth founded here Nancy's Very Own Foundation, the first feminist private foundation in Canada, which provided much-needed leadership to increase philanthropic giving to women and girls.

Many fundraising events were held in the house for organizations based in Toronto that had no access to other large houses. The organizations included the Canadian Voice of Women for Peace, the Canadian Women's Foundation, Casey House, the DisAbled Women's Network, Intercede for Domestic Workers, the International Institute of Concern for Public Health, LEAF, The Linden School, the National Action Committee on the Status of Women, Skyworks Films, and the Toronto Institute for Human Relations. Fundraisers for women in politics included those for Susan Fish, Nancy Jackman, June Rowlands, and Barbara Hall.

A concluding paragraph, introduced by the stately phrase "To this house came," offers a list of women—some famous, some not—who gathered at Roxborough Drive to advocate for social justice and make history together. And a final line, again in bold type, affirms, **"This plaque has been placed on a piece of Ontario granite as tough and enduring as the women it commemorates."**

If, curious by now, you walk past the boulder and stand outside 184 Roxborough Drive, you will see what the realtor's brochure in 1980 described as, "from the street...a traditional three-storey Georgian mansion." Its 9,000 square feet, with an interior "transformed by the addition of a large, ultra-modern wing at the rear," would offer ample room for the diverse gatherings of women it hosted. Communal space included a sun-bathed living room with floor-to-ceiling windows overlooking a wooded ravine; an "adjacent, sunken, conversation area"

Left (top): Unveiling of the Heritage Toronto plaque commemorating Canadian feminism and the work done at 184 Roxborough Drive, Toronto, on October 16, 1999, by women named on the plaque.
Left (bottom): Nancy Ruth and Mary Eberts on the granite boulder after the unveiling of the plaque.

that could be combined with the living room "to make a perfect entertaining area"; and on the lower level, but also above ground with views of the ravine, a large recreation room. Certainly, this house could accommodate, in the understated words of the citation, those "organizations based in Toronto that had no access to other large houses."[2] It could offer up space for plotting strategy, organizing opposition, raising money, and creating new political and social entities. It could also make room for the celebrations that happen when women work hard together and succeed in bringing about social change.

But why, at the age of thirty-eight, single, and only recently returned to Toronto after years of living out west and abroad, would Nancy Jackman (as she was at the time) buy a mansion in Rosedale, one that lawyer-activist Mary Eberts would call a "great clubhouse and meeting place?"[3] And how did Nancy and her friends turn this clubhouse-mansion into a hub of feminist activity? Who was Nancy Jackman? What shaped her and led her to become a leader in Canada's feminist community? The granite boulder offers no answers, its plaque focusing instead on the *collective* of women and what, together, they accomplished. Nancy herself is a strong believer in the value of collective action, so the emphasis is fitting. All the same, she does have her own story, one that includes wealth, hardship, passion and loneliness, generosity, and frailty, as well as granite-like toughness and endurance. In the chapters that follow, I hope to do justice to that story.

Footnotes for this chapter can be found online at:
http://secondstorypress.ca/resources

Nancy Ruth with a favourite bumper sticker, "BACK OFF I'm A Goddess," Toronto, October 16, 1999.

Nancy Ruth being held by her mother, Mary
Coyne Rowell Jackman (1904–1994), age 38,
outside the family home on the day of her
baptism in 1942.

Chapter 2

NANCY RUTH JACKMAN: CHILD INTO WOMAN

As a child, it was clear to me that what the world respected was about the values my Father held, the values of amassing capital, the value of doing unto others as they would do unto you, the values of progressing forward and upward in a class-based society. The values my Mother taught me had to do with reaching out beyond your own class, the value that women were submissive to men even if they raged inside, and that the family mattered a great deal. But as I was growing up, I was aware the values my Mother had were not ones that were respected and I wanted to be respected. And it wasn't just that, I actually lusted after the power that I saw my Father's values could bring and...I was rude and contemptuous of my Mother and her worth.[1]

JANUARY 6, 1942—The Feast of the Epiphany in the Western Christian tradition, the day the Three Wise Men arrived in Bethlehem to present their gifts to the Christ child. On that day, Mary Coyne Rowell Jackman and Henry Rutherford (Harry) Jackman welcomed their fourth child

Henry (Harry) Rutherford Jackman
(1900–1979), age 55, father of Nancy Ruth.

and only daughter, Nancy Ruth Jackman, who was named in honour of Mary's great-grandmother, Nancy Greene, and whose middle name came from Harry's mother's surname, Rutherford (Harry's sister was also named Ruth). Nancy's birth on a Christian feast day was fitting, given her family's strong connections to the Methodist Church and her own future within the United Church as a commissioned minister. Yet her relationship with the church would be a troubled one, not least because its privileging of "wise men" would leave her alienated from its practice and doctrines, just as her own wealth would make the church question her capacity for obedience.

At the time of his daughter's birth, Harry Jackman was a member of parliament, having been elected in 1940 to represent the Toronto riding of Rosedale, where he and Mary lived after their marriage. He was a member of, and finance critic for, the National Government Party, one of the predecessor names of the Progressive Conservative Party of Canada and the government's official opposition at the time. In 1945, the party settled on its new name and he was re-elected under the banner of the Progressive Conservative Party, serving in the House of Commons until his defeat in the 1949 election. He was thus away in Ottawa for much of Nancy's early childhood. "I remember him coming home once and picking me up in the front hallway and my saying to Mummy, 'Who is this man?' What the hell did I know? He came home now and then."[2]

Harry came from English and Scottish stock, immigrants to Ontario in the 1830s, some of whom arrived with the British army and were given land grants to farm, while others found careers in subsequent decades as schooner captains, grocers, and salesmen. A wealthy uncle financed his study at Osgoode Hall Law School and Harvard

Nellie Langford Rowell (1874–1968),
maternal grandmother of Nancy Ruth,
circa 1910.

Business School, after which he set about with a fierce drive to make his name and fortune in Toronto's financial industry. By the time of Nancy's birth, he was not only a member of parliament but on his way to securing a place in Toronto's establishment; his career would see him working successfully as an investment manager and building his own substantial business in the insurance and financial services industries.

Mary Jackman, by contrast, had grown up in the same Rosedale where she and Harry made their home—a leafy enclave built around ravines and filled with stately mansions that were occupied by many of Toronto's leading citizens. Rosedale has been described as a "community of old wealth...of the movers and shakers of the various professional worlds of English-Canadian culture: lawyers, doctors, editors, brokers, bankers and board chairmen."[3] The daughter of a prosperous and well-established family, Mary knew privilege from her birth. Her father Newton Wesley Rowell (who died before Nancy was born) was a Methodist lay minister; a prominent Ontario politician in the provincial Liberal Party and later in the federal Union Government formed in World War I; a lawyer and, for a time, the Chief Justice of Ontario. Her mother, Nell Langford Rowell, also from a staunch Methodist family and daughter of a Methodist minister, graduated in 1896 from Victoria College at the University of Toronto, placing her within a small minority of women university graduates in her day. Both of Mary's parents were involved in significant international organizations—the League of Nations and the Young Women's Christian Association (YWCA), for example—as well as in pan-Canadian organizations such as the Canadian Institute of International Relations and the Institute of Pacific Relations. Mary's views and values, embedded in the way Nancy was raised, were shaped by her own parents' national and international engagements.

When, as a girl, Mary travelled to Europe with her mother and father, she visited art galleries and developed a keen appreciation for modern art (which her daughter would later share). She was sent for her schooling to King's Hall in Compton, Quebec, where she gained fluency in French and was chosen as head girl. Like her mother, she graduated from Victoria College (1925), after which she pursued leadership training at Selly Oak in Birmingham; postgraduate studies at the London School of Economics; and further French studies in Paris.

Both Mary Jackman's parents were deeply engaged with the Methodist Church throughout their lives and Mary was brought up to be equally engaged. The daughter of a prominent and high-performing family, she strove to live up to their expectations—for example, what was known in progressive Protestantism as the "social gospel," the imperative for Christians to create "God's kingdom on earth" by working to alleviate social injustice. During her university years she was an active member of the Student Christian Movement (SCM), a Protestant organization focused on economic and social justice and mission work, and she was employed full-time as women's secretary by the SCM from 1928 to 1929, a job she would have liked to continue after her marriage but gave up because of the societal norms of the time.

Mary's correspondence with Harry before their marriage reveals her doubts that she would be able to reconcile her own values and sense of self with those of the man who was so ardently courting her. Not only was she a young woman shaped by her family's Methodism, but she had also had experiences that challenged the conventions of her upbringing and of the day. She had worked, travelled, encountered other cultures, and she had attracted the love of Roy Lee, a Chinese minister from Australia whom she had met at Selly Oak but whose proposal she ultimately declined. An accomplished young woman, she later struggled to find an outlet for her gifts within the confines of marriage and motherhood as they existed in her day. And she urged her only daughter towards an independence that she herself was never able to achieve.

In spite of her lingering doubts, Mary Rowell married Harry Jackman in the Metropolitan United Church in 1930, ushering in fifty years of a union that would be marked by recurring turbulence and unhappiness on the part of both husband and wife. Mary's commitment to a life informed by "social gospel" principles had a profound effect on her daughter. At the same time, Nancy grew up within a traditional patriarchal household and would struggle to reconcile her mother's values with those of her powerful father.

Nancy's brother Henry Newton Rowell (Hal) was born in 1932; Frederic Langford Rowell (Eric) in 1934; and Edward John Rowell in 1940. Because of the difference in their ages, they were viewed by the family during Nancy's childhood as "two sets"—the "boys" (Hal and Eric) and the "children" (Nancy and Edward). All four were raised in an atmosphere of privilege, with household servants (cook, maid, part-time laundress, and seamstress), material comforts, and cultural and sporting activities typical of their social standing. All went to summer camps and graduated from elite boarding schools. Hal attended Victoria College at the University of Toronto as his mother had done, obtained a law degree at Osgoode Hall, followed his father into business, and later became lieutenant governor

Jackman family in 1943 at Overdown Farm
near Kleinburg, Ontario. Top L to R: Mary
holding Nancy Ruth, Harry holding Edward.
Bottom L to R: Hal, Eric.

of Ontario. Eric took his BA from Trinity College at the University of Toronto, earned a PhD in human development at the University of Chicago, and moved from an early career in business to be a practicing psychologist. Edward studied philosophy at Victoria College, earned a teaching certificate from the Ontario College of Education, and worked for a few years as a schoolteacher in Ottawa and Ghana. Soon after, he broke with family tradition by converting to Roman Catholicism and ultimately becoming a priest within the Dominican Order.

Nancy grew up in what her brother Hal describes as a "male-dominated household, very competitive."[4] Describing her feelings about her father years later, she comments, "He used to reward my brothers when they got good marks or did well in athletics.… They'd get a record, a book, or something. I never got those things."[5] The perks, Nancy said, were "tied to performance" and "I resented that. I thought my father should love me anyhow."

The household was not only male-dominated but characterized by a constant undercurrent of tension between Nancy's parents. The diaries and letters of Nancy's father, published in sixteen volumes by son Hal, record numerous instances in which Harry felt slighted by his wife. In his editorial comments Hal notes the "many references" in his father's diaries to "disappointments in his home life."[6] In 1951, Harry writes, "Admittedly I am not very happy in my marital relations with a fine person but not a teammate."[7] Two years later he complains, "Am I nothing in Mary's heart but a good provider?"[8] Harry's diaries reveal a man striving to build a financial empire and moving in refined social circles but ill at ease and much less socially adept than his wife. Mary, by contrast, was deeply engaged with her church, with SCM and community work, and

Nancy Ruth, age 10 (1952), with her father.

with numerous cultural pursuits, including building her growing trove of paintings by some of Canada's leading artists. In 1930, before she married, she was given $25,000 by her parents to do with as she wished and it was with her own funds, not her husband's, that she bought art.[9] In the years following her mother's gift to her of a first edition of *A Room of One's Own*, Mary also assembled the finest collection outside of Britain of first editions by Virginia Woolf and other members of the Bloomsbury group, and by Virginia and Leonard Woolf's Hogarth Press. This collection is now housed in the rare book room of Victoria University.

Each partner in the marriage can be seen to disdain the pursuits of the other: in his wife's eyes, Harry valued wealth over spiritual well-being and social responsibility, while in Harry's eyes, Mary cared more about the church and about spending "his" money than she did about the effort he expended in building his family's fortune. In his notes to his father's *Letters and his Diaries*, Hal refers to the ongoing conflict between Mary's SCM "idealism" and Harry's "commercial values."[10]

Many years later, after her mother's death, Nancy Ruth produced a film in tribute to her mother that included, among other revelations, Nancy's memories from her teenage years of bruises on her mother's body and of seeing her father push her mother down the stairs.[11] In the same film, her brother Edward recalls frequent instances of hearing their father abuse their mother verbally at the dinner table, lashing out and belittling her in front of the family. Nancy herself recalls as a child "being rude and contemptuous of my mother's worth" and longing to share in the male power of her fathers and brothers.[12] Only much later would she understand and reframe her experience, as she explains in a 1990 address:

> I am a feminist because of the relationship I saw and felt between my Mom and my Dad. My Dad and my three brothers were typical of their day—they were completely wrapped up in their own affairs and they expected the women around them to be likewise. They expected and demanded that our household revolve around their needs and activities. And everything in society reaffirmed their belief. Women's place was in the home, women were to do right by *their* men, and doing right by them meant keep quiet, run the house perfectly, look great all the time, and don't make waves or demands…. Watching my Mother give in to the men in her life made me very angry—and that anger wasn't directed at the cause of the problem but at my Mother, who was the victim of the problem. I couldn't understand why she'd do it! I couldn't understand why she let these men treat her with less consideration and respect than they would have shown to strangers in the street. I resented women like her, and had enormous contempt for Mom. I was angry at her because she was one of those women who give in as a means of keeping the peace and maintaining the harmony of the house.

This is their way to survive!

And so when I felt rage bubble up inside me at what was obviously an unfair situation, I blamed women, and I believed it was my Mom's fault that things were the way they were. Well, the good thing about ignorance is that there's always the chance you'll bump up against truth and enlightenment and eventually I did. Today I have a much better understanding of both my mother and the many, many other women like her who did what they could to cope in those days.[13]

These hard truths, however, were still years away from Nancy's understanding. As a child she would work hard to win her father's approbation and to succeed on his and her brothers' terms.

Nancy's education, like that of her brothers, was commensurate with her family's wealth and social standing. At age three she was sent to Windy Ridge Day School, a private school then under the direction of W.E. (Bill) Blatz, a leading child psychologist who gained renown for his child-centred theories that focused on children's need for security and independence as central to human development. When she was four, she attended the Institute of Child Study at the University of Toronto, a nursery school also heavily influenced by Dr. Blatz's theories (in 1951 Windy Ridge would merge with the Institute of Child Study, which was renamed the Dr. Eric Jackman Institute of Child Study in 2010 in honour of a gift from the Jackman Foundation, of which Eric is the president). She entered Rosedale Public School at age five but at age seven was enrolled at a private girls' school in Toronto, Bishop Strachan School (BSS), as a weekly boarder—mainly, she recalls, "because my parents were travelling."[14] Thus began what would be, by Nancy's account, many unhappy years boarding at a succession of schools.

At age five she was also sent to her first summer camp for a week, and recalls, "I was terribly homesick. I hated it."[15] Homesickness for her mother is a recurring theme in her childhood memories, whether she was at camp or at school just a few kilometres away from the family home in Rosedale. There are few records of her years at Rosedale Public or BSS, aside from accounts Nancy shared later in her life. She recalls, for example, one day when she was attending Rosedale, "I remember school boys taking my favourite teddy bear out of my arms and stomping it into the slush and snow. I was devastated." She also recounts with some pride, "When I came home from school, if Mommy was out, I would go visit Thelma, the laundress, whom I saw standing starching my father's collars. I

Thelma Wall, Finnish laundress/ cook to the family, enjoying a beer on Pine Island, Go Home Bay, circa early 1950s.

Mary and Harry in 1958 in their cottage living room.
The cottage on West Wind Island, Go Home Bay,
Georgian Bay, Ontario, was purchased in 1949.
Murals by some of the Group of Seven can be seen
on the walls. The murals are now in the National
Gallery of Canada.

Top: Nancy Ruth on West Wind Island, age 8, in 1950. Left: Nancy Ruth, age 6, standing with the Ridout cottage behind her. Bottom left: Nancy Ruth, age 17, with A.Y. Jackson, on South Pine Island in 1959. Bottom right: Mary, age 55, and Nancy Ruth, age 17, with A.Y. Jackson on South Pine Island in 1959.

remember going upstairs and later asking my mother why she did not have a chair to sit on. This is the first instance of me demonstrating a social conscience."[16]

Nancy describes herself in these early years as a "stuttering, obese child who didn't fit in at school," and as an adult she pointed to this early experience of marginalization as another catalyst for her development of a social conscience, commenting that it taught her "to notice and protect others who were different."[17] Of her five years at BSS (1949–1954), she recalls, tongue likely in cheek, "I learnt how to do hospital corners on the bed sheets, sew bags for my chapel veil. Learnt how to genuflect, it was the thing to do."[18] BSS is in fact an Anglican girls' school (junior kindergarten through high school) that prides itself on its academic rigour and success in university preparation. But for young Nancy, it was an alien environment where she stood on the sidelines, unable to find a place for herself.

Nancy struggled academically and only many years later realized that she suffered from learning disabilities, something not well known or understood in the 1940s and early 1950s. Although she was never diagnosed, she believes that she suffered from dyslexia. She was slow at reading and embarrassed when made to read aloud in school. Not only did she (along with Edward, who was also a stutterer) have to go to speech therapy classes for years, but she was also assigned to remedial reading classes, which made her feel "like I was a dummy." As she recalls, "between being chubby, not having confidence, and stuttering, I disliked schoolwork."[19] As an adult, she finally succeeded in academic environments that emphasized hands-on and experiential learning, but she floundered in traditional educational settings.

One source of pleasure for Nancy during these

childhood years was the family cottage at West Wind Island on Go Home Bay in Georgian Bay, Ontario, purchased by her father at her mother's urging in 1949, when Nancy was seven. The family had rented another cottage in the area the previous summer to see if the locale suited them. Mary and her childhood friend Alida Starr Martin had visited West Wind as girls, and Mary's uncle Professor Arthur Langford had a cottage in the Inner Bay. The cottage appealed to Mary Jackman in part because of its connections to Canadian painters from the Group of Seven. Its former owner, art patron Dr. J.M. MacCallum, had built the cottage in 1913 and murals in the living room included paintings by Arthur Lismer, Tom Thomson, and J.E.H. MacDonald. A.Y. Jackson and other artists such as Lismer, Charles Comfort, Will Ogilvie, Sophia Hungerford, and Jack Nichols were frequent cottage guests during Nancy's childhood and would take her mother, other guests, and Nancy on sketching picnics. Writing in his diary in the summer of 1953, Nancy's father describes a seventieth birthday party for A.Y. (Alec) Jackson at the cottage, at which "[Alec] reminisces about the early days of Canadian art and our island where the Group of Seven in a very real sense had its birth."[20]

Harry's diary also has a number of references during these years to Nancy's growing prowess as a swimmer. He writes in the summer of 1952, for example, that "Later we went swimming from island to island and Nancy Ruth must have swum at least half a mile. She is getting on very nicely after her month at Glen Bernard Camp.... She seems to have no sense of fear and goes right ahead doing anything that anyone else is doing."[21] We may see in this passage a girl eager to please her father and to keep up with her athletic brothers. If both camp and school were

Right: Nancy Ruth skiing near King's Hall, Compton, Quebec, circa 1955–1956. Below: Nancy Ruth on Billy Boy, in "Winter Repose" at the family farm, "Overdown 2," age 14, 1956.

"Winter Repose"

Nancy and Billy Boy '56

places of deep unhappiness for Nancy, these opportunities to spend time with her family and to excel at physical activities offered some respite in her troubled childhood.

But the return to school each fall was inevitable and both Nancy's parents were concerned by her lack of academic success at BSS. In her first term there the school principal wrote Mary Jackman a letter assuring her that "Nancy is all right, I think. She is quite good at school, you know. I think her fussing with you is just a child's way of getting attention and pity.... Altogether I think you would be wise not to worry about Nancy at present; she really is getting along quite happily."[22] Nancy's academic results, however, did not bear out the principal's optimism; her report cards from BSS and from later schools she attended might even suggest that she was a classic underachiever. She is described, for example, as "often inattentive"; "lazy"; "capable of a much higher standard"; a pupil who "could do better work if she took greater care."[23] The picture that emerges is of an innately bright child who—for reasons that may be a combination of emotional immaturity, learning disabilities, unhappiness, rebellion, or lack of trying for fear of failing—does not perform at the level of which she is capable. In January 1954, at the beginning of what was to be Nancy's last term at BSS, her father complains in his diary that "Mary renounces all the teachings of Bill Blatz and the St. George's Institute of Child Study by promising Nancy a pony if she gets 70 percent in her schoolwork."[24] The incentive failed and the following September her parents tried a new approach, sending their daughter, now aged twelve, to the eastern townships of Quebec to attend Mary's old school, King's Hall, Compton (KHC).

Nancy remembers being deeply unhappy at the new school:

Because my birthday was in January, I was seen to be young there. I was placed in a separate residence from the girls I knew from Toronto. From day one, I hated it. I sleepwalked. As a consequence, I was moved downstairs with the even younger students in case I fell downstairs and hurt myself. This was simply intolerable to me.[25]

In the diary she began keeping when she left for King's Hall, Nancy writes, "I have arrived just by the skin of my teeth. I nearly missed the train. Packing was horrible. So is the life here so far."[26] On October 9 she continued to record her unhappiness. "My bike arrived today. I have never been so homesick." By November 1, her academic difficulties were beginning to surface: "Mark sheet went up, I came 16/20 with 60% what a flunk." When end-of-term exams began in December, she writes, "Exams were Scripture which was a sin and literature was a stinker."[27]

The diary entries from that first term also reveal a pattern of rebellion and misbehaviour that was to characterize Nancy's two years at King's Hall: "Got -10 for telling a lie, -5 for drawing in prep."[28] Recalling this experience years later, Nancy writes, "Most importantly, I did not understand why the rules at Compton were different than the rules at BSS. Why doing something at BSS, like stealing the communion wine or putting the thermometer on the radiator, were mildly disciplined. At Compton, these were harshly disciplined. I was bored with the constant discipline of mending the Prefect's laundry, scraping gum off the dining hall tables, marching 13 miles to the Vermont border in a snow storm."[29]

The picture that emerges from these years is of a high-spirited and active young girl who was easily bored and found it hard to settle down to her studies. She confessed to her diary repeatedly that she has failed to study, that she wrote letters or doodled during prep time, and that she was disappointed in her academic results. On the playing field, by contrast, she often excelled and noted with pride that she made the first team in both soccer and softball. She seemed happiest when she was skating, skiing, or doing other sports such as gymnastics. On October 6, 1954, she writes that "I was the best on the rings today in gym"; on October 14, 1954, "We did handstands on the horse today, what a thrill."

For Nancy's parents, however, her athletic prowess was not enough to offset her poor conduct record and her failure to shine academically. In December of her second year, she commented in her diary that she "did dreadfully" on her exams[30] and, after she travelled home to Toronto for the Christmas break, recorded an argument with her "old man" about the importance of his not judging people by their report cards.[31] She returned to King's Hall for one final term after Christmas, but by then it was clear that her mother's hopes that she would excel in this setting were not going to be realized. As Nancy says many years later, "The principal, Miss Gillard, highly recommended to my mother that I not return. What joyful news was this?"[32] In contrast with her later school experience, Nancy remembers that she had "no friends from those days" at King's Hall, Compton.[33] They had been difficult and lonely years that did very little to give her security and confidence as she entered adolescence.

Back in Toronto in the summer of 1956, Nancy hoped to resume her studies at BSS. Although she had not done well academically, she had formed a number of friendships, setting a pattern of active social engagement coupled with

A studio portrait of 16-year-old Nancy Ruth, as she says, "trying to look sophisticated!"

(and likely compensating for) academic mediocrity that continued throughout her schooldays. Her mother always encouraged her to make friends at school and bring them home, especially if they were foreign students with no other place to go.[34] Her father's diaries from her time at BSS describe several instances when Nancy had school friends over for birthday parties or to go to movies or ride ponies (one of her favourite activities). And BSS had the further appeal of the known and the familiar. Yet the school would only take her as a boarder, and she "couldn't bear going into boarding" for a whole term at a time.[35] Branksome Hall, however, another private girls' school in Toronto, agreed to take her as a weekly boarder and that compromise was struck. In the fall of 1956, at the age of fourteen, Nancy entered Grade 10 at Branksome Hall School (BHS), boarding during the week but allowed to go home on weekends.

If, to paraphrase Wordsworth, "the child is mother of the woman," we can trace in Nancy's teenage years interests and traits that stayed with her throughout her adult life. In both her diaries and her later accounts of her youth, we see a person with an intense need for friendships and a capacity for strong and generous affections. We see someone who has a keen appreciation for the arts—theatre, dance, opera, film, painting—regularly making notes about shows or performances and her response to them. We also find an interest in politics, including active participation in the Young Progressive Conservatives club in her later teen years. And at the same time, we witness the "demons" that would plague her on and off through the ensuing years: a recurring lack of confidence in her capabilities; an inability to control her appetite and maintain a healthy weight; a longing for a meaningful vocation coupled with uncertainty about what contribution she could make.

Nancy's academic performance at BHS continued the familiar story from KHC: she knows that she should study but finds any excuse not to do her homework and is usually disappointed in her grades. Once again, she was a discipline problem, frequently receiving "order marks" (disciplinary sanctions) for breaking school rules, including on one occasion going out with other boarders to see Elvis Presley at Maple Leaf Gardens (when they were ostensibly having dinner at Nancy's house).[36] After a gap in the diaries for 1957 and much of 1958, she writes on January 12, 1959, "I am finally a day girl—and I started a diet." Yet her escape from boarding did not enable her to break now-established patterns. On February 26, 1959, she records in her diary, "Hell, why aren't I doing my homework like I should be, and I have the time too, but I suppose that I hope that I will get through like I have been doing for the last two years, in fact all my life but I know sure guns that I won't." A couple of months later she laments, "I certainly would like to know what the hell is the matter with me. I must work hard enough to go to college so that I can learn what is the matter. But I must work real hard.... I am still a fat slob who isn't doing what the doctor wants, and just not giving a damn about anything."[37] A month later, when exams are in progress, she writes, "I stayed up until 3 a.m., trying to learn Physics and Geography...ate another pound of turtles, my face is all breaking out, and I have gained 4 lbs."[38]

Some of Nancy's suffering during these years can be read as normal adolescent angst; she wants to fit in, to be attractive, to be liked, and to see a purpose ahead for her life. She records frequent daydreams in her diary—of marriage to a British lord or of becoming a famous surgeon and saving the life of a child she had borne and given away to its father and his new love. One day she might write, "I keep thinking about a Naval career,"[39] on another, "I now want to go to Bulgaria and live as a peasant for two years,"[40] and a few days later, "Sang [alone in her room] with Ella Fitzgerald and Tony Bennett. I wouldn't mind being their private secretary."[41]

Nancy also confides to her diary her sexual fantasies and passionate crushes—on male and female teachers and on boyfriends and girlfriends. She notes a number of times that she was still a virgin and wonders in early 1960 if she "could be a lesbian."[42] Nancy's confusion and unhappiness were to some extent typical of adolescent experience, but her mother was concerned enough about her daughter's behaviour—which included yelling at both parents, lighting fires in wastepaper baskets in her bedroom, and eating countless Turtle chocolates—to send her to a psychiatrist, Dr. Ruth Franks, who lived near the Jackmans and was a family friend. In her diary, Nancy mentioned therapy sessions throughout these years, sometimes finding them helpful and other times not. She seemed to welcome a chance to confide in an adult who would not judge her, and yet she remained frustrated at her inability to break out of cycles of negative behaviour.

This behaviour included continued and bitter fights with her family. Whether she was at boarding school and home only on the weekends, or living at home full-time, Nancy's teenage years were marked by recurring conflict and outbursts. On February 24, 1959, she writes, "Mom and I fought badly. She says no car. I won't apoligize [sic]." A week later she complains, "The whole damn family revolted me, and I told them so, why is it that when I walk into this house I become miserable."[43] On March 25 of the same year, she "got a lecture [from her mother] about how inconsiderate I am towards parents and the maids," and on March 28 she predicted that she will "probably be having a row with Dad soon as he says he's about to break."

Harry Jackman's diaries from this period describe his continuing frustrations with his daughter. On February 8, 1959, he writes, "Church and dinner at home with all the family, except Nancy, who is away in Collingwood skiing. What a waste of time. Saturday she has to be at school and Sunday she drives the Ford station wagon about a hundred miles each way and is dead tired. No work is accomplished. Where is sweet reasonableness?"[44] On March 24, 1959, he confides to his diary, "My little daughter, to whom nothing seems right and who has not learned to co-operate with the inevitable, rather gets me down when her mood is bad."[45] When we recall Nancy's resentment that her father seemed to reward his children only in return for their achievements, a passage from Harry's diary during this period takes on particular significance:

> Yesterday Mary and Hal gave me their candid impressions of the wrong way in which I handle Nancy. Presents should not be just prizes, but given for love alone. Also they say I am chiefly interested in the children for bringing honour to my name. Hal says that Nancy is a jewel. Mary says that she is very like me. Perhaps they are both right.[46]

Yet her father's moment of insight does not seem to shift Nancy's dynamic with her family and she continued to labour under feelings of being misunderstood and unappreciated. She also continued to lash out, at her mother in particular, until many years later when she had gained greater insight into the constraints of her mother's life.

Interestingly, Mary Jackman seemed to understand the complexity of Nancy's dynamics long before Nancy did herself. On June 2, 1959, when Nancy had just finished Grade 12 at BHS, Mary wrote in a letter to her daughter:

> I'm sorry to be away from your last closing and sorry too to leave just when you had been talking to me, more as a friend than an enemy. I hope we'll have another hair-brushing session again soon.
>
> Meantime, please try not to spurn your naturally "sweet" self as per your photograph, which should prove to you how sweet you look.
>
> I remember how surprised I was to see Charles Comfort's portrait of me because it appeared to me like a strong courageous person—which I did not feel I was.
>
> On the other hand, I know you are, and I admire you for it.
>
> I am aware now that at too early an age you took up the cudgel for your Mother in defending the rights of a woman to express her opinions etc. This tended to make you aggressive and combative, but especially I fear made you scorn the "sweet" ineffective character-type in which you placed your mother.
>
> I hope now that you have been living at home and seen more of us—that your opinion will level out a bit, and that you can recognize that sometimes a mild, unresponsive attitude is not necessarily weak....
>
> Much, much love from your old-not-so-sweet Mum.

Mary Jackman clearly discerned in her seventeen-year-old daughter a strength of character that she admired, seeing behind Nancy's "combative" exterior an insistence on the validity of the female voice in a family dominated by its men. Though Nancy could not yet recognize a different type of strength in her mother, Mary hoped that in time she would learn to do so.

These adolescent years, while difficult for Nancy in many regards, were also ones in which she had a vibrant social and cultural life. In January 1958, when she was halfway through her second year at BHS, her father notes in his diary, "Mary and I go to Branksome Hall Parents' Night, which is very interesting. Nancy is very popular with her schoolmates and liked by her teachers, but they say they cannot get any work out of her."[47] In sharp contrast to her lonely years at King's Hall, Nancy kept up—often at the expense of her schoolwork—what sometimes seems to be a frantic round of social engagements, skiing trips, shopping expeditions, and visits to plays, movies, and galleries. Her diary is filled with accounts of her friendships and what they meant to her. On March 20, 1959, for example, she writes about having coffee with a friend with whom she "talked and talked and talked," one whom she can "really trust." She goes on, "I have told her about my miseries at K.H.C...things I have never told anyone else." On numerous other occasions she dropped in at friends' houses, inviting them to the family's farm or Georgian Bay cottage, or over for dinner at her home. Many of Nancy's friends later in her life have remarked on her intense desire to be with people, and this trait was evident when she was young.

The catalogue in her diaries of plays, films, and concerts that the teenage Nancy attends is also extensive. Her

Nellie Langford Rowell (Nancy Ruth's grandmother) with her daughter, Mary Coyne Rowell Jackman, 1955, outside Nell's house at 5 Cluny Avenue.

mother was an avid art patron, so she had many opportunities to go to galleries and to meet artists who were guests in the family's home. She took trips with her mother, to the Detroit Institute of the Arts (April 1959) where she admired the Diego Rivera murals and the Picassos, as well as to the Brussels World Fair and to London and Edinburgh in the summer of 1958. In the "My Trip" diary she kept on this journey, she faithfully records visits to the theatre, concerts, and galleries. The Edinburgh Festival was on and she commented after attending a production of T.S. Eliot's *The Elder Statesman* that it was "most enjoyable" and "had a lot of meaning for me in facing one's wrong deeds, and the rebellious son to father."[48] She found the Byzantine art exhibit "magnificent," admiring its mosaics and "outstanding" jewellery.[49] Her mother wrote home to her father, "Nancy has been great fun and good company."

One art form that held a strong appeal for Nancy at this time was photography. She acquired a good camera and mentions her picture-taking on various trips. In the spring of 1960 she was overjoyed to learn that she had won a prize in an international high school student photography contest to which she had submitted slides from her 1958 Edinburgh trip: "To-day I received a letter saying that I had won third prize, a bronze medal for my picture on the castle up near Appin, Argyll, Scotland, and honorary mention for another photograph. I yelled when I read the letter, and was terribly happy."[50] In the fall of 1960, when she had enrolled at Jarvis Collegiate in another attempt to pass the examinations needed to qualify for university entrance, she wrote, "I would like to do photography."[51] A letter written to her uncle Fred, transcribed in her diary but annotated as "never sent," describes her love for skiing and "good parties" and then adds, "Another great interest is photography but unfortunately my parents don't encourage that form of art."[52] She dreamed of going to New York City and becoming a news photographer like Margaret Bourke-White, but her parents would not consider letting their nineteen-year-old daughter go off on such an adventure.[53] In later years she continued to search for suitable artistic outlets for herself.

Nancy's lifelong interest in politics also took shape during those teenage years. Although her mother's family were prominent Liberals, under Harry's influence the Jackmans were firmly in the Progressive Conservative camp. After his time in federal politics, Harry remained active in the PC party, including as a fundraiser, and continued for many years to contemplate another run for office. Three of his children—Eric, Hal, and Nancy—later made their own attempts at being elected, though none of them succeeded. As a teenager, Nancy was active in the Young Progressive Conservatives (YPC), serving as a delegate at their convention in November 1959 and attending meetings from time to time at Toronto's Albany Club. In June 1960, she writes in her diary, "Am bored with history—love Y.P.C.'s."[54] In the fall of that year she was elected third vice-president of the Rosedale YPCs and spent time at their office typing lists and stuffing envelopes.[55] The letter to her uncle Fred confides that, besides photography, "My other great passion is politics, conservative or liberal I don't care, but since I am on the executive of the Rosedale Young Progressive Conservatives I suppose I am a Tory."[56] And a lifetime Tory she would remain, to the bewilderment of some of her feminist friends, though she has sometimes chafed at ideological differences with the Party.

One striking omission from her teenage diaries is any sense of Nancy as a deeply religious person, although religion would later take a central place in her life. She does remember her depth of feeling when she joined the church, on April 4, 1954—"It meant a lot to me"—yet during her adolescence, as often as not she mentions sleeping in on Sunday and missing church, to her parents' chagrin.[57] In September 1960, she records in her diary a conversation with a friend in which she explained that, as a non-Anglican at King's Hall, Compton, she was not allowed to take communion and that after KHC "every time I saw people in the United Church go up for communion I thought that they were being sacreligious [sic]—e.g.: Daddy."[58] Having come from an ecumenical family, she found this exclusion at KHC troubling and felt that it alienated her from the church. She ends her diary entry by writing, "I still feel closer to God in nature alone." And looking back years later, she recalls that as a teenager she also turned to poetry as a spiritual outlet, reading and making up verses in the ravine behind her house instead of going to church.[59]

Nancy's three years at Branksome Hall School, while happier than those at King's Hall, Compton, were no more academically successful. Her difficulties still appeared to stem from a complex tangle of rebelliousness, a fear of failure if she truly tried to compete with her older brothers, and a desire to punish her father for the pressures that he put on her to succeed. She failed to pass her exams at the end of her senior year there and in the summer of 1959 she and her mother took a driving tour of Maritime universities in hopes that she might gain entrance to one of them in the fall of 1960. Unlike Ontario, admission to Maritime universities did not require completion of "senior matriculation," or Grade 13 as it was also called until it was phased out in 2003. Nancy spent the academic year 1959–1960 taking classes at Thornton Hall, a private high school in

Toronto, preparing to take her exams again the following spring. Her diaries for this period record the same pattern of struggle in school: "I can't do the Algebra";[60] "Was made a fool of in Botany, Zoo and History because I didn't know my work";[61] "Mrs. Broom told me that I would probably not be in her History class next term. I only got 30% on my mid-term report";[62] "Did a little Chem in the morning, only to fail in the afternoon."[63] In the middle of that term she writes, "I go to see Dr. Franks on Wednesday, so maybe she can straighten me out and get me to work at school"[64]—but no change was forthcoming.

In June 1960 Nancy took her "junior matriculation" examinations—the exams that at that time yielded an "ordinary level" high school completion certificate in Ontario. She earned her certificate with what would be considered a "low pass" and her father writes in his diary of June 20, 1960, "Nancy passed her junior matriculation with an average of 54%—not enough to assure her acceptance by the University of New Brunswick, but an application has nevertheless been made."[65]

Meanwhile, Nancy's parents had promised her, on completion of her junior matriculation, a long-wished-for trip to Europe as part of a tour with other young people— some of whom she knew and some she first met on the trip—and she set out for this "European Odyssey Tour" in early July. Once again she kept a trip diary in which she recorded her group's voyage by ship from New York City across the Atlantic, followed by their progress through major cities in England, Sweden, Denmark, Germany, Switzerland, Austria, Italy, and France, then back home by ship to New York and by train to Toronto, where she arrived on September 10, 1960. Nancy seemed to be in her element on this two-month journey, filled as it was with adventure, major cultural attractions, and ready companionship. On July 8, for example, the single day she had in New York before embarking, she and a friend managed to visit the Museum of Modern Art, the Metropolitan Museum, the Guggenheim, and take in two movies before they boarded the ship that evening!

In each place they visited, Nancy records excursions with various members of her tour group to the Tate Gallery, Tivoli Gardens, the Louvre, the Venetian Academy, the Sistine Chapel, theatres in London, performances of *Aida* and *La Traviata* in Rome and of *La Bohème* in Paris—"It was very good and I cried again in the last act."[66] There was even skiing in Interlaken as well as a bus trip through the Alps. She describes days and nights of congenial company—songs and card-playing on the bus, and evenings spent in taverns discussing history, politics, and religion. The person revealed in this summer 1960 trip diary was one who thrived on social engagement, cultural stimulation, and constant activity—indeed, the person who would come into her own in Nancy's future, although not until she had reached full adulthood and independence.

Perhaps the one dark moment in Nancy's European trip was her receipt of a letter telling her that she had not been admitted to the University of New Brunswick.[67] She records only that bare fact, but its significance had to be clear to her. Most of her friends would be heading off to university in the fall, but she would be left behind to attend another year of high school and try once again to gain her senior matriculation certificate. Shortly after her arrival back in Toronto, where she was met at Union Station by her mother and father and remarks drily in her diary that they "are still the same parents,"[68] she enrolled at Jarvis Collegiate Institute, her local public high school.

On her first day there she saw a boy she knew and remarks in her diary that he was "the only person I saw that I knew at Jarvis—& I was so thankful to see him I almost kissed him in the middle of the hall." She adds that she is "a bit scared for tomorrow but I am sure it will be all right." And she ends this entry with a note of regret that all her friends were going off to college and "I really feel left out of things."[69]

By the following month, Nancy was back in the familiar cycle of malaise and binge eating: "I worked myself into a very bad state of depression and ate six pieces of chocolate cake. This was all about me at Jarvis. I am happy at Jarvis, but I honestly don't think this is the right thing for me mentally—I would think Huron College-Western [an undergraduate college affiliated with the University of Western Ontario] would be excellent as a failure there would be so much more worthwhile."[70] It is poignant to see her, at the age of eighteen, reduced to assessing her prospects in terms of relative degrees of failure rather than potential success. A few weeks later she writes, "I listen to La Boheme in my room because it is easy for me to relax with it. The exams are in two weeks & here I sit enjoying myself immensely not doing homework."[71]

Nancy's year at Jarvis Collegiate unfolded in much the same way as her year at Thornton. She kept herself busy skiing, visiting with friends, and going to meetings of the YPC. She found her academic subjects difficult but procrastinated with homework assignments. And she often daydreamed of finding the perfect husband. While it is disconcerting to see this future champion of feminism place her hopes on marriage as her pathway to a meaningful life, we have to remember that she was a child of her time in this regard. Living as she did inside a world of male privilege, she could not yet imagine her own ability to shape an independent future. On March 7, 1961, she writes, "Haven't opened a French book all day, and can't say I care. All I have on my mind is going to England next year. Having a romantic—to all senses—time and I would love marriage to some suitable man." In mid-August she writes bleakly, "I failed all four of my senior matrics" and records the results for each: French Au[thors], 40 per cent; Zoology, 40 per cent; French Comp, 33 per cent; and Botany, 38 per cent; with an overall average of 37.75 per cent. She then notes beside the tally, "no comment."

The dreamed-of trip to England, perhaps not surprisingly, was not in the cards for that year. Within a month Nancy was enrolled at Ryerson Polytechnic Institute (now Ryerson University) in Toronto, where she set out to study business administration. She begins her diary entry on a positive note—"I have had 4 days at Ryerson and quite enjoy it"—but by the end of the same lengthy diary entry starts to equivocate—"My year is going to be a very hard one without a great deal of work. I somehow feel that this isn't the best idea, but even now I am trying to make an excuse for next May."[72] She liked her English class, which had been the case in her former studies, and in fact enrolled in a night course in English at the University of Toronto that fall. Accounting, however, she found "incomprehensible"—a troubling indication since she was pursuing a business major.[73] Two days later she is already signalling defeat: "Any homework I have done has been in English. I am not going to pass."[74]

Nancy maintained contact with friends from Branksome Hall who were attending university in Toronto, as well as with some of her Jarvis classmates. Her diary throughout the academic year mentions badminton games, skiing trips, parties, and numerous evenings out at the theatre and movies. She joined the Ryerson Judo Club and made friends on campus, recording typical student activities like hanging out in the student centre playing cards and coming fifth in a bridge tournament—only a few days before her first-term exams. Her drive to be active and socially engaged remained on display as a central part of who she was.

During that year Nancy continued to fret about possible careers and her lack of preparation for a meaningful profession. One weekend when she had gone out alone to Overdown, the family's farm, she writes, "Daydream about being in the air force and impressing them with my knowledge, and complaining about not being able to advance in rank because of a lack of a degree."[75] Other daydreams continue to conjure up a future where her problems are solved by meeting the right man and being swept into marriage: "Finally, I got around to thinking...that after I had quit my summer job in London, I would go to the continent with a chap—English—perhaps named Peter, and we would get married and have a wonderful honeymoon. Both of our parents are shocked to an extent; but both families are respectable so it sort of ends happily."[76] If her fantasies gave her some comfort, they also troubled her: "Why why why, am I such a dreamer—it's bad for me—Doc Franks says I have to [sic] much time to think about myself—this is true." Interestingly, she ends this passage with consideration of another possible future: "Social work—no—not for me."[77]

Relationships with her family continued to be troubled during Nancy's Ryerson year, as she records quarrels with her brothers and deep resentment at the way she was treated by her father. In one outburst she writes, "Daddy,

Daddy why can't you listen without making remarks. Your four children are queer in different ways—and I am one of them—DAMN YOU FAMILY—YOU ALL LAUGH AT ME!!!!!!!"[78] If there was one change, it is found in her relationship with her mother, toward whom she began to show more affection and appreciation. As she describes one evening at home, "Tried on Mother's black crepe dress w/ train…. Then Mom & I tried on all the evening dresses and saris, great fun."[79] She records on Monday, January 8, 1962, that she had gone to church "for Mom" the previous day, and in the spring she mentions that she routinely went to a weekday meal with her mother at the Metropolitan United Church: "This is the first Wednesday I haven't eaten at the church with Mom in a long time."[80] She seems to have begun recognizing her mother's efforts to intervene on her behalf, including persuading her father to support her for the coming year in London. Nancy's maternal grandmother, Nell Rowell, lived near the family in Rosedale all those years and, when Nancy visited her to say good-bye before she left for Europe, she notes that her grandmother "made me promise I'd look after Mom as Mom looks after her—and I said I would."[81]

It is clear from Nancy's diaries that the London stay was agreed to well before she completed her year's study at Ryerson. Nevertheless, she did complete the year, and with results that were somewhat better than her grades at her previous schools. She did well in both English and economics and when her first-term marks were reported, she writes, "Great Guns—I came first in Economics out of 360 odd."[82] She passed two out of four subjects, with an overall passing average of 69 per cent. But, as she had predicted, the two subjects with which she struggled proved impossible for her to master. On June 2 she notes, "I wrote the exams in reasonable nervous comfort with the knowledge that I would fail my Accounting and Mathematics of Finance." Her first year of postsecondary studies was over, and it took almost seven years before she at last earned a university degree as a mature student at York University.

The year at Ryerson did give her leadership opportunities with the Ryerson chapter of the YPC, where she was elected president "by two votes" in March 1962. She and her YPC friends were active in the federal election that spring, the first in which Nancy was so directly engaged. They held poll captains' meetings, canvassed neighbourhoods, put up lawn signs, and drove voters to the advance polls. The Progressive Conservatives, however, did not fare well in the 1962 election. Nancy's candidate in Rosedale lost, as did most of the PC candidates in Toronto, and John Diefenbaker's government was reduced to minority status.

On the same day that she recorded these disappointing results in her diary, however, Nancy also writes with what must be some jubilation, "Now I'm off for a year. It's hard to believe."[83] Her dream of spending a year abroad will finally be realized. Now twenty years old, she will travel with her parents to Russia and Scandinavia that summer and then take up her stay in London as a young woman on her own.

Footnotes for this chapter can be found online at: http://secondstorypress.ca/resources

Nancy Ruth in her cherished Saks 5th Avenue
taffeta dress with her mother, Mary Coyne
Rowell Jackman, wearing her engagement
diamond brooch, in the early 1950s.

Chapter 3

"I WISH I COULD BE SOMETHING"

THE 1960s for Nancy Jackman were years of continued searching, as she grappled with the classic questions of young adulthood: "Who am I? What shall I do with my life?" Her diaries of that time were often achingly honest about what she saw as her failures and limitations. They were also full of yearning. In the late fall of 1962, after she had taken up residence in London, we find her alone in her room, listening to a recording of opera singer Joan Sutherland and commenting in her diary, "Wow, what a woman. I wish I could be something."[1] This decade would in fact open up three major avenues for her emerging self-hood in the form of a profound religious awakening, an equally profound encounter with feminism, and her first passionate love affair with another woman. At the same time, she continued to grapple with questions of voca-tion, of how to be something. Her friends were finishing their education, choosing careers, and settling into their professions while she remained unsure about what useful contribution she could make.

In the summer of 1962, following a month with her

Nancy Ruth with her parents in Moscow, summer 1962. The trip was arranged through the USSR Ambassador to Canada as Harry was President of the Art Gallery of Ontario when Russia lent artwork to the Gallery. Harry Jackman, 4th from L, then Nancy Ruth and Mary Jackman.

mother and father in the USSR and Scandinavia and a few days staying with them at the Dorchester Hotel in London, Nancy saw her parents off for their flight back to Canada, noting that evening in her diary, "The good-bye was brief & no tears." Mary Jackman had booked her a room at the Young Women's Christian Association (YWCA) across from the British Museum until a space at the William Goodenough House became available. That afternoon she walked across the street to the British Museum, alone for the first time, and writes that she "felt quite somebody to walk up those steps all by myself. Still hasn't clicked on me that the parents have left." Her sense of a fresh beginning is captured in the words with which she ends this diary entry: "bed w/o chocolate, [with] an orange & a new life."[2] She was twenty years old and possibilities abounded. Yet her "old self" was still in residence. Try as she would to eat oranges instead of chocolate, to apply herself to her studies, to have confidence in her self-worth, she had not left behind the conflicted person she brought with her to London.

Nevertheless, although London in 1962 had not yet entered what came to be known as the Swinging Sixties, the city still offered Nancy a feast of pleasures in the arts. In addition to the plays, concerts, galleries, and auction houses that had become a fixture in her life, she relished going to jewellery exhibitions and collections at the Victoria and Albert Museum, as well as trips down Bond Street, Regent Street, and around the Goldsmiths' Hall. Jewellery was a passion she shared with her father, whose diaries are filled with allusions to gemstones admired and purchased; she pursued that passion further some years later when she studied jewellery-making at George Brown College and worked as a jeweller in Amsterdam. In her mid-seventies, after a trip to Korea, she donated her collection to the World Jewellery Museum in Seoul.[3]

Inspired by her mother's love for her Bloomsbury book collection and for contemporary art, Nancy also hunted for treasures at art sales and auctions. Her parents had given her an allowance of three hundred dollars a month—"heaps of money" as she calls it—so she was free of financial worry for a time, with change to spare.[4] One of her first indulgences was to purchase, for nine pounds ten shillings, an umbrella from the luxury goods shop of Swaine Adeney Brigg, complete with a gold-plated band on which she had her initials engraved. It's easy to picture her as a young woman feeling splendid with her first taste of independence as she strolls down Piccadilly using her very own monogrammed umbrella as a walking stick. She had no compunction about receiving an allowance or living on her family's wealth; indeed, she had long viewed a portion of that wealth as her rightful due. "I knew I had money in King Vaughan Farms [the fund her father had set aside as a future inheritance for his children]," she recalls, "so why not some of it now?"[5]

Nancy's characteristic drive to build a social network was on full display in these London months as she connected with friends from Toronto as well as British friends of her parents: Ken and Ruth Case, Lord and Lady Pender, as well as others in their well-to-do circle who invited her to weekend house parties in Kent and hunt balls in other parts of England. When she was invited to her first house party, she agonized that she has "made an ass of myself" by asking "what will I wear etc."[6] One friend of special importance was a former prefect from Branksome Hall, now living at the FANY Club in Sloane Street, someone she "had a crush on" in school.[7] Her diaries brim with accounts of the time they spent together and Nancy's longing for them to share a flat. This intensity prefigures later relationships she will forge with key women in her life, but in this case her friend was wary of the attachment and clearly wanted to maintain some distance between them; at the end of one evening they spent together Nancy records in her diary, "She doesn't want to live w/ me as she's afraid of her influence & responsibility towards me…. She keeps stressing that you can only love the opposite sex etc. She doesn't realize the full extent to which she is all I've got…. Hell—she says 'be.' Be what?"[8] Loving and being are intertwined in Nancy's mind; she is searching for an identity but still uncertain of what she could be aside from a person who loves and is beloved.

Despite the despairing tone in this diary entry, Nancy did find a flatmate to move in with after her summer stay at the William Goodenough House was over. Marian Hebb, whose boyfriend, Dennis Kelly, was a friend of Nancy's brother Eric, agreed to let Nancy share her bedsit at 45 West Cromwell Road; she lived there for the last few months she remained in London. Shortly after Nancy moved in, Marian wrote to her mother that, "A young society type Canadian student has been staying with me for about a week. She has been sent to Europe by her parents to become 'sophisticated'—which she is decidedly not.... She is very wishywashy about what she is going to do and is very anxious to get in with the 'right' people."[9] The room Nancy shared with Marian had two single beds, a gas ring for cooking, and a bathroom down the hall where they had to put shillings in the meter to get hot water. While the conditions may seem spartan for a "young society type," Nancy recalls that she "didn't want to be by myself" and that she wanted to save her money for a "rainy day."[10]

Marian remembers Nancy as someone who was easy to live with but appeared to be "young and vulnerable and quiet," qualities she found "at odds with" the person she admires and knows her to be today. At the same time, she recalls that Nancy was "always very busy" and had an intense social life: "she seemed to have all these connections and was running off to this and that and balls and whatever." The two young women got along well but did not become close; in retrospect, Marian realizes that they had a great deal in common, "but I don't think we knew it then."[11] Marian eventually returned to Canada and made her career as a writer, book and magazine editor, and lawyer, and she and Nancy later crossed paths as sister feminists and supporters of the Writers' Union in Toronto.

Nancy's "busy-ness" in England included a hitch-hiking trip with friends to Scotland to attend the Edinburgh

International and Fringe Festivals, which she had gone to with her mother when she was sixteen. Looking back, she calls this second visit to Edinburgh "quite an adventure." She and friend Martha Corrigan got locked out of their youth hostel when they returned after midnight one night and were picked up by the police, who let them spend the night in a jail cell. On this same trip they hitched a ride from a man who invited them to "come home for tea." Accepting his invitation, they found themselves on a grand estate complete with peacocks strutting on the lawn and were served a sumptuous spread in the man's "well-appointed large living room looking out on a loch."[12]

In October, Nancy began auditing classes as a special student at the London School of Economics (LSE), where her mother and her brother Hal had studied before her—her LSE attendance was one of the two requirements her parents had set as a condition for supporting her time abroad. Throughout the fall she complied as well with their other requirement—that she participate in therapy sessions with Dr. Percy Backus. Dr. Backus was a Canadian psychiatrist living in London who was recommended to Mary Jackman by her former psychoanalyst, J.A. Hadfield, who had seen Mary in 1926–1927, the year she had spent in London and Selly Oak as a young woman.

Nancy's diary reveals that she was lukewarm about her courses on Commonwealth governments and comparative politics at the LSE. On October 4, just before the term began, she writes, "School tomorrow. Ugh." On the following day she fears that, "This will be another Ryerson of not knowing anyone." She attended lectures sporadically, barely making class on time, dropping in on the wrong lecture by mistake, or leaving early because "I decided I couldn't face that man on Commonwealth govs., he's so insipid."[13] On one occasion she chose to go to Sir Arnold Plant's class "because of his title and because he must be good to get it."[14] She was still not prepared to be a serious student, yet she continued to fret about this failing: "I do wish I [would] sometimes do some thinking. I'd quite like to write a paper.... Oh the joys of doing nothing aren't pleasant. Work Jackman work!!! Yet I won't."[15] Throughout her life she both admired intellectual achievement and questioned her own powers of thought, leading her to choose women as friends and lovers who were, in her words, "smarter than" herself.[16]

Like her courses at LSE, she found limited value in the sessions with Dr. Backus. Of her first visit she writes, "He seems a nice enough man. Sympathetic. I am afraid I made Dad into too much of an ogre."[17] On her next visit she tells him that she "always wanted to hurt Dad."[18] After her session on September 3 she considers that "today we got nowhere," and a few days later remarks, "didn't get much further, but somewhere at least."[19] By early October she was confiding in him that she was "afraid to go back to Canada" because she "would have to face going to Shaws [secretarial school] or something as horrible as that"; she took comfort, however, in his assurances that she was smart: "This was a good feeling, because I have begun to wonder about my I.Q."[20]

Nancy complains in her diary at the end of October that Dr. Backus "keeps harping on my early & continuing resentment of authority" and that he "knows nothing of my sex inhibitions or much of my desire for power."[21] She began to skip appointments—"I missed Dr. Backus this morn again"—and when she went, felt that they were accomplishing little.[22] Of her last session with him before she left London at the end of December she writes simply,

"Dr. Backus & left happily w/ no judgements anywhere."[23] In the report that he submitted to her parents just over a year later, however, Backus showed considerable insight into his young patient. He wrote that, while Nancy had been sent to him because of "her obesity, and depression associated therewith," he quickly realized that she was "sincerely and deeply concerned about all that had contributed to this state of affairs, and it became evident that the symptom of obesity was one expressive of a deep seated hunger for something she had not found in life." He concluded that "I have not the slightest doubt that Nancy inherently wants to give herself to something worthwhile in the human field" and that "apart from a happy marriage, the giving of herself to training for leadership and encouragement in some form of public service would develop her innate potentialities and bring her more enduring fulfilment than any other way of life."[24] His understanding of his patient may have been incomplete, but he was prescient in seeing her capacity for future leadership and her hunger to "give herself to something worthwhile."

Although the original plan had been for Nancy to spend a full year in London, sometime during that fall she persuaded her parents that she would be better off moving to France in the new year and enrolling in a special course, French for foreign students, at the University of Grenoble. The location would have the added attraction of allowing her to ski in the French Alps. Despite London's charms — evenings at the Royal Opera House and Royal Albert Hall, ample art shows, and the theatre that she loved so dearly — she felt that she was going nowhere. She had found neither the sense of purpose nor the close relationship she had hoped for. Most of the young people she spent time with were doing second or third degrees or had launched their careers, while she was simply auditing courses, half-heartedly at that. It is no wonder that in October she confides in her diary, "I'm still feeling so bloody inferior and lack self-confidence."[25] A month later, grasping at romance as a path to fulfillment, she writes, "I must get thin to get a man. I want so much to be loved."[26] But at the same time she continued to dream of finding a respectable vocation. Fearful that she has been unable to succeed at any studies above the level of secretarial school, she exclaims in her diary, "Oh God, somebody please think me worthwhile to employ at a decision making position. I refuse to be a typist etc. Damn Father for reducing my capabilities to this level."[27] Her stay in London had taken her no closer to finding a future career and she was ready now to move on.

While Nancy was glad to be leaving England—"my God, it's cold, & the smog"[28]—she confessed to a friend how afraid she was as she contemplated making a new start in France.[29] Worried that she would be homesick for her family if she stayed in London for Christmas, she decided to join a group of twelve Canadians from London House and William Goodenough House on a ski trip to St. Anton, Austria, before going on to Paris and then Grenoble. They set off by minibus on December 21, arriving in St. Anton on the 23rd. Nancy went to midnight mass on Christmas Eve—"nice, but I wasn't homesick"[30]—and skied most of Christmas day. She was not an expert skier and took lessons over the following days, spending her nights socializing in the local *rathskellers* with her travelling companions.

Nancy reached her "age of majority" while she was in Austria, hosting her twenty-first birthday party on January 3, 1963, three days early because the group was leaving St. Anton on the fifth. She ordered a birthday cake at a nearby hotel where she and her friends gathered

Nancy Ruth
on her 21st
birthday, 1963.
She was skiing
in St. Anton,
Austria, with
other Canadian
students
studying in
London.

for dinner, followed by a show of Tyrolean dancing in the rathskeller downstairs. When the orchestra struck up "Happy Birthday," the cake was brought in "with all the gang singing for me." She writes in her diary that night that "I think people enjoyed themselves, but I was never in the mood except when I cried when they sang happy birthday" because "I *love* being the centre of attention." For this special birthday her mother gave Nancy her own moonstone jewellery that her daughter had long admired, while her father gave her a fine 2.5-carat emerald that he had brought back from Bogota. She was at first pleased when she learned of her father's gift a few days earlier, until she realized that she "wasn't getting a settlement" that would furnish her with the financial independence she had hoped for but he was unwilling to grant.[31] By January 6, Nancy had moved on to Lech, Austria, to visit with school friend, Pam Bond, and her family. Her diary entry recounts another day of skiing, this time with a cold and sore throat, and concludes, "Tossed & turned w/my nose dripping until the end of my twenty-first birthday."[32] It was an inauspicious close to her official entry into adulthood.

The following weeks took Nancy to Vienna, where she was enthralled to hear Elisabeth Schwarzkopf sing in *Der Rosenkavalier*. Looking back years later, she recognized the allure that the diva had for her in that role—a strong woman dressed in a white satin suit, wearing silver shoes, playing a man—noting, "Talk about unexplored lesbianism!"[33] She played her recording of the opera over and over again while she was in Grenoble—"I would CONDUCT it with my white baton and felt fabulous."[34] By January 19, she was in Paris, where again she met old friends from Canada, including Sheila Shotton, a future broadcaster with the CBC who later that spring persuaded her to take a road trip through the south of France and the Camargue. Nancy remembers walking miles in Paris to retrieve from customs a large Christmas fruitcake that her beloved Jackman cousin, Rae Adams Carroll, had sent: "it was covered in thick marzipan with a Georgian Bay tree on it" designed by artist Illy Gepe, Rae's landlady—and it reminded her intensely of home. She spent her days in Paris walking along the Seine to see the booksellers—buying a large, engraved, red morocco leather-bound copy of *Paradise Lost*—or visiting cafés famous artists such as Gertrude Stein, Alice B. Toklas, Simone de Beauvoir, Pablo Picasso, and Ernest Hemingway had once frequented; by night she went to avant-garde movies or to the opera.[35]

When Nancy moved on to Grenoble she took up residence first in shared student housing and then in a room in a workers' apartment building. Years afterward she recounts that she "hung out with the foreign students, especially one English guy, Clive Kendall, who didn't want to learn French either…! All I remember about the French classes is that I used to be able to say quack quack in 13 languages."[36] She came down with her first bout of pneumonia, spitting up blood; she wanted to go to a doctor but didn't because "I couldn't explain my health problems in French."[37] Iris Nowell writes in her biographical sketch of Nancy that she "spent weeks alone recovering in a tiny cold room" and then found companionship with prostitutes near the town centre with whom she and other foreign students had supper on the weekends: "The prostitutes had no johns on Sunday nights, no relative's homes to go to, and like Nancy they were lonely and welcomed female company… one imagines Nancy thinking of her strait-laced parents and gloating over her wonderful little peccadillo."[38]

With her course in Grenoble drawing to a close—she

left a week before it ended, hoping that her mother would not discover her delinquency—Nancy headed back to Paris and London for a couple of weeks before flying home to Toronto on April 6. Two days later she records in her diary the outcome of the 1963 Canadian federal election in which her brother Hal ran in their father's old riding of Rosedale and was soundly defeated by Donald Macdonald, a future minister of finance: "Not a Tory seat in Toronto. Dreadful situation w/ a minority Liberal government."[39] She made the rounds of Toronto friends and family and, having lost some weight as a result of her illness in France, basked in the compliments she received: "I wore a new navy chiffon cocktail dress & my moonstone jewelry. I looked well and knew it…. [An old friend] came up the steps & w/ his arm around me said he had never seen me looking more lovely. I really must get thin now. It's such fun."[40]

Before long, she persuaded her parents to bankroll the tax-free purchase of a white Volkswagen bug for her to pick up in Paris where, as promised, she set out with Sheila Shotton on their adventurous drive through the south of France. Of that time she recalls, "I think Sheila and I just motored around, drinking wine and drinking in life."[41] They spent time with Roma in the Camargue—Nancy still has a pair of gold-coloured hoops that she was given by a Roma woman in exchange for her pair of dangling tin Buddhas—and traipsed as they pleased through châteaus, galleries, vineyards, and ruins.[42] Nancy's parents, however, still hoped to turn their daughter to more serious purposes. Her father sounds a note of irritation in his diary that spring after Nancy has returned to Europe: "I receive a letter from Nancy, who wants to have a bigger allowance to live better. She wants to meet people in Europe, not just see places."[43] On June 8 he frets, "The thoughts of the opportunities our Nancy has had, but her strong will and lack of self-discipline has overridden our objections."[44]

Around that same time, Nancy's mother sent her information about international youth work camps run by the World Council of Churches and Nancy agreed to sign up for a camp on the Greek island of Lesbos, joining a group there in the summer of 1963. She kept no diaries for this time but wrote home regularly, and her father comments several times in his diary about the "fine letters" the family received from Greece, even suggesting that his daughter "could easily become a correspondent for a newspaper."[45] According to Nancy, the WCC camps "were an attempt to build bridges between youth of different cultures, languages etc. with manual labour the common thread…. So we built a school library for the Greek Orthodox Church. Early to rise, dig the foundation, mix cement, carry bricks, build the walls, make the window frames etc…. I suppose my interest later in the Holy Spirit was a result of this time, and going to orthodox church services."[46] Nancy also vividly recalls a brush with religious sexism "rooted in thousands of years of history" while in Greece. The local Greek Orthodox bishop shocked her with his answer when she asked why the old men up on the olive grove hills wore long wool socks with baggy pants. Putting his arm around her, he said, "My child, don't you understand? When the Christ child comes again, he shall be born of man. The bag is to catch the Christ child when he arrives."[47]

At the end of what turned out to be a productive and satisfying summer, Nancy's parents agreed to support a further stay in London until the end of the calendar year, conditional upon her resuming her sessions with Dr. Backus. Her return to London coincided with the marriage of Edward Samuel "Ted" Rogers, Jr., then an

up-and-coming Canadian broadcasting magnate, to Loretta Robinson, whose mother was a Woolworth and whose father was the British MP for Blackpool

Nancy Ruth, 4th from left, at a World Council of Churches work camp in Lesbos, Greece.

and future Lord Martonmere. Nancy stayed at The Savoy and remembers pulling up to the hotel after driving from Athens in her VW jammed with her worldly goods and marching herself into "a very different world." Hal Jackman was a groomsman and the wedding at St. Margaret's, Westminster was a spectacular affair. It was followed by a reception at the Robinsons' house on the Mall, where four thousand yellow roses had been delivered from Covent Garden. Nancy "had never seen anything like this" and when she went upstairs to the washroom located in Mrs. Robinson's dressing room "couldn't resist" opening a cupboard where she found "so many beautiful and exquisite

Nancy Ruth and Mrs. Gerald Campbell at
a party before the marriage of Loretta Anne
Robinson and Edward (Ted) Rogers, Jr., in
London, England.

Nancy Ruth with members of the
wedding party of Loretta Robinson and
Ted Rogers in London, England on
September 26, 1963.

peignoirs." This glimpse of upper-class British luxury was intoxicating to Nancy, but for most of the wedding she "hung out with the other Canadians."[48]

For the rest of her autumn in London Nancy resumed her round of social and cultural events, going to auction houses, riding horses in Richmond and Hyde Parks, and joining the Royal Commonwealth Society "so I could spend the weekends out of London."[49] She also kept her promise to see Dr. Backus, who wrote to Mary Jackman a few months later, "On her return to me in the autumn we were faced with a fixed period in which something was to be achieved in anticipation of her return home to a situation full of misgivings regarding her future." In his opinion, because of these constraints, the time he spent with Nancy was "of very limited value." He continued to believe that her struggle with controlling her weight "is not really one of diet at all but one of a deeper unsatisfied hunger in herself, in her spirit."[50]

Finally, on December 12, 1963, Harry Jackman records in his diary, "Nancy is home after eighteen months abroad, looking fine. She has a number of treasures from Sotheby's and Christie's. She has also acquired a library of objects d'art and jewellery, including Fabergé."[51] What she has not acquired, however, is a direction for her life. She recalls of that time, "Well, I think I was a useless young woman, with nothing to do and no degree etc. so I went to secretarial school. I hated it. This was not my image of my life."[52] The threat that she saw hanging over her in London had now materialized. Unable to propose a convincing alternative, she was forced to enroll in the secretarial training that she had been determined to avoid.

Her rescue from this unhappy fate, however, arrived quickly and from a most unexpected source: "Then this brochure came in from the World Council of Churches about this work camp in Bali Indonesia. I had no idea where Bali was & I didn't care, nor did I care that there was a war in Vietnam."[53] Harry Jackman writes in his diary on June 8, 1964, that "Nancy has received her acceptance in a ten-month tour of duty at the ecumenical work camp in Bali. She wants to go."[54] Interestingly, she writes to Dr. Backus that spring about her plans, and he replies to her that "the prospect of you taking up some special work in Indonesia can be of inestimable value to you.... The big thing is to find real fulfilment in some experiences that are related to higher values."[55] Nancy's time in the Greek work camp had been a prelude to her year in Bali, Indonesia, which would indeed connect her to "higher values" and would turn out to be a life-altering event.

Over the years Nancy has often, and with relish, told the story of her awakening to Christianity in Bali. In a 1989 interview with Eleanor Wachtel, for example, she recounts that the work camp experience was first of all, a humbling one: "It knocked some of the arrogant, WASPish, high-flying Rosedale stuffing out of me.... I began to ask, in the global picture, who am I?" She goes on to say to Wachtel, "I woke up one morning and understood that God loved me."[56] Describing the experience to Iris Nowell in 1996 she recalls, "The feeling was one of pure peace and joy."[57] As she remembers the experience over fifty years later, she believes that it was coloured by her encounter with Bali's Hinduism, which was "foreign from my United Church theology." In the village church services she attended, for example, she encountered a strong conviction that "God could intervene in nature" and thus came to "believe in the power of the Spirit" in a direct way that she had never done before.[58] We do not have her contemporary account of this transformative event because for the first eight months of her time in Bali she put aside her custom of keeping a diary, "having hoped that my Sunday letters home to my parents would do."[59] But on April 24, 1965, she writes, on the first page of a new journal, that she is not satisfied with the letters as a record and so will once again take up her diary.

She recounts in the early pages that her transcendent religious awakening is now "some months ago," a time of great happiness when she "felt I would be prepared to give my all, and everything if Jesus asked."[60] Not surprisingly, the passage of time along with the challenge of living in close proximity to twenty other young camp workers had dampened her initial fervour. She reflects, for example, that "I have come to a much deeper relationship and understanding of God than ever before, but my initial enthusiasm of wanting to return to Canada and do work for people my own age in the church seems to have disappeared."[61] Living conditions in the camp were fairly primitive—bamboo huts with earthen floors, wooden slat beds with kapok mattresses and pillows, and kerosene lamps—and the work camp members were disparate in background and age. They came from ten different countries, with the youngest twenty and the oldest thirty-two. Reading material was limited, Western pleasures, food, and entertainment were frowned upon, and some of the manual labour they were assigned to do was of questionable value, for example, building frog ponds to breed giant frogs for the Chinese market, frogs that never materialized.

Two-and-a-half months away from the end of camp, Nancy devoted many of her diary entries to reflecting on her months in Bali and analyzing the strengths and shortcomings both of the camp structure and of herself and her fellow workers. She is frank as is her wont, but she is also impressively even-handed. Indeed, there is a new note of maturity in her pages as she acknowledges that group members are getting on each other's nerves but assumes her own share of responsibility—"my presence is no doubt a hindrance now instead of the joy it was."[62] She is also more outward-looking than she had been in her earlier diaries, writing with compassion about the difficult life circumstances of some of the other workers—"How fragile we all are."[63] During much of the time she spent living abroad, her companions were similar in background and socioeconomic status. In Bali, by contrast, she lived in a Hindu community with very different people; ten of the group were Christians from Indonesia and the others were Christians from Japan, Switzerland, Germany, England, the USA, Ireland, and Canada. Her horizons were significantly expanded by this experience.

Some of her core beliefs were also challenged during her time in Bali. She was more conservative than many of her fellow workers and felt conflicted when their arguments for social justice, for example, pitted workers' rights against those of management.[64] Although she may have complained—as she does on one occasion, "Oh to be back w/ people who think, rightly or wrongly, as I do"—she was being stretched in new ways to reconsider her social and political framework.[65] And her diaries show that she was now taking more note of political turmoil in the world around her than she had done in the past. The mid-sixties were a time of widespread conflict in southeast Asia and, living as she did in Indonesia, she gained a heightened awareness of this conflict's causes and its consequences. After an evening when she was in charge of leading prayers, she writes that she has prayed for "the political troubles of Viet Nam, India & Pakistan, Malaysia and Indonesia &

This page: A postcard, with a photo of Nancy Ruth, written on June 21, 1965, to her grandmother, Nellie Langford Rowell, from a World Council of Churches work camp in Bali, Indonesia.

Opposite, top right: Nancy Ruth, centre, putting in the floor of a lime factory at Lukluk, Bali (Indonesia), June, 1965. Bottom right: Nancy Ruth, far right, with a gamelan orchestra, welcoming World Council of Churches workers to Denpasar, Bali (Indonesia), 1965.

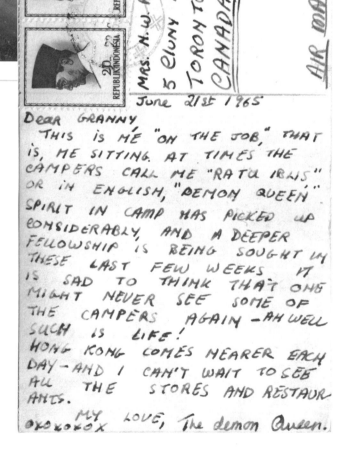

MRS. N. W. ROWELL,
5 CLUNY AVE.,
TORONTO, 5,
CANADA

AIR MAIL

June 21st 1965

DEAR GRANNY
THIS IS ME "ON THE JOB," THAT IS, ME SITTING. AT TIMES THE CAMPERS CALL ME "RATU IBLIS" OR IN ENGLISH, "DEMON QUEEN." SPIRIT IN CAMP HAS PICKED UP CONSIDERABLY, AND A DEEPER FELLOWSHIP IS BEING SOUGHT IN THESE LAST FEW WEEKS IT IS SAD TO THINK THAT ONE MIGHT NEVER SEE SOME OF THE CAMPERS AGAIN — AH WELL SUCH IS LIFE!
HONG KONG COMES NEARER EACH DAY — AND I CAN'T WAIT TO SEE ALL THE STORES AND RESTAURANTS.
MY LOVE,
OXOXOXOX The demon Queen!

the Dominican Republic. I hope my wish that the leaders of these countries would not let pride hinder their peace-making attempts was heard not only by God but by the Balinese who are so insular."[66] During Nancy's time in Bali, Indonesia was in political turmoil. She recalls that most nights there were killings in the villages as war raged between President Sukarno's army and the communist rebels: "A village mayor's wife, whose husband had been killed, was sent back his testicles in a box. I had not heard of such violence and torture."[67]

Alongside the evidence of a political wakening in her diaries, there are also frequent and lyrical descriptions of her surroundings. On April 29 she writes, "Last night it was so hot that Swari, Asri, and I walked down to the beach to an old out-rigger and sat...watching the sun go down. There are definitely moments when the sun rests at night and you see the dark outlines of the small fishing craft at sea, their lights becoming brighter and brighter as the darkness grows. The palms wave and whistle to the winds."[68] On May 6 she exclaims, "How lovely the sun-sets are at Lovina [the northern coastal town where they are currently building school furniture].... The sun falls & the lamps from the small fishing boats make an arc of light from shore to shore."[69] The following evening she sat outside writing in her diary and notes that "The sun is just starting to set and each time I raise my eyes the sky & clouds have changed their tones and hues. The boys...are practicing football safety falls in front of me—slowly they become tumbling black figures."[70]

The quiet, reflective quality of these passages is echoed in other sections where Nancy writes of her Christian com-mitment. She has been a reader of literature for many years but now chooses to read and note down passages from religious writers, such as twentieth-century Trappist monk Thomas Merton and seventeenth-century metaphysical poet George Herbert. On April 30 she writes, "To quote from Thomas Merton's journal *The Sign of Jonas*, 'One reason why we are less fervent than we ought to be is that we cripple our own spirit by taking ourselves too seriously. We expect too much from ourselves when we ought to expect everything from God on Whom we utterly depend.' How true that is and yet for such a long time I insisted on being utterly self-sufficient. God how wonderful you are. I cannot truly live w/out you."[71] She was finding in religion a passageway out of the narrow self-absorption that had for so long confined her. Yet, at the same time, she recognized what a fragile hold she had on this newfound state of being: "If I can only keep my faith—have it to help me throughout life's way.... I hope when I go home that I can start nightly bible readings & prayers after dinner."[72]

While she was by no means freed from the self-doubt and recriminations that plagued her through her adolescence and young adulthood ("I do not seem to have the force of mind to continue and self-discipline myself. What a lazy bastard I am—and always have been"[73]), Nancy's Bali diary entries display a greater confidence that she was capable of charting a new course for her life—and of reaching toward those "higher values" of which her psychiatrist spoke. In the final few weeks, she successfully resisted the implse to leave camp early, even though the daily work was no longer meaningful and many of the camp members had grown bored and quarrelsome. Her father and mother visited her for a few days in January on a stopover on their way back from an Institute of International Affairs conference in India, prompting a comment from her father in his diary that "Nancy is a brick to stick it out

Nancy Ruth, in her French lace dress made in Hong Kong for her visit to the Canadian High Commission in New Delhi. There she is with Mrs. Norah Michener and Monsignor Knox on July 20, 1965.

ten months, considering what she is giving up."[74] A month later he writes, "We have received a number of letters and conversations complimenting Nancy on the form-letter on Bali which she circulated broadly among her friends, and also on her maturity."[75]

A copy of the form letter written at the end of January 1965 still exists and it concludes, "This experience I shall never forget, nor shall I regret. There are of course difficulties such as lack of privacy in communal living, and nothing but the rice paddies to turn to for a change. Bugs, rats, etcetera, sometimes become intolerable, but all is working out successfully, and I hope the World Council of Churches feels this is successful enough to allow others to join in future camps in developing countries. I cannot help but remember the expression 'I sought for happiness and happiness eluded me, I turned to service and happiness found me.'"[76] She had come to believe that not simply religion but a religious life in the service of others might offer the path to self-fulfillment that had so far eluded her.

On July 10 Nancy writes, "Much has happened since I last wrote [June 21]. Camp has ended and I am returning to my beloved country."[77] She was now visiting her parents' friends Roland and Norah Michener in New Delhi, where Roland was serving as Canada's High Commissioner to India. After two weeks with them, she moved on to Tehran, then to visit friends in Athens, Geneva, Lausanne—where her friend Bips Graalaek is "astounded at my new faith"[78]— Marseille, London, and Dublin before arriving back in Toronto. Her last diary entry for this whirlwind period of travel until she takes up pen again in February 1966 is the one for August 3, but her father records that on September 1, "After dinner, Mary and I met Nancy returning from her ten months in Indonesia at Malton airport. She seems in good spirits."[79] And on September 13 he writes, "Nancy has been accepted for a two-year course, mostly theology, at Covenant College."[80]

When, in later years, Nancy tells the story of her religious awakening in Bali and her return to Canada, she delights in adding, with a laugh at her own presumption, "I knew I had to return to my country and bring Jesus to Canada. It was a vocation.... I still carried enough of my Rosedale arrogance that I had no inkling that the presence and spirit of Jesus might already be here."[81] She also had little inkling that to serve in the United Church, as she hoped to do, she would need advanced academic credentials — and she had still not finished her high school senior matriculation. But Mary Jackman knew the principal of Covenant College, the Reverend Dr. Harriet Christie, through the Student Christian Movement (SCM), and Dr. Christie agreed to admit Nancy into the first year of Covenant College's diploma program on probation, after which an academic committee would decide if she could continue and under what conditions. A year later, when the committee met, it stipulated that after her first year she would have to complete courses in logic and English at a university summer school in order to be admitted into the program's second year.[82]

The college where Nancy chose to do her theological study was established originally as The United Church Training School for women who wished to be commissioned as deaconesses within the church. Although women had occasionally been ordained as ministers in the United Church of Canada (UCC) during the first half of the twentieth century, in the 1960s there were still limited roles for them within the UCC; primarily in the areas of Christian education, visitation of the sick and elderly, and some contributions to church services, and most sought to be commissioned in the diaconal order. Covenant had started accepting men in 1962, but women students remained in the majority when Nancy attended in 1965–1967 and there was a strong emphasis on communal life, with all students required to live in residence. Here Nancy at last found a community where she felt she truly belonged, where she was deeply engaged in her subject of study, and where she achieved solid academic success—in part, she recounts, because she had her first opportunity for the small group instruction and experiential learning that she believes was key to her ability to learn.[83]

When she resumed her diary on February 26, 1966, Nancy describes her decision to enroll at Covenant as "due to lack of education for church work." She admits that her first term "had its vicissitudes," including her alienation of some of the other students by her "loud mouthed attitudes,"[84] but she has made good friends, among them Ghanaian Comfort Baifie. She later became godmother to Comfort's son Kannin and visited the family in Ghana a number of times over the years.[85] Another new friend was second-year student Virginia (Ginny) Dobson, who had been assigned as her "big sister." Ginny was not only a Progressive Conservative like Nancy but had spent a year teaching English in Indonesia, which drew the two young women together. Ginny says of Nancy at that time, "My family didn't have the kind of wealth that Nancy's family had, but I was not intimidated by her rich background. Many of the other women at Covenant College had rural backgrounds, and didn't quite know what to make of Nancy—particularly because Nancy loved to shock people with outrageous statements and foul language! At Covenant College!" Yet, Ginny adds, "With Nancy, if you spend time one-to-one with her, you get to know the Nancy who is sensitive, kind, extremely bright, observant, warm, sharing, questioning. We became friends."[86] Ginny and Nancy in fact remained lifelong friends, and Nancy visited Ginny several times in India after she married and moved there in 1970. Ginny's social activism in community organizing and supporting single women in Rajasthan has been recognized worldwide and has been an added bond between the two women.[87]

Along with new and compatible friendships, Nancy affirms in her diary that she has at last found the right academic program and a clear sense of vocation: "Throughout this term I've been stimulated by theology. I can only see my future as the service of God—no matter what the ministry."[88] A few months later she records with pride, "Well, the year is almost over and I have gotten a B+ average which I never expected in my fondest day dreams. Also I was awarded prizes in Old and New Testament."[89] Nancy's next year at Covenant College was equally successful, ending in her graduation at the top of her class on May 8, 1967—a resounding victory for someone who had long doubted her academic ability.

A hallmark of Nancy's second year, aside from her success as a student, was the relationship she formed with the Reverend Gwenyth Hubble, only the third woman to be ordained (in 1939) as a minister within the Baptist Union of Great Britain. During her career in England, Gwenyth had served as assistant general secretary of the British Student Christian Movement; principal of Carey Hall, a women's missionary training college in Birmingham; and a member of the World Council of Churches Committee on the Life and Work of Women in the Church. After her retirement to Canada in 1966, she was engaged by Covenant College as a visiting lecturer, teaching introductory survey courses in the New Testament. She also started, and led for several years, a highly popular series of Bible study classes for the Ecumenical Institute of Canada.[90]

In her history of the Centre for Christian Studies, the successor institution to Covenant College, Gwyn Griffith notes that Gwenyth Hubble "had a significant impact on many of the students" at Covenant: "Gwenyth was a big woman in both stature and personality, and she exerted power."[91] Another portrait of her character in the book *Women, Work and Worship* describes her as "a strong, gentle, compassionate yet challenging, perceptive and wise Christian woman. She was often quite frank and open about her shortcomings and spoke of her struggles to overcome them, especially those she thought might prevent her from being effective. In doing so she communicated courage and confidence to her associates."[92] Nancy found Gwenyth "a person of great depth, and someone I can relate to well";[93] a few weeks later she writes that Gwenyth has told her "perhaps she'd been sent by God to Covenant this year to help me. To think that God would do such a thing like that for me & thru such a wonderful person."[94]

Gwenyth had clearly taken the aspiring young churchwoman under her wing, and we can imagine Nancy's hunger for the kind of affirmation that such a caring and accomplished elder could give her. The older woman's powerful personality and her own frankness about her personal struggles struck a chord in Nancy, drawing her to someone with a certain commonality of experience but at the same time the greater wisdom and perspective that come with age. Reflecting on her feelings for Gwenyth, Nancy says, "I haven't a close relationship to God, and I find it difficult to articulate what it means to be a Christian

Reverend Gwenyth Hubble, Nancy Ruth's New Testament professor, mentor, and friend. Covenant College, 1966.

in contextual situations. But Hubble is near—have no fear. I love her very dearly."[95] And many years later, when she is asked who her greatest mentor has been, it is Gwenyth Hubble whose name Nancy invokes: "She respected, encouraged, believed in me when others doubted me. She pushed me to push myself toward things that seemed undoable by me. Most importantly, she had expectations of me that I would work for the good of others, not primarily myself."[96]

A few months after her 1967 graduation from Covenant College, Nancy was able to record another academic milestone. She had not only completed the university courses Covenant had required her to take but had also continued to enroll in additional university courses: "Tonight is a big night in my life. I wrote an examination in the 'Recent Trends of Western Civilization' in Atkinson College Hall, York University," York's college for mature students. She goes on to say, "When I walked out of that hall 20 minutes before ten, I left Atkinson College, and I completed my first year of University. It is a day that I suppose I thought I would never reach. It was only when I was walking into the door of my apt. a few minutes ago that I realised what I had done. *It is good not to have quit on this one.*"[97] For someone who longed for the respectability of academic credentials but who routinely gave up, dropping out or quitting for fear of failing, the completion of a full year of university studies while juggling concurrent coursework at Covenant and York represented a significant turning point.

Nancy takes time in her diary to thank "many people" for helping her reach this happy moment: "Covenant College for getting me started last summer in York University. The excitement of the learning and the instruction of all the teachers that have influenced [me] in the past year. Gwenyth Hubble and [Gwenyth's friend] Laura Pelton who have helped me through difficulties. My parents who have financially supported me, and especially my Mother who has put up with the new learning that has made me feel so 'right' and 'important.' My father whose praise I still seek, and who gives it to me when I stand first in the class."[98] This last comment is both telling and ironic, in light of Nancy's conviction that much of her previous failure has stemmed from her rebellion against her father, to punish him for withholding his love from her if she did not excel.

Another significant change for Nancy was that, for the first time in Toronto, she was living in her own apartment. In this same diary entry, she recounts an evening a few months back when Gwenyth took her to dinner and suggested that she get an apartment in the building where Gwenyth and Laura Pelton lived, at 245 Roehampton Avenue, Eglinton and Mt. Pleasant: "I was utterly flabbergasted that these people should care so much. This was too good to be true and I never expected it to materialise. They want to help me mature!!!"[99] Through her mother's advocacy, Nancy's parents agreed to the move and an increased allowance to support it, conditional on the continuation

Nancy Ruth (top row, 4th from L) with students and teachers, Covenant College, 1966. Her friend, Ginny Dobson Shrivastava, is in the bottom row, 2nd from R.

of her BA program in political science at York. When her program at Covenant College ended in May, she was thus able to move into an apartment rather than back home to Rosedale. Nancy went with her mother to choose furniture for the apartment—some antiques, including a dining room table, chairs, and a glass cabinet, all of which she still has—as well as her graduation present of stainless steel cutlery.[100] Though she was no longer one of Gwenyth's students, she was now her neighbour and able to maintain close contact with her friend and mentor, taking her grocery shopping and sharing cups of tea.

Nancy's diary ends with her August 1967 entry, and she does not write again until she starts a new journal in late December 1968. Those intervening sixteen months were important ones and included an "awakening" as critical to her development as was her discovery of God's love in Bali—her August 1968 encounter with feminism at a World Student Christian Federation conference in Turku, Finland. It was also in Turku that she met Dutchwoman Trudy van Asperen, with whom she had her first serious love affair after Trudy moved to Canada with the Canadian SCM.

Between September 1967 and May 1968, Nancy completed the second year of her three-year BA program at York. Even though she was now living independently, her life remained tightly intertwined with her family. Her father's diary in May 1967 recounts her parents' pride in her scholastic achievement: "Mary and I go to Timothy Eaton Memorial Church for Nancy's graduation ceremony from Covenant College. She heads her class, and wins a prize. Miss Hubbell [sic] speaks very highly of her—the outstanding personality in her class."[101] Yet in August he laments Nancy's "explosion of hate and bad manners at

Nancy Ruth's graduation portrait from Covenant College, Toronto, 1967.

dinner last night," adding the following day that "Nancy, at Mary's bidding, apologizes to me for her conduct of the other evening."[102]

Harry's diaries of this period cite numerous conflicts with all four of his children and also chronicle his pre-occupation with ensuring that the fortune he has now accumulated be maintained in perpetuity. He wonders in May 1960, at the age of fifty-nine, "What would be the effect on me of the gradual realization that none of my sons cared to carry on the financial 'empire' I have built up?"[103] He clearly sees the line of business succession running through his male heirs, both in Nancy's generation and in ones to come. Early in 1967 he frets that Nancy "has no suitors" even though she will turn twenty-five in a few days: "It is probably a mistake to follow the natural instincts of one's heart by dividing one's estate equally among one's children. Eddie presented a problem with his likely vow of poverty [when he entered the Dominican order]. What purpose is served by giving Nancy a fortune if she does not marry?"[104] With his focus on ensuring the succession of his estate through his descendants, Harry was distressed by Nancy's remaining unmarried and childless.

Two of Nancy's brothers had married by this time—Eric to Deone Griffith in June 1959, and Hal to Maruja Duncan in August 1964. Eric and Deone, who divorced in 1968, had two children—daughter, Tara, born in 1962 and son, Tom, in 1965, while Hal and Maruja had three during this period—sons Henry and Duncan born in 1965 and 1966, and daughter, Victoria, born in 1967. When his granddaughter Tara arrives, Harry writes, "It is strange how a son gives rise to more hope and joy than does the birth of a daughter. I am surprised I am not even more enthusiastic than I am over the birth of my first grandchild."[105] When

Eric and Deone's son was born almost three years later, Harry records his elation: "Tom is our first grandson.... It is a fine thing to have a grandson!"[106] Later that same year, after his second grandson, Henry, was born and he continued to feel profound regret over Edward's desire to become a Roman Catholic priest, Harry writes, "Eddie believes that his life challenge is to become a priest in the Dominican order.... If he were the only son it would be a disaster for me, but with Tom and Henry, there should be salvation—what a strong, blind impulse is the perpetuation of life through children."[107] It is noteworthy that Harry's concept of "perpetuation of life" includes neither his daughter, Nancy, nor his granddaughter, Tara. It is the male succession that matters.

There is little doubt that some of Nancy's anger toward her father stemmed from her knowledge that, while he loved her and was often generous in his financial support, she did not figure into his plans for the future of his business empire. The outburst in her London diary when she voices her dread of secretarial school—"Damn Father for reducing my capabilities to this level"—was a clear indication that she found him at least partly to blame for the vocational dead end she had reached. Yet years later, when questioned as to whether her father ever proposed taking her into the business, she recalls that "Dad had introduced me to women in finance throughout the years, something most dads didn't do. He introduced me to women politicians, to Cairine Wilson the first woman senator, [to women] engineers, pointed out how many of my female cousins were lawyers etc. There is no doubt that he saw his children, his seed, as leaders.... When I returned to Toronto in 1978, age 36, I took the stock brokers course. But by then, Hal was well ensconced and father was out of the business, so I never got in."[108] One of the most poignant entries in Harry's diaries, given the frequent and ferocious battles between father and daughter, is his admission in the fall of 1969 that "Nancy is probably more like me than any of the children. I love her dearly and am heartbroken that she will not work towards an objective which will give her some satisfaction."[109] Harry may have seen in his daughter his own strength of will and drive to achieve, yet he was frustrated by her lack of direction as to what she might achieve in her life.

It is possible that Harry Jackman, torn between love for his daughter and the patriarchal conventions of his era, entertained the idea of a role for Nancy in his business empire but never found his way clear to making room for her. He notes the importance of primogeniture—the right of the first-born son to inherit the family's estate—in a diary entry of 1967: "Only recently, I looked up the history of Russia to confirm that the nobility amounted to nothing until primogeniture was set up."[110] A couple of months later he writes, "Just as countries must have capital accumulation, so must families if they are to grow and prosper. While I shared some of my most important assets with the four children equally, it is perhaps well—although not as I would have had it—with only one son carrying on in the financial tradition. Lucky to have one such son."[111] His first-born, Hal Jackman, is that son and he did indeed succeed his father in controlling the family's financial empire—as Hal's son Duncan did in later years.

Harry's mention of sharing some of his assets equally with the children refers to his establishment in 1956 of a holding company, King Vaughan Farms, in which he placed one half of his financial assets in the form of shares, with the rest of his assets remaining within his business or for his personal use. As part of this estate planning, those King Vaughan shares were left to appreciate in the fund and were designated to go in equal portions to his children upon his death. Nancy was keenly aware of her father's plans and when she at times frets over not having control of her own "fortune," it is the King Vaughan Farms holdings to which she is referring.

Although Hal captained his business after his death, Harry envisioned a role for his other children in the newly established Jackman family foundation—all the children, that is, except Edward if he carried through with his intention of becoming a Catholic priest. In Hal Jackman's explanatory gloss on his father's diary of 1965, he notes that the Jackman Foundation had been incorporated in 1964 with a gift of $150,000 from Harry. By December 1965, with Edward still in training to enter the Dominican Order despite his father's attempts to dissuade him, Harry transferred the bulk of Edward's inheritance—"25 percent of the value of the children's ownership [in King Vaughan Farms]"—to the Jackman Foundation. Hal explains that the transfer agreement "provided for the securities to be returned to Edward if, in the opinion of the Foundation's trustees, Edward was no longer subject to the vows of poverty or chastity."[112] He insists that his father's reaction to Edward's decision to become a priest "was based not so much on anti-Roman Catholicism, but on the fear that the substantial values that he had placed in Edward's name might go to other than his issue or to those not of his choosing."[113] Whatever the underlying motive, Harry was adamant that he would not let his hard-earned fortune fall into the hands of the Roman Catholic Church and be used for their purposes rather than his own and those of his descendants.

When the Jackman Foundation convened its first annual meeting on April 30, 1966, at the family home in Rosedale, Mary, Hal, Eric, and Nancy were all there. The foundation's directors had initially consisted of Hal, Mary, and Harry, but the family members agreed at this initial meeting to replace Mary with Nancy. Harry comments that night in his diary that Eric, who wasn't a director at the time, was nevertheless "not silent" at the meeting and questioned the use that had been made of Edward's inheritance to augment the foundation's funds. It seems that, while Harry had made Hal aware of his decision with regard to the disposition of Edward's funds, he had left Eric in the dark. Harry's account credits Hal with defending his father's decision-making authority by pointing out to the others that "all the assets have been derived from my exertions."[114]

A family drama ensued, with Eric asking what Harry saw as "irrelevant" questions so that father and son "nearly have a scene." This interchange, clearly distressing to Harry, prefigured further conflicts over the foundation and the division of assets within the family in years to come. In 1969, for example, Harry complained that Edward had written him "a horrible letter" arguing that his money should not have been put into the Jackman Foundation and that "he feels ordained by God to get it back so that he may do what he thinks God wants him to do with it."[115] Just as troubling to Harry at that same time was that "Nancy threatens to consult a lawyer in regard to her assets." He found Nancy's threat to be a great affront, arguing in his diary that "In the formative years of my estate-building, I gave each of my children a quarter interest in well over half my assets, which greatly increased in value, so that they are all worth some millions in liquidating value if our investment companies were realized upon."[116] Yet the assets had not been liquidated, nor had Nancy received the settlement she hoped would provide her with financial independence, and she was now pressing harder to gain control of the funds that were designated for her in the future.

Against this background of patriarchal authority, of Nancy's desire for financial autonomy, of her elder brother's increasing influence within the family business, and of her own sense of being shut out from a meaningful role, it is not surprising that Nancy's first encounter with feminism had such a profound impact on her. During her time at York University, she became a member of the York SCM led by her friend Lynda Newmarch. In the summer of 1968 she travelled to Finland as part of York's SCM delegation to attend the World Student Christian Federation General Assembly.[117] She recalls the momentous occasion in an essay published in 2010:

> For the first time in my life, women hit the agenda. My feelings of isolation and unfocused anger began to disappear. My immersion into feminism filled me instead with excitement and passion.
>
> The 1960s were a time when protest movements, Nehru jackets, Mao caps, pot, the Age of Aquarius, and folk music flourished in North America. Lesbian singers like Meg Christian achieved acclaim. Liberation theology from South America was hot. And it was the male students from South America who dominated the World Student Christian Federation conference. But in the midst of these vociferous men there surfaced a group of American women who invited the other female participants to come and share their vision.
>
> I went by myself. I was curious.

The American women there had been part of the Black integration struggle, student revolutions on campuses, opposition to the Vietnam War, and the growth of alternative communities. They were resisting the domination of men in leadership. They protested the limited roles for women. These American women introduced me to feminist ideas and analysis. And feminism changed my life.

For the first time I felt included in a group that valued me. Feminism caused me to reinterpret history. I began to see how wrong the dominant ideologies and problem-solving techniques were. What I had been taught at university was imbued with patriarchal assumptions. What I had been taught in my family about women's roles was stifling. I wanted more.

In Turku I encountered feminism. I was empowered by it, and I became deeply committed to its vision.[118]

Once again Nancy underwent a dramatic awakening, this time to a secular vision that would end up derailing her plans for a life inside the church. Both awakenings held out to her the gift of acceptance, of being valued, first by God, and now by inclusion in a group of women whose worldview made sense of much that had perplexed and troubled her. At this moment, she tells us, not only her sense of isolation but also of "unfocused anger" began to disappear. One striking contrast between her experiences in Bali and in Turku is that the former left her with a feeling of "pure peace and joy," a state she found difficult to sustain outside Hindu culture and inside a culture of Western rationalism, while the latter stirred up an anger she was finally able to understand and channel.

That anger had been evident since her childhood, and it surfaced again as Nancy began to campaign against the dominant ideologies that surrounded her. A significant irony is that she first encountered feminism in a foreign country and not closer to home. She was, after all, the granddaughter of Newton Rowell, who successfully argued the 1929 Persons Case before the Judicial Committee of the British Privy Council, then the highest court of appeal for Canada. That case led to women being acknowledged as "persons" under Canadian law and thus eligible to serve in Canada's Senate. Yet Nancy was almost forty years old before she learned this piece of family history.

As she tells the story to a newspaper reporter in 1989, the truth came out when Nancy invited a retired United Churchwoman to lunch eight years earlier "to discuss the church's attitude toward women clergy. Partway through their discussion the woman—Bea Wilson—said to Jackman, 'You don't know who you are, do you?' and then told her about her grandfather's role in the famous Persons Case." The reporter went on to quote Nancy's account of this revelation: "I remember my rage that women were of so little consequence in my family that nobody had ever mentioned the Persons Case, that half the population makes Newton Rowell famous but it wasn't important enough in my family."[119] Bea Wilson's question, "You don't know who you are, do you?" resonated on several levels. Nancy's drive to "be something"—to find a vocation and a meaningful identity—consumed her throughout her young adulthood. She struggled during that period with the distinction between being "something" and being "somebody"—a Jackman, with the privileges of her family's wealth and social standing, yet a female Jackman shut out of her father's business empire. For her to learn—more

Portrait of Newton Wesley Rowell in the robes of the Treasurer of the Law Society of Upper Canada, 1935–1936.

than a decade after her meeting with feminists in Turku—that, unbeknownst to her, she was descended from a champion for women's rights in Canada was a shocking and painful discovery; her rage comes as no surprise.

The sisterhood Nancy connected with in Turku—a group of feminists who operated within the framework of the World Christian Student Federation—included the woman who would figure prominently in her future, both as lover and as cherished friend. Geertruida Maartje, (Trudy) van Asperen was Nancy's contemporary in age and held a master's degree in religious philosophy from the University of Utrecht. She was active in the Student Christian Movement and a few months after she and Nancy met, she was offered the position of International SCM Study Secretary to the Canadian SCM based in Toronto. Interestingly, forty years earlier Nancy's mother had been women's secretary at the University of Toronto SCM. Although Nancy did not begin her next diary until December 22, 1968, it is intriguing to find in Harry's diary for December 8 of that year the following entry: "Mary, Frederick [Eric], and I go to the Metropolitan Church. Nancy takes part in the discussion from the pulpit. The subject is her SCM conference in Finland. She was very good. She also sings very well with a sweet voice, and is making progress on her diet. She brings home a Dutch girlfriend for dinner."[120] The Dutch girlfriend was Trudy, who after her arrival in Toronto had stayed with Nancy until she could find an apartment of her own. Nancy recalls how Trudy enjoyed sparring intellectually with her father at the dinner table, reminding him that Karl Marx had said that the ruling classes had more in common with each other than with their own countrymen. Nancy "could hardly contain her laughter" at this "perfect shot" at her father—but Harry was not amused.[121]

When Nancy picks up her diary two weeks later, it is to make the brief entry: "Lite another advent candle in remembrance of Trudy." By now her new friend has become a major presence in her life. Yet, uncertain how their relationship would evolve, she laments her own inability to maintain an even keel: "I cannot let love go free—I cannot hold that quicksilver loosely in the palm of my hand—I clutch."[122] One night during that period, Nancy recalls that while she was having her hair dyed by a gay friend named David from the SCM and kept talking about Trudy, David

Trudy van Asperen in Berlin. Nancy Ruth met Trudy in Turku, Finland, in the summer of 1968 at the World Student Christian Federation General Assembly.

turned to her and said triumphantly, "Don't you understand what has happened? You have fallen in love with a woman. You are a lesbian!" She remembers being shocked by this revelation and spending many nights thinking about it.[123]

In the early months of 1969, Nancy's feelings oscillated wildly between hope that she had found her life mate and fear that Trudy, who had never before had a sexual relationship with a woman, would not fully return her love. In March she writes that she and Trudy were "taken as lesbians" at a gay friend's party, that she wishes they were, but that Trudy is "very threatened"; a couple of days later she confesses that she "really pushed Trudy on lesbianism."[124] By late April, she was convinced that she and Trudy were in love with each other, but in early May Trudy told Nancy that she had misinterpreted her expressions of affection and that "she didn't want to sleep with me."[125] At this point, they were in a motel north of Sudbury on the first night of their cross-Canada driving trip to Banff for an SCM conference; by the time they reach Banff they had become lovers.

Over the coming months Nancy recorded a deeply tender and erotic relationship between the two women and years later she affirmed that relationship as one of the most important in her life, adding that Trudy "was the person who made me know I was a lesbian."[126] Nevertheless, their future together was constrained by the social conventions of the time. The year in which they became lovers, 1969, saw the Stonewall riots in Greenwich Village, which many consider a turning point in the campaign for gay and lesbian rights in the United States. Yet Toronto's bathhouse raids, which also provoked mass protests on the part of LGBTQ activists and began to shift public support in their favour, did not happen until 1981, even though sex between men in private had been decriminalized through changes made to the Criminal Code by Pierre Trudeau's government in 1969. In the milieu of the late 1960s, whether in the US, Canada, or Europe, to be "out" was to face being shunned by mainstream society; in the religious Netherlands the situation was even worse than in Canada.

Nancy pressed Trudy for a commitment to their relationship, but both women were aware of the price that would be exacted if they lived openly as lovers. Trudy invited Nancy to stay with her when she returned to Europe to study for her PhD in theology, but on May 25 Nancy writes, "I tell her that for me to live w/ her in Europe is to enter into a marriage contract. She tells me that's too much to ask of her—she couldn't be in her field of work etc. & how would we live. I told her the economic question was irrelevant even if Dad disinherited me. T. defined her love for me as wanting to make me happy—but knowing that she couldn't.... We decided that neither one of us wanted to break the relationship & that we had to work on the parts of the relationship that were feasible. Oh—I so want to be loved and love in a lasting relationship."[127]

During the two weeks in June that they spent alone at the family cottage on Georgian Bay, they fantasized about the possibility of a life together but could only imagine it within a conventional framework: "We played games & dreams by saying 'If I was a man and you were my wife.' It was wonderful fun—but oh so sad too. I came to believe that Trudy really would marry me if I was a man & that she would ask me to marry her if she was a man."[128] Later that month, the day after Trudy has left for Berlin, where she lived for the next two years, Nancy writes to her friend Roger Perkins, who has become a confidante,

> Trudy left last night for London and Rotterdam. It was very sad, and after both of us trying not to cry all day, by going to the museum etc., we both cracked at the airport gate. I cried most of the night, and of course all the way home in the car. Why is it that two people who love each other cannot be near each other on a permanent basis? Trudy and I spent two blissful weeks at the cottage. Perhaps it was the closest thing I'll ever have to a honeymoon. And for Trudy it too was wonderful.[129]

Although Nancy grieved for what she was losing, she also confesses in the same letter, "I think in the end I realized that for myself, I too wanted to have children and a husband, and was not free enough to accept society's condemnation by living with Trudy."[130] Almost forty years later, in an article titled "The senator is out," *Herizons* magazine (fall 2008) celebrated Nancy—now Nancy Ruth—as Canada's first openly lesbian senator. Society's condemnation certainly lessened over that time, but Nancy's determination to live an authentic life also steadily strengthened during the intervening years.

With marriage to Trudy an unattainable dream, Nancy was faced yet again with the question of what she would do with her life. In May 1969, at the age of twenty-seven, she completed her BA in political science at York University, but she graduated with only a C+ grade average and her studies at York did not bring her the same satisfaction that those at Covenant had: "I hated [it]." Although Atkinson, Nancy's college at York, was focused on part-time studies and many of its students held down full-time jobs, Nancy remembers being "the oldest student and they were so young in so many ways."[131] At the same time, as she recalls, she took some comfort in not graduating with a B average because to her mind it meant that she "would never have to do graduate work" since her undergraduate record would not qualify her for admission to graduate school.[132]

A career within the church remained a possibility, but Nancy would need further training beyond her diploma from Covenant and her BA to attain a senior position. At one point she considered attending Union Theological Seminary in New York City as an "unclassified student" but that plan never materialized.[133] Trudy wrote to her—a letter that "upset me"—to advise her not to go on studying and Nancy quotes Trudy's words in her diary: "Since you say you're not a student & I think you're right—why go in that direction?"[134] Jewellery-making continued to hold a fascination and indeed seemed to be on par with a career in the church; she watched the film *The Agony and the Ecstasy* and wrote afterward, "Pope says to Michelangelo to get on w/ his work. And I. God I must too. Is it jewellery or Church work?"[135]

The unexpected answer to this question of "getting on with her work" was that she went to Jerusalem to live with SCM friend Donna Runnalls—in the future, Runnalls became the first female dean at McGill University, in the Faculty of Religious Studies—who was there doing research for her PhD thesis on Josephus. Nancy had alluded to a possible trip to Jerusalem a couple of times in her diary over the summer but was very concerned with Gwenyth's health after she was diagnosed with a malignancy. In mid-July, however, they received news that Gwenyth's cancer was "treatable & she has a life expectancy of 20 yrs," so this barrier to her plan was removed.[136] Harry Jackman, not surprisingly, despaired at his daughter's choice: "Nancy has elected, for no reason other than that she has a friend in Jerusalem, to go there and spend or waste a year in some form of Bible study, as to which she never expects to be an authority. Another year wasted, and at 27, when time is very precious."[137] On September 18 he writes, "Nancy gets off to Israel at 5:00 p.m. on a charter flight. One hopes that she is doing more than temporizing with life."[138] Whether she was temporizing or not, he continued to support her financially ("Daddy gave me my allowance until the end of January").[139]

"Temporizing" is a fair description of Nancy's motives at this stage. She records in her diary that she really has "no reason" for going to Jerusalem; at one point she even jokes that she is "going to Israel so I could go to Berlin."[140] On September 2 she writes in a letter to Trudy, "I can't tell you why I am going, nor can I answer your question of what do I hope to get out of it."[141] In part she saw the trip, which Trudy violently opposed—largely because it was only two years after the Six-Day War and she feared for Nancy's safety—as a way of "leaving Trudy" now that Trudy has left her.[142] She seems to be casting about for a grand gesture, a means of escape from the emptiness of her life after her passionate love affair and her lover's departure. It is not unlike her leap to Bali as an escape from secretarial school a few years earlier. The headiness of her success at Covenant College was behind her; her degree from York had turned out to be a disappointment; and she still had no serious career prospects. Trudy, by contrast, was now working on the PhD that would eventually lead to a successful career in academia, and Nancy felt the gap between their achievements acutely. She hoped to continue their relationship—in whatever form that might take—but did not want her life to be subservient to Trudy's.

After a round of good-byes to family and friends, including Gwenyth, Nancy flew to London where she was picked up at the airport by the Reverend Dr. Marie Isaacs, another friend she had met at the Turku conference. Like Gwenyth, Marie was a minister within the Baptist Church of England, the fourth woman to be ordained, in 1962; like Trudy, Marie became Nancy's lover, but only years later, after Trudy had married. While staying with Marie in Deptford, in the east end of London, Nancy spent time with Marie's friend Tim Curry, who was currently onstage in his first major role, acting in the West End production of *Hair*, and who later gained fame for his role as Dr. Frank-N-Furter in the *Rocky Horror Picture Show*. One evening she donned her "hippie clothes" and went to see *Hair*: "It was good fun and of course I loved dancing at the end. Had a drink later with Tim and then home."[143] She bought the new Beatles album *Abbey Road*—she and Trudy shared a love for the Beatles, citing their lyrics often in the letters they exchanged—and went shopping on the King's Road, visiting "hippie fashion houses. Quite fun, but I didn't buy anything, either because the clothes were too small or too expensive."[144] And after a week in London, she left for her much-anticipated reunion: "Was happy all the way to Berlin & then at customs I got flip-flops in my stomach."[145]

Nancy's anxiety was soon allayed when she and Trudy resumed their relationship as lovers. She stayed with her for two weeks, during which time they explored Berlin, went to Munich to visit Trudy's sister Marit, quarrelled, made up, made love, quarrelled again, and generally behaved like two people who care deeply for each other but cannot resolve the tensions between them.[146] On Nancy's final morning in Berlin, "T arrived to wake me w/ the white rose that has been growing for the last few days in the garden." A petal from that rose remains pressed in the pages of her diary fifty years later. Again, their parting was emotional—"We sat in [the] airport & cried together & said we loved one another & we do"—but Nancy was comforted by Trudy's promise to visit her in Jerusalem.[147]

On October 14, 1969, Nancy arrived in Israel for what would turn out to be a seven-month stay. Donna Runnalls met her at the Tel Aviv airport and took her to the apartment in Jerusalem they would share; Nancy's first reaction, recorded in her diary that night, is that "it's hard to believe it's Jerusalem. It's just another apt!—& rather unfinished in terms of paint etc."[148] The next morning, however, she set out with her usual zest for adventure to explore the old city: "Strange smells, women in Arab dresses, others veiled. Dark narrow streets. Money changers & store keepers always wanting to say hello, won't you come & see my store." One store she was particularly keen to visit was owned by a member of the influential Nashashibi family, a

Palestinian friend of Trudy's and Donna's from their time in Jerusalem in the mid-sixties with the World Student Christian Federation. When Nancy and Donna arrived at the shop, they learned that Mr. Nashashibi was currently in Amman, so they visited instead with his wife, sister-in-law, and four children, none of whom spoke English. Donna attempted to speak Arabic but was "frustrated by her inadequacies" while Nancy had "great fun waving my arms about & using sign language." She ends her diary entry that evening with the comment, "Miss you T—but life is exciting."[149]

Over the next few months Nancy registered to audit courses at both the Hebrew University of Jerusalem and Hebrew Union College—on subjects such as introduction to the Bible, Jewish history, and the Old Testament. None of the courses proved especially satisfying; she complains in a letter to Trudy that she has just been to Hebrew Union College to see if they were offering any Bible courses in English because "the introductory one at the university was such a bore that I walked out. There are about 200 people in it, mostly American freshman, and the professor spent the first hour trying to justify a critical literary approach to the Bible!" She goes on to say that "all the available courses at this time are terribly elementary (even for me) if they are being taught in English."[150] Deciding that she should try to learn Hebrew, she enrolled in an *ulpan*, a school for the intensive teaching of Hebrew, but soon decided she was "not serious enough" for the discipline of a foreign language.[151] Later she took a course in biblical geography at an evangelical college and found it "exciting beyond belief. It helped make sense of so many of the Bible stories."[152]

In a letter written to Maruja Jackman a little over a month after her arrival in Jerusalem, Nancy confesses, "I go to school half-heartedly—because I have nothing else to do that interests me at present." Over the past summer she had confided in her sister-in-law about her relationship with Trudy and she now told her how painful she was finding their separation. She was uncertain whether they would ever live together and knew that "I bloody well have to live my own life, and if that at the present means learning Hebrew to do graduate work in bible, then I'd better get on with it. But here I sit, doing little work…and knowing full well that if Trudy says 'come,' I'll go, no matter where it is!"[153] In her diary entry the night before this letter to Maruja was written, she makes the same admission of her inability to resist Trudy's influence, and yet she also castigates herself for being "stupid, as I need a definite 'mission' outside Trudy."[154]

While she was in Jerusalem, Nancy did look for other "missions" or occupations that could both provide a purpose in her life and offset her absorption with Trudy. She had not ruled out graduate work in theology and in early January she writes to her SCM friend Roger Perkins that "a friend who builds hotels in New York and Tel Aviv is convinced that I should leave 'religion' for a while, and take up business." Nevertheless, she adds that she has "made the foolish mistake" of applying to Union Theological Seminary, though she is "quite convinced that they won't accept me."[155] And even while thinking of a religious career, she worries in her diary that "I can't see myself in a congregation or working for the Church, I'm too involved emotionally w/ it."[156]

She seriously considered the advice to "take up business," writing to Trudy in January 1970 that "I have been thinking for some weeks now of going home and immediately getting a job either in brokerage or insurance.

Nancy Ruth wearing her Middle Eastern rings in Jerusalem in April, 1970.

Just yesterday in a letter I've put out a half-hearted feeler to Father and Hal."[157] That spring, just before leaving Jerusalem, she tells Trudy that she has written to Hal, "a serious letter" this time, "asking him to find me a job on the market or get me into one of the training programs come June first." Hal responded, however, that "because of the market decline etc. all sorts of people are being laid off & the big companies have cancelled their training programs." Further, Hal's letter "goes on at length that I should try another field of business—in which my family is not connected—in which I will be respected for my own merits."[158] There is considerable irony in Hal's advice, given that his own success—talent and hard work notwithstanding—was built within the family business and he benefited substantially from his family connections.

With a business career on her mind and a flagging interest in her studies, Nancy shifted course rather dramatically in early 1970. She had spent a great deal of time with Nashashibi in his Via Dolorosa store, sharing dreams over cups of coffee and games of shesh besh, and had grown very interested in his shop, where he sold Bedouin jewellery and clothing along with other merchandise. On January 26 she writes to Trudy, "So it was last Friday that I decided to work for Nash (voluntarily). The idea is that I will try and clean up the shop a bit, and perhaps give him a few ideas on how to sell…. I have introduced the idea of making key chains from all his odds and ends—which seemed to please him. Also suggested we get new paper for the shelves…. He is getting a welding machine in the back of his shop, and will make iron things, lamps etc. I am very glad of this, as he will at last be back in his 'art.'" Nancy notes that the members of her *ulpan* were sorry to see her go—"which was rather nice"—but she wanted to devote her remaining time in Jerusalem to what seemed to be a more productive enterprise. She even imagines partnering with Nashashibi in an export business: "Nash offered to send me lots of nice stuff if I was to open up an 'oriental' shop in good old T.O.…. I wrote a very nice letter to a cousin [Chris Barron] yesterday who is a partner in a small brokerage firm. I said nothing about wanting a job, but that I was about to try my hand at business here (if only he knew). This is just to keep my bridges built and well open." Her change in direction has clearly lifted her spirits; she tells Trudy that "today I am happy again after some weeks of the opposite in all its manifestations."[159]

Over the next few weeks, Nancy continued to assist Nashashibi in his shop and attend occasional lectures in the classes she was auditing; she also carried on her active social life, touring the region, going to discotheques and student clubs, travelling to Ramallah for oranges with John Landgraf, an American working on his PhD in archeology with whom she later hitchhiked through Turkey to Istanbul, and, along with Donna, hosting friends for dinner and card-playing. Increasingly, however, she was preoccupied with Trudy's pending visit—and with the question of whether Trudy would bring her friend Antoine with her when she came. Antoine was not yet a lover but was a precursor to other relationships Trudy would have before her marriage in 1973. Nancy understood that Trudy's right to have male lovers and ultimately to marry and have children was part of their tacitly agreed-to arrangement, but she nevertheless found the prospect difficult to accept. On February 13 she writes in her diary that she has "been getting excited about T. coming. Unfortunately, I put myself back into the position of wanting to 'serve' her. To live with her without a life of my own. This upset me—not just because it would be bad for me—but because I dream of impossibilities."[160] These "impossibilities" included the prospect of a partnership between equals, in which Nancy herself had the kind of successful career that Trudy was poised to attain. They also included Nancy's hopes for a lifetime together with Trudy, a dream she could not let die.

Trudy arrived in Jerusalem on March 7—without Antoine, to Nancy's delight. He joined them ten days later but stayed with other friends, not in Nancy's and Donna's apartment, so the threat he presented to their intimacy evaporated. Trudy shared Nancy's single bed; they were very quiet, never sure whether Donna realized the nature of their relationship and never confronting the matter: "Both T. & I wonder if Donna knows or is suspicious—but for a change, T. doesn't seem to care."[161] After a passionate reunion their first night together, Nancy was immensely reassured: "All my ideas about 'what next' were 'foiled' by T. taking the initiative. What a fool I am, not to have thought she might! So goes life. It's wonderful."[162] The next three-and-a half weeks were filled with long conversations, shared meals alone and with friends, visits to a *kibbutz* and to Greek and Roman Catholic churches, and a "fantastic" Hebrew University production of *Twelfth Night* where "Shakespeare truly came alive."[163] Their only serious quarrel arose after a night on the town when Nancy danced with a number of Israeli men—both to Beatles tunes and to traditional Greek music—in an "exhibitionist style" that angered Trudy.[164] Nancy is adamant in her diary that "I have no intention of stopping dancing & to do so only when T. is present is…is love? Her jealousy in such things is not good."[165] They talked through their differences, however, and their time together was happy for both of them.

Three days after Trudy and Antoine left Jerusalem, Trudy writes from Berlin that she is happy to be home again but sorry to be "without my best friend." She continues, "I find myself waking up at night, talking to my trunk…wondering why you are so far away and why you don't answer at all. Wish you were here." Further, she tells Nancy that she has "decided that I should make every effort to get the thesis finished as soon as possible, so that some decisions can be taken concerning our future as soon as possible."[166] Nancy is elated by this news, writing in her diary that "it was a lovely letter & kept me happy for hours."[167] She was now mentally preparing to leave Jerusalem and to stop off for a time with Trudy in Berlin before she returned home.

The opportunity to leave came when John Landgraf offered to travel to Europe with Nancy via Cyprus and Turkey. They set off from Tel Aviv to Haifa by train on May 12, then took a boat from Haifa and landed in Cyprus the following day. Nancy maintained a detailed chronicle of their trip over the next three weeks as they hitchhiked around Cyprus for several days, went by boat to Rhodes and on to Turkey, then hitchhiked across western Turkey stopping in Ephesus, Aphrodisias, Priene, Miletus, Pergamon, Troy, and Istanbul. They often slept "rough" in farmer's fields but at times found rooms with village locals. The trip was rich with visits to archeological sites, which were of great interest to them both, and with the human adventures that come with such travel—in Aphrodisias, for example, Nancy writes, "So far the people…have been magnificent. Not a truck driver who has us for a long time hasn't bought us tea or their yogurt drink."[168]

Nancy and John parted ways on June 4 in Istanbul, where she arranged to ride the rest of the way to Germany in a minivan with an Australian couple. When she next wrote in her diary on July 3, Nancy was preparing to leave Berlin after a three-week stay with Trudy in the basement of the Netherlands consulate where Trudy was renting an apartment. The two of them went to the beach and horseback riding in the Berlin forest, did "some smuggling into east Berlin," and rode "little bicycles up the Kurfurstendamm." Nancy describes their visit as "successful" but perhaps "a little too long."[169] She pressed Trudy for assurances that they would find a way to live together, which Trudy gave her, yet Nancy found herself asking for "constant confirmation."[170] Trudy encouraged her to sleep with men, as she herself planned to do. There was still much to be resolved about their future life together but for the time being, Nancy had to consider once again what kind of job or further training to undertake. In the first letter Trudy writes after Nancy's departure, she tells her friend, "Having you here was very good. I feel we made some progress, which is good. I am still concerned, though, that you should find some kind of work which is fulfilling for you."[171]

Harry Jackman's entry in his diary for July 13 echoes Trudy's observation: "Nancy arrived home from Jerusalem after nearly a year's absence. She is looking fine; her weight is about the same. Unfortunately she is no further ahead than a year ago as far as career is concerned. She will be unhappy unless she embarks on something useful."[172] Everyone agrees on her problem, but no one, least of all Nancy, has a ready solution. Ironically, it seems that her father has begun to take seriously the prospect of a future in business and finance for his daughter just as she has swung away from the idea. She writes to Trudy on July 25 that "When Dad and Mom were down in the States last weekend, Mom said Dad was telling everyone that I was going into a financial career, so when I mentioned jewellery the other night—there was a long pause, and comment—don't do anything further without speaking with me! What a guy."[173]

A career as a jewellery designer and maker had indeed begun to figure prominently in Nancy's plans. It represented, as she saw it, "a trade that I didn't need to speak a [foreign] language with," a way for her to combine work with travel to foreign lands.[174] As a jeweller, she could work in Holland while living with Trudy, now her uppermost goal. Despite her father's injunction, by September she had enrolled in a jewellery arts course at George Brown College in Toronto. Her letters to Trudy over the coming months are full of anecdotes about the course. At the end of her first week, for example, she writes, "Can you believe it's taken me from 8 a.m.–4 p.m. for 4 ½ days to cut a square, triangle and hexagon 3mm wide by 40 mm long! Fantastic eh! Well it's coming, but I had to redo my square this morning as I filed too low on the center edges. I keep remembering you on discipline…! It's quite fun though, and I am enjoying it—so far. Patience Nancy. One push of the file too hard, and you've got 4 hours of work to repeat."[175] She not only enjoyed doing things with her hands, but her love of beautiful jewellery had blossomed over the years and she now seemed to have a pathway to a useful occupation that would give her professional fulfillment.

In addition to her jewellery work, Nancy actively engaged once again with the SCM and even joined a group who went to Montreal to attend the annual shareholders' meeting of the Canadian mining company Alcan to protest their building of a dam in Mozambique.[176] She also spent time with Gwenyth and signed up for one of her Ecumenical Institute Bible study classes.[177] Rather than live

Nancy Ruth and Trudy van Asperen in
Saintes-Maries-de-la-Mer, France, circa 1970.

with her parents, she boarded with Hal, Maruja, and their children in their house on Crescent Road in Rosedale, sending affectionate stories to Trudy of her young niece, Victoria, and her nephews Henry and Duncan: "Duncan has just come up, and asked if I will still take him to Holland or Chocolate Land with me sometime. Yes I will, but am having difficulty explaining that the buildings etc. aren't made out of chocolate."[178] Not only did Maruja remain a trusted confidante, but Nancy got on well with Hal for most of the year, although the family tension over money was building once again. Eric resented Hal's predominance in the family business and felt that he was being taken advantage of. Harry was determined to protect the financial holdings he had built up over a lifetime but was under increasing pressure from Eric and Nancy to "cash out" and distribute to them what they believed was their fair share of the family wealth, their quarter interest in King Vaughan Farms. Nancy describes to Trudy a family "board meeting" where the foundation auditor, "as soon as he saw the family problems coming out made the most preposterous excuse to leave the board room!" Nancy goes on to say, "No one knows what Eric will do now. Hal doesn't want to write him anything, because it might be used against him in court. Father is King Lear-ing again, and Mother keeps saying, 'but it's not your money.' What a joy to be home again."[179]

If the current family drama was less than joyful, it was offset by the pleasure Nancy found in her jewellery course. Although the course lasted almost a full year, she stayed with it more faithfully than with any project she had undertaken since her theology studies. Early on, however, she recognized a weakness: "Oh Trud, the designing is going to be so difficult. We were asked to design something for a 40 mm brass sq. I sat for 4 hours with pencil in hand and couldn't produce anything. Even going to design books didn't help all that much."[180] This sense of inadequacy continued to plague her as she pursued her new craft; nevertheless, she did well in the program and completed many of her classes with distinction. She came first, for example, in her gemology exam and passed the course with an overall 79 per cent average: "that's an 'A' around George Brown."[181] Further, she took pride in the fact that she had earned her father's respect for the work she was producing. He writes in his diary, "At her jewellery class she made a fine little round brass box with a tightly fitting lid—very good craftsmanship" and "I visit Nancy's class exhibit of jewellery at the O'Keefe Centre. She has two exhibits, which were good."[182] Nancy recalls that the two exhibits her father admired were "an arched and hammered silver disc with a bezel of aventurine, held up by a round dark green velvet cord through silver findings" for her mother and "clip-on earrings set with a sparkly black stone" for Gwenyth Hubble.[183]

The academic year at George Brown was punctuated by two visits with Trudy—a skiing trip together in Switzerland at Christmas and, in March 1971, a trip to Utrecht, where Trudy had moved to take up a job teaching philosophy at the University of Utrecht while she continued to write her doctoral thesis. Their plans to live together in Holland were taking shape and Nancy enrolled in Dutch classes—with great enthusiasm but with the same limited success she had with other attempts to learn a new language: "I am very stupid in this language of yours."[184] By late winter 1971, they had found a house to buy together in Utrecht, at 22 Donkerstraat, and begun to exchange excited letters about renovations and furnishings.[185]

Their plans were almost derailed, however, when Trudy wrote that she was involved again with Albert van den Heuvel, a married man and a prominent figure in the World Council of Churches with whom she'd had a previous affair. She and Albert "want to try to see each other again as soon as possible. I don't know when that will be nor do I know what the content of a possible 'arrangement' might be. It may not be anything more than that: trying to be together as often as possible." Trudy goes on to say to Nancy, "I'm writing because I am not sure what it would mean in terms of us being together…. At Christmas you said that you did not want to disavow what had been so important to me for over six years now. Still, it would be different if you had to live with it, rather than knowing it as something that happened in the past…. Love, I don't know what to say. Would you want to come and see how things work out, say till Xmas? I cannot decide for you…. Forgive me for all the pain. Please, don't cry or do anything rashly. Try and understand that it hasn't changed my feelings for you."[186]

Nancy replied to this news within a couple of hours of receiving it, and with a fair measure of equanimity. When Trudy confided to her about Albert during their skiing trip, she had understood that the relationship was an important one and in her letter reminds Trudy that at the time "I wanted to do everything in my power to get you and Albert together—so why should I have changed my mind?" Further, she assures Trudy that "I love you just the way you are—with all your complexities, with your ability to sustain your love for Albert and still care for others. I love you because you are honest with me, and because you seek my well being as well as your own. Hey, I just love you because you are my friend." The decision she quickly reached was that "I'd like to take you up on your offer till Christmas.... I would like to come, not because there are no viable alternatives for me here, but because it's someone for you to talk to or cry with when you want—or to yell and scream to too. I would like to come because things haven't really changed that much, that is, expectancy is becoming a fulfilment. What confidence I can give you re my 'having to live with it' we'll just have to wait and see."[187] In light of her passion for Trudy, the support she envisioned offering would be a supreme test of her powers of friendship.

Nancy wrote very little in her diary the year that she was back in Toronto, likely because she kept up a voluminous correspondence with Trudy and retained copies of all her own letters. One of her few entries is that of June 26, 1971, just ten days before she leaves for Europe, where she confesses to being "increasingly anxious about seeing T," adding that "I am going, thinking of returning after Xmas.... I have cold feet—even though I think I am no longer in love. Yet—the Albert letter made me cry with some despair. Do I no longer need her at all? I am frightened—very frightened."[188] Her confusion and ambivalence are understandable, given the investment she had made in the relationship over the past two years and the uncertainty of its outcome.

Nancy did in fact live with Trudy in Holland for a full year. Before her arrival, Trudy was able to arrange a placement for her at Kootje Kennemans, a jeweller in Amsterdam, where she commuted each day in her blue Peugeot to work in their cellar, making cufflinks, wedding bands, and amethyst drop earrings for Trudy.[189] She remembers the year as "exciting and at times painful." She and Trudy rode horses in the forest as they had in Berlin, went on bicycle rides along the canal, drank delicious sweet coffee with gingerbread, took trips to the south of France, and made visits to van Kranendonk Duffels jewellers to start what became Nancy's exceptional collection of art deco jewellery.[190] Yet Albert's visits were difficult for her and for Trudy; each time he came Nancy had to arrange to stay with friends and Trudy was often upset by his behaviour. On November 10, 1971, Nancy writes in her diary, "Evidently he can't or won't divorce his wife. Poor T., she loves him so much." In the end, Nancy recounts, "We broke up because I couldn't bear the pain of Trudy sleeping with men like Albert."[191] Neither could she envision a future career for herself as a jeweller because she continued to feel inadequate as a designer and "wasn't going to make cufflinks for the rest of my life."[192]

Nevertheless, Nancy embraced much of her year in Holland. Writing of the time years later she says that Trudy was "the love of my life, a soul mate.... It was a relationship of much hope. Her family welcomed me etc., her mother knitted me sweaters, her sister has remained a lifelong friend." And, as has been the case since her adolescence, she found it "fun to be part of another culture," adding that "Trudy included me in everything, with all her friends from the university too." She helped edit Trudy's PhD thesis on Marxist philosopher Ernst Bloch, written in English and completed in 1973—"Hope and history: A critical inquiry into the philosophy of Ernst Bloch." She was also the matchmaker who brought Trudy together with the man she would eventually marry. Lucas Reijnders, considered to be the Ralph Nader of Holland, had dedicated a book to Trudy without ever having met her, on the strength of his admiration for her published works. When Nancy organized a birthday picnic, complete with hotdogs, on the beaches of The Hague, she included Lucas on the invitation list. A year after Nancy returned to Canada, Lucas and Trudy were married and at her wedding, Trudy wore one of the jade art deco necklaces that Nancy had given her.[193]

The extraordinary friendship between these two women endured until Trudy's death from breast cancer in 1993. In the summer of 1972, however, Nancy brought an end to her dream of a life together with her soulmate. Her thoughts were already turning back to her friends and family in Toronto when she received the news that her mentor and beloved friend was dying—Gwenyth Hubble's cancer had returned and was deemed to be terminal. Nancy flew home to be with her and was at her bedside at the Wellesley Hospital when she died on August 17, 1972.[194] She mourned and honoured Gwenyth, and started to think again about a life in the church.

Footnotes for this chapter can be found online at:
http://secondstorypress.ca/resources

Chapter 4

SEARCHING FOR MINISTRY

When I went to theological college in the sixties, church history included a lot of things, but not how we women have ministered throughout the history of the church.[1]

WITHIN HOURS of receiving a phone call from Gwenyth's friend Laura Pelton, Nancy was on a flight home—carrying the painful knowledge that she would not return to Holland and her life there with Trudy. She went straight to Wellesley Hospital from the airport and was with Gwenyth when she died early the next morning. Exhausted from travel and grief, she slept through the moment of her cherished mentor's death, leaving her feeling "like one of those disciples who couldn't stay awake."[2] But as she walked home that morning along Rosedale Road, she broke into song, celebrating Gwenyth's life through the words of Cat Stevens' "Morning Has Broken."[3]

Gwenyth knew that Nancy had come home to be with her and she may have remembered with gratitude all the times her young friend had taken her to the hospital for radiation treatments during the summer of 1969, when she was first diagnosed with cancer. Dr. Harriet Christie, speaking at a memorial service in Toronto later that fall, recalled her own final visit to Gwenyth in the hospital, when Gwenyth said to her,

> You know, I have been thinking that now my life is over and all I can do has been done, I will spend the remainder of my time in contemplating God. There isn't anything more I can do about the past, and I look with gratitude and joy to the future. Therefore, I thought I would let my mind dwell on God. But you know I found I couldn't think about God without thinking about people. Every time I tried to think about God and my relationship to persons and friends, I found I couldn't hold them apart.[4]

Nancy had been important among those friends, steadfast in her devotion to this trailblazing female minister, and would surely have been in Gwenyth's mind and heart in those final days of her life.

In the days and years to come, with Gwenyth as an exemplar, Nancy continued her search for a vocation within Christian ministry. Gwenyth herself faced opposition to her ordination in the 1930s—a speaker at her London memorial service remarked that the "Baptist establishment of the day hesitated and temporised about admitting her to the ministerial list"[5]—but her ordination and successful career in the church held out promise for the younger woman. One of Gwenyth's successes, achieved after she retired to Toronto, was the program of Bible study classes that she organized and taught through the Ecumenical Institute of Canada. During the time that she led those classes, from spring 1966 until a few months before her death, nearly

1,500 people, most of them women, registered for the weekly morning sessions, including "ministers' wives, Salvation Army officers, Roman Catholic nuns, deaconesses, furlough missionaries, married women young and old—a remarkably representative cross-section religiously and socially."[6]

Kay Hockin, then staff associate of the Ecumenical Institute, wrote in a bulletin that

> Miss Hubble's death in the summer of 1972 left her many friends not only with a sense of loss, but particularly for those who had found new dimensions to life and its meaning through the Bible studies, with a deep desire to continue the activity which she had initiated. The staff of the Ecumenical Institute picked up administrative chores and leaders were found to continue the courses which were to have been carried by Gwenyth herself.[7]

Hockin went on to note that Nancy Jackman was one of those leaders taking on, with Sister Annette Mattle, the course in Galatians that Gwenyth had been scheduled to teach.

Back in Toronto and engaged in teaching a Bible study class, where she felt a "drive to do good work for Gwenyth," Nancy decided to enroll in further biblical studies to update her knowledge.[8] With her BA from York University in hand she now qualified for admission to Emmanuel College, The United Church of Canada's theological college affiliated with Victoria University at the University of Toronto. Her coursework at Emmanuel could have led to a master of divinity degree had it not disappointed her with its lack of connection to her personal and spiritual interests: "In Emmanuel I was introduced to German Rationalism, Barth, Tillich—all that stuff." But she felt that these subjects had nothing to do with the spirit; "with the spirituality under which I had received my conversion [in Bali] and my understanding of God. I thought I was in wacko land."[9] She also found systematic theology—an approach to the Bible that organizes all its teachings into categories by topic—completely "irrelevant" to her interests. Further, in the curriculum she studied there was "no feminism," a major omission given her growing interest in examining religion through a feminist lens. Although she "liked the history and bible courses," she "hated the systematics," reporting with some disgust that in her systematics course she only opened Karl Barth's *Dogmatics in Outline* for the first time the night before her end-of-term examination; even though she found "it was tedious," she managed to "ace" the exam.[10]

By early 1973, unhappy with her experience at Emmanuel College, Nancy began to look again for a meaningful occupation. She was back living with her parents at 35 Rosedale Road, in a self-contained apartment recently created for her on the second floor of their home in what had been the "boys'" wing. Her father records in his diary on February 3, 1973,

> Nancy for lunch. She is worried about a job. When she applies at age 31, people can never understand that she has never worked at a steady, paying job before. The fact that she is "rich" sometimes means that a needier person gets the position. She is full of energy and ability, but has no direction, as I told her some years ago. We must get her experience and a useful place in life.[11]

That "useful place" showed up within just a few months, when the United Church advertised a position at its Naramata Centre for lay training in the Okanagan Valley in British Columbia. The centre was looking for someone to lead a new fundraising campaign, and when the CEO came to Toronto on a business trip he arranged to interview Nancy over his lunch hour. As she recalls the occasion, "Ivan Cumming was interested in meeting me for the job. I picked him up at Church House, 85 St. Clair East, and took him back to my apartment for a fish lunch." Ivan was impressed at her initiative and her decision to take him home to a lunch that she had spent effort preparing. "Anyhow, we got on, Ivan was charismatic and I liked him."[12] Ivan liked the high-spirited Nancy in return and offered her the job—which would be the first paid position she had ever held. She accepted his offer with no hesitation; it was her chance at last to establish her professional worth.

On August 2, 1973, Harry Jackman records in his diary, "Nancy left for Naramata and her new job with the United Church. She feels the challenge and responsibility of her first important job. She bids farewell with tears in her eyes.... She has very little proven record, not much persistency, but a strong, enthusiastic personality."[13] Harry goes on to say that "She must have lost 40 pounds, and looks very beautiful." His remark was one of many in the diaries that referred to Nancy's weight, and, as mentioned, her psychotherapy sessions in London were intended in part to help her deal with her "obesity." She had struggled and continued to struggle throughout her life with social expectations of female beauty defined by body size, with the seeds for this conflict planted in early childhood.

For now, a newly slim Nancy was off to take up work for which she had great zeal but little experience or training in a setting far from her home base of Toronto, moving across the Rockies to what seemed to her another country; "like the end of the world."[14] Opened in 1947 by the United Church as the Christian Leadership Training School and soon named after the town near where it was sited, the Naramata Centre covered twenty-three acres on the eastern shores of Lake Okanagan. It was a bucolic retreat where lay people and clergy could go to be trained as leaders, pursuing professional growth and spiritual renewal. During Nancy's time there the centre was also engaged in meeting a diverse array of local human service needs, offering, for example, counselling courses for community social workers and a training program for foster parents. It further served as a halfway house for a nearby psychiatric ward as well as hosting music workshops, family camping, and Christian education programs. Writing to friends in South Africa, Nancy enthusiastically described this range of programming and commented, "One of the exciting things about being at a place like Naramata is that it doesn't have just one direction but in fact several directions…we're into a million things and there's probably a million things I haven't mentioned."[15] For Nancy, the centre was both a haven and a proving ground. Many years later she would look back and recount with gratitude that her three years at Naramata "changed my life."[16]

Her new boss, on the other hand, may have wondered at times what he had signed on for. Within a day of her arrival, when asked what she wanted to do first, Nancy said she wanted to buy a car. As she tells the story, she had been to see Ryan and Tatum O'Neal in *Paper Moon* the night before she left Toronto and loved the film, with its "flogging of bibles to widows and saving up to buy a thing that spun on the hood of his car." Rex, the centre's financial administrator, drove her into the nearby town of Penticton, where they visited Ford and Chevy dealers, "but the image of O'Neal's car with the thing whizzing around just wouldn't leave my mind." So, she shyly asked Rex if there was a Mercedes dealership and he promptly took her there: "I had transferred every cent I had, $8,000, to the Royal Bank in Penticton. The Mercedes dealer had a second-hand white diesel 240C, with red leather seats, $6,000. I couldn't resist. I blew my wad on it." Her purchase completed, she drove her new car off the lot and straight back to the main building at the centre, where she parked in full view of the dining room. "Everyone was there having lunch, and my boss, Ivan, said, omg, look what she bought. I think it blew everyone's mind."[17]

Nancy's impulsiveness and trademark flamboyance are on full display in this story, yet Ivan was a match for her. She recalls that the first time he asked her to go to a 10 a.m. meeting in Vancouver she assumed that she would fly but he soon set her straight: she would get up at 4 a.m. and drive the six hours there. "I realized this was the way things were done. That took some of the smartass Toronto stuff out of me."[18] Most importantly, Ivan introduced her to group dynamics and team decision-making and cultivated her sense of self-worth. Even though it "was difficult to always catch the new balls that Ivan kept throwing in the air...my leadership skills were developed here more than anywhere else in my life."[19] As she relates her Naramata years in an interview with Iris Nowell,

This was my introduction to the whole field of human relations...and through this discipline I worked and lived in an environment that valued people. If you were doing something difficult and a staff member gave you clear and succinct evaluations, you learnt and grew. There was the assumption that you could always grow…. It made me a deeper, richer, better person.[20]

Elaine Peacock, Nancy's only female colleague on the Naramata staff, recalls that when her fundraising duties allowed time for it, Nancy joined in as part of the program design and delivery team. The centre's winter session, for example, brought young people aged eighteen to thirty to the centre to live and learn in community and to pursue topics of interest to them. One year, at the request of a group who wanted to study third-world development, Nancy created a simulation game drawing on her Bali experience. She set her simulation on the impoverished tropical island of "Narabanana," and participants were asked to do research and explore what actions they might take to improve economic and social conditions on the island. According to Elaine, the participants "learned reams" and "it was great for them," while it was a chance for Nancy to do "something that she would not have been able to do before she came to Naramata."[21] Ivan also encouraged the Naramata staff to enroll in a part-time MA in applied behavioural science at Whitworth College (now Whitworth University), a private Christian college in Spokane, Washington. They commuted for four-day weekends and a week in the summer, and Nancy went on to complete her MA in 1977, thriving in the context of applied and hands-on learning.

The Naramata years were a time of challenge and growth for Nancy. She had little training for what she was called on to accomplish as a fundraiser, but she embraced her assignment with the "energy and ability" that her father admired in his daughter. Though inexperienced herself,

Nancy Ruth's home in
Naramata, BC, 1973–1979.

Nancy Ruth with her one-and-only Mercedes-Benz
diesel car with red leather seats, Penticton, BC,
August, 1973.

Nancy was able to call on her father for expert guidance since he was himself a veteran fundraiser for many of his own charitable causes. Harry's diaries over the next year chart his earnest efforts to support his daughter's success. Before the end of August he sent her a half-hour tape recording as well as a seven-page letter outlining his advice about how she should proceed with her work. At the same time, he fretted about whether she had been handed an impossible assignment: "I spent most of the morning studying the Naramata literature in an endeavour to understand Nancy's job and responsibility. I fear she may have taken on something for which she has no adequate experience—a $1,250,000 capital building fund-drive."[22]

In September Harry flew to Penticton where Nancy, resplendent in her Mercedes-Benz, met him at the airport and took him to the house she was then renting from the centre, although she later paid fifty-five thousand dollars for her own house on a point of land in Lake Okanagan. He happily shopped with her in Penticton for household items, pruned her willow trees, and, by the time he left, had "made notes for her in a special notebook, outlining an organization for her campaign."[23] Advice, of course, wasn't all that Harry had to offer; later that same month he notes that the Jackman Foundation had made a gift to the campaign of five thousand dollars for a room to be named after his mother, Sarah Ann Rutherford.[24]

With her fundraising campaign launched and her confidence growing, Nancy decided to spread her wings even further. In the spring of 1974, she applied to the British Columbia Conference of the United Church for admission to the diaconal order. Through a series of blunders, the Conference turned down her application at the last minute, too late for her to warn her mother who had flown out to BC for the installation service. Mary Jackman was understandably "heart-broken," as were Nancy's friends at Naramata. Only later did Nancy learn that "I was not accepted as 'they' thought I wouldn't obey the courts of the church" because "I was wealthy and could walk out anytime. Such discrimination."[25] This fear of Nancy's independence was reprised years later when she sought political office and evoked concerns about whether she would be able to bring herself to submit to "party discipline."

The national protest mounted by Nancy's supporters ensured that her application was approved the following year. On May 4, 1975, she was "commissioned to the office and work of Deaconess" in Victoria, BC.[26] Her mother was once again present, this time for a service that emphasized feminist liturgy and language, largely in response to Nancy's influence. For Nancy, however, the celebration was tainted by her bitterness at the injustice done to her the preceding year: "By that time I didn't care much."[27] Nonetheless, she remained in the order for a few more years until further administrative missteps by the church in the early 1980s finally led to her resignation, though not yet to the end of her search for a vocation within the church.

Nancy's work for the Naramata Centre took her to rural and city churches in both Alberta and British Columbia, where she visited congregations to ask for their support for the capital campaign. On one such occasion she described the centre's important work and its need for more classrooms, renovated bedrooms, and expanded space for family camping. In her appeal for donations she told the congregation,

I was attracted to come to the Okanagan and work at Naramata Centre because it is a place where you are accepted, not only by your staff members but where it is clear that you are accepted by that which is greater than yourself.... For many who come to Naramata Centre, whether they are children or senior citizens or somewhere in between, the high ethical ideal of the scripture, "To love thy neighbour as thyself," is out of the range of possibility until they turn again toward God.... Naramata Centre is an institution that cares about God's mission, about God's grace, about God's love.[28]

Despite Nancy's passion for the centre's work, meeting her campaign goals continued to be a challenge. Her father worried that she did not have the traditional resources of a capital campaign—in particular connections to wealthy people in Alberta and British Columbia—that were needed to ensure her success. On a trip to Vancouver, he took her to meet Larry MacKenzie, a former senator and former president of the University of British Columbia, to ask for advice, but confessed that "Larry cannot offer many constructive suggestions re Naramata Centre fundraising. He and I are too old to know the present generation of rising, energetic young businessmen. Mary and I are both concerned about how worthwhile is Nancy's present fundraising job unless it is backed by a very strong committee, which is presently not the case."[29]

Nancy stuck to her project for three years, raising some but not all the required funds. Along the way, Elaine Peacock recounts, she sometimes discovered other needs that the centre should be addressing and took the initiative to raise money for those needs. In one instance, she was approached by families who had children with disabilities

Lois Campbell, Marie Isaacs, and Elaine
Peacock at Nancy Ruth's home in
Naramata, BC, 1974–1975.

and felt limited in their ability to participate in Naramata's programs. In response, according to Elaine, "Nancy raised funds and persuaded the centre, and they established a summer staff position which was precisely someone hired to work in the morning hours with children with disabilities on a one-on-one basis. It was a marvelous thing.... It didn't actually raise money that went into the general funds of the Centre, but it raised money to help with that significant program need."[30]

Nancy also helped shape training programs at Naramata, seeking, for example, to "stimulate feminist thinking" by connecting with the National Action Committee on the Status of Women and by bringing in a Women's Kit from the Ontario Institute for Studies in Education. Among the books she placed in the Naramata Resource Centre were Rosemary Ruether's *Liberation Theology* and *Religion and Sexism: Images of Women in the Jewish and Christian Traditions*; Jill Johnston's *Lesbian Nation: The Feminist Solution*; and Alice Hageman's *Sexist Religion and Women in the Church*.[31] Her awareness of sexism within the established church was by now highly attuned and was matched by the energy she applied to agitating for change. Throughout her future work, one of her strongest traits has been creating change by linking people with people and with ideas.

During her years at Naramata Nancy began her second serious love affair, this time with an ordained clergywoman. In September 1974, the Reverend Dr. Marie Isaacs, whom Nancy had first met at the 1968 WSCF conference in Finland, flew over from England for a visit. Like Gwenyth Hubble, Marie was a minister in the Baptist Union of Great Britain, the next woman—with a gap of twenty-three years—to be ordained following Gwenyth herself. During

Marie's visit, the two friends camped in a tent in the Rockies and became lovers, a four-year relationship that Nancy calls "a mistake from the beginning."[32] The extensive correspondence between the two women over those four years shows a greater intensity of affection on Marie's part than on Nancy's, with Nancy warning Marie early on that "I cannot commit myself to you in the manner you seem able to commit to me."[33] Nevertheless, this relationship ultimately took her back to London in 1977 to live with Marie for a time and find work within the Anglican Church.

In the summer of 1976, Nancy's contract with Naramata was not renewed: "I think Ivan Cumming got tired of me. And probably I wasn't bringing in enough money. I saw it as being fired."[34] She chose to stay on in her house there for a few months and then to rent the house out when she took up residence in Spokane and completed her MA. She recalls that her then seventy-three-year-old mother was a "great sport" when Mary came to visit her daughter at her student digs in Spokane. Nancy was sleeping on the floor on a foam mattress and using garden chairs and a card table for furniture. Mary stayed with Nancy and they "enjoyed tooling around in the Mercedes to various hippy type events as well as to the university gallery."[35] After her graduation from Whitworth College in May 1977, Nancy soon left to join Marie in London, leaving her friend and colleague Lois Campbell in charge of her stock ledgers and house rental.[36] Harry writes in his diary on June 27, "Nancy leaves for six months in England, hopefully to get a job. She is very emotional about leaving her parents and…has a hard time holding back tears."[37]

Nancy was indeed able to land work in London, though for the most part on a volunteer basis. She was engaged by the Archbishops' Council on Evangelism (set up by the Anglican Archbishops of Canterbury and York) to be a member of a team of assessors responsible for studying a congregation in York—St. Michael le Belfrey—that had grown remarkably in a few short years from a handful of parishioners to a congregation of over eight hundred. According to a letter of reference written by the council's executive secretary,

> her contribution was absolutely critical to the whole operation. Her background experience in group awareness and management styles enabled the whole team to focus quickly on those areas of that large and lively work in York where unappreciated tensions were involved. Since our work was at once analytical and enabling (and, incidentally, since one of the pressure areas had to do with the ministry of women in a local church), what Nancy had to give was more than relevant. Her own easy style with people, her ability to give of her best in a mixed team, her obvious enjoyment of the task despite its involving all sorts of new and partly uncongenial angles, all added up to our feeling a big debt to her for her willingness to assist.[38]

This consulting work allowed Nancy to apply her recently acquired organizational development skills as well as her keen interest in feminist critique, both areas of expertise she continued to hone over the coming years.

Nevertheless, London held no attraction for her as a permanent place of residence. She had fled its damp cold and smog fifteen years earlier and was no more enamoured of living in the city than she had been as a young woman. She soon used her connection with Donna Runnalls, her former roommate in Jerusalem who was now dean of religious studies at McGill University in Montreal, to help secure a visiting New Testament lectureship for Marie at McGill, and the two of them went off to Montreal for the winter term of 1978. Not content to be idle, Nancy sought employment for herself and was able to secure a short-term contract as an organizational development consultant with Dominion-Douglas United Church. Once more she earned positive reviews from her employer, who cited her "remarkable ability in dealing with people of diverse experience and interests," her strengths as a "doer," and her high level of enthusiasm and energy.[39]

Within a few weeks of the couple's arrival in Montreal, however, Nancy learned that Marie was becoming involved with another woman, a young graduate student. Even though Nancy had never felt the depth of passion for Marie that she had experienced with Trudy, she didn't see the breakup coming, having assumed that the two of them would continue to work on their relationship and find a way to stay together. When term ended in April, Marie went off to Egypt with her new lover and Nancy returned to London, uncertain of her future there. The flat at 44 Great Percy Street near King's Cross, which she had bought for Marie, was lonely; she found herself depressed and thinking about suicide. She walked for hours through the city parks and along the Thames, at a loss as to what she should do, until a chance encounter with a woman in a wheelchair—gaily sporting a balloon—shook her out of her self-pity: "I thought, fuck this, this woman can cope, so can I, and started packing for Canada."[40] She was heading back to a life in Toronto that would see her start her own consulting firm, come into her financial inheritance, join forces with Toronto leaders of the Canadian feminist movement to bring about significant political and social change, run for political office, begin her campaign for feminist philanthropy, and ultimately receive an appointment to the Senate of Canada. Her flash of awareness as she walked beside the Thames—*this woman can cope and so can I*—held more truth than she could possibly have dreamed.

Nancy's return home in the summer of 1978 included a detour to British Columbia to attend a United Church conference and visit with Naramata friends, but by September she was back in Toronto for a seminar led by Jack Gibb, a renowned pioneer in humanistic psychology and the "grandfather" of organizational development. By October she had bought her first Rosedale house, at 22 McKenzie Avenue. She had not yet given up on finding her vocation in some form of church ministry and over that summer applied unsuccessfully for the position of national field worker with the ecumenical Inter-Church Committee for World Development Education.[41] But the church's reluctance to admit women to positions of leadership—indeed, the silence in official church history about women's long tradition of ministry—and the embedded sexism within Christian teaching and practices were a growing source of discontent.

At this stage in her journey, however, Nancy remained attached to her personal experience of Christianity and was not ready to give up on her search for a community of faith. Despite the contradictions between her feminist convictions and the patriarchal structures of organized religion, she fought to create a church in which she felt at home. Such a church might make space for the irreverent or the outrageous; Nancy not only trained as a clown but "introduced clown ministry to Toronto in 1978," sometimes riding the subway in a clown costume and occasionally conducting a "clown service" at area churches.[42] After one such service at Willis United Church in Drumbo, Ontario, the minister wrote to praise her for helping his congregation "look at their worship ministry to each other in a fresh way."[43] It was just the kind of difference she still dreamed of making in the church.

When Nancy moved permanently to Toronto in 1978, she rejoined the congregation of Metropolitan United Church and in the mid-1980s she took on a role there as interim associate minister. By then, she had tried her hand at other professions, most notably as an organizational development consultant, and she had begun her crusading work to embed women's rights into Canada's legal system. The Christian church, however, retained its hold on her for almost a decade after her return home, and, in the end, she mourned its failure to make room for her own call to ministry.

Footnotes for this chapter can be found online at: http://secondstorypress.ca/resources

Chapter 5

"THE PITCHER CRIES FOR WATER TO CARRY"

The pitcher cries for water to carry/
and a person for work that is real.

—Marge Piercy[1]

She kept on finding ways to do stuff that mattered.

—Elaine Peacock[2]

ELAINE PEACOCK, a colleague at Naramata and a lifelong friend, recalls Nancy's frustration at being turned down for positions "because she was wealthy and didn't need to have a job." Elaine understood that her friend "needed to have a job because she needed to be doing something, not because she needed the money."[3] Nancy's yearning to "do stuff that mattered" had been evident since her early teen years and she felt the drive for community in any campaign she undertook. She continues to believe in the oft-quoted axiom of Margaret Mead: "Never doubt that a small group of thoughtful, committed individuals can change the world. Indeed, it is the only thing that ever has."[4] In speeches she has delivered throughout her life, she

Carol Gradenwitz (Dr. C.J. O'Connor) at West Wind Island, Georgian Bay, Ontario.

constantly returns to this theme: "When it comes to truly making a difference, don't do it alone.... The power of numbers can move mountains. And when you have friends and allies beside you, it makes the activist's journey a lot more enjoyable."[5] Nancy's next few years in Toronto not only brought her new friends and allies, but the joy of working alongside them on behalf of causes in which she deeply believes.

Nancy returned to Toronto in the fall of 1978 with skills and credentials she had lacked five years earlier. She was now trained and well-versed in the field of organizational development, and at the Jack Gibb seminar she attended that fall she met Carol Gradenwitz, a woman with whom she quickly established both a personal and a business partnership. Carol moved in with Nancy in her McKenzie Avenue house in Rosedale, bringing her business, Gradenwitz Management Services, Inc., with her.[6] Nancy was soon listed as vice-president on the company's letterhead and a seminar leader in its promotional brochures, heading up sessions on standard topics such as managing time and running effective meetings, as well as in more specialized areas such as the care and nurturing of volunteers within a church setting.

In addition to her role in Carol's business, Nancy set up her own consulting firm for non-profits and named it, fittingly, given her own love of lateral thinking, "Creativity—The Human Resource." Under the firm's auspices she promoted a wide range of organizational development training sessions, including her own services as Muffin the Clown. She chose the name because she was "round and had good things inside" and she adopted the persona because "it allowed my shyness to dissolve."[7] Muffin, her promotional brochure explained, "believes that making the unexpected happen, or turning things a little upside down, helps us hear God's word more clearly."[8]

Writing to her friend Kay Macpherson about the origin of clowning in her consulting business, Nancy told her,

> I started on a clown career by chance. I went to the annual congress of the Association for Creative Change.... They had a pre-caucus workshop on clowning. I loved it. It was marvellous. It was legitimization for me to do everything I always wanted to do. It was a time of great joy for me.... It was not fatness, religion, or anything else that put me into clowning. It was simply my own zest and joy of life. The experience being as positive as it was, I then decided that I should choose clowning as a technique in management consulting.[9]

Nancy Ruth and Carol Gradenwitz (Dr. C.J. O'Connor)
as "Muffin" and "Puffin," circa 1979.

She was sometimes hired to bring clowning to Toronto-area churches, and she saw in the established church the greatest potential for her clown work to make a difference. In this same period she actually hatched the idea of writing a book about clowning in the church, outlining its historical precedents as well as why it should be tried and how to get it started. While the book was never published, she amassed a substantial body of research on the topic.

Nancy's Covenant College friend Ginny Dobson Shrivastava, whose sister Liz Dobson worked as a research assistant on the proposed book, speculates that Nancy was drawn to clowning for a number of reasons: "clowning is a way to relate to people who don't necessarily fall in the category of good churchgoers...a kind of marginal movement, but one which Nancy would have been attracted to. Because of course she had a sense of humor and has a sense of humor, and also likes to perform, so the clown was a kind of natural...it also reached out to people who were put off by more traditional forms of hearing about love and forgiveness...it was reaching out to the marginalized, the unchurched, the perhaps sad, battered and blue of this world."[10]

Reflecting on the dynamics of her friend's personality, Ginny adds that the clown persona may express a dichotomy in Nancy's own makeup—"it's a happy face but sad inside"—although she goes on to say, "Maybe 'sad' isn't the right word.... Maybe it's 'tumultuous.' A happy face but in turmoil inside? I don't think Nancy is a sad person, but there is something there, isn't there?"[11] Clowning was "performance art," which let Nancy step outside conventional restraints and give full play to her creativity and iconoclasm. It also appealed, as Ginny remarks, as a way of "ministering to the marginalized"; in time, when Nancy took up a formal position in the church, she developed a growing impatience with the failure of organized religion to place enough importance on such ministry.

Whether the clown face disguised sadness or inner turmoil, Nancy herself points to the freedom from her own limitations that clowning offered her: "It allowed me not to have to be a woman born of a certain station in life and gave me a mask through which I could connect with people in a more honest way, rather than to keep the pounds of protection I've carried most of my life." And, while her letter to Kay Macpherson underscores the "zest and joy of life" she found in clowning, she also donned her clown costume as a way to fight off bouts of depression. In those early years back in Toronto, when she was at times feeling, to use Liz's words, like one of the "battered and blue of this world," she would don whiteface and go play with a ball while riding the Bloor Street subway. "Sometimes," she recalls, "I'd bounce it over to somebody else and startle them, make them smile and then I'd smile. See if I could make them smile."[12] This image evokes a Nancy almost twenty years younger, sitting in a park in Grenoble telling dirty jokes with her friends and relishing their attention—"I made a fool of myself but got laughs."[13] Her capacity to laugh and to invoke laughter—as fool, healer, friend—has been one of her most remarked-upon and enduring traits.

Though she now lived separately from her parents in her own house, Nancy's return to Toronto meant a re-entry into the Jackman family fold. On January 6, 1979, her thirty-seventh birthday, her parents hosted a party for about 150 guests at Toronto's Badminton and Racquet Club, to celebrate Nancy's return to Toronto as well as her brother Eric's homecoming after seventeen years in Chicago.[14] Harry's diary in the ensuing months records numerous

Christmas, 1974, the Jackman family.
Top row, L to R: Hal, Edward, Nancy
Ruth, Eric. Bottom row, L to R:
Harry, Mary.

family events—a visit to Nancy's house on McKenzie Avenue and to Eric's new house around the corner on Drumsnab Road; dinners at 10 Cluny Drive in Rosedale, where her parents had moved in 1976 and where Nancy has lived since her mother's death, or at Overdown, the family farm; birthday parties; lunch with Nancy at the National Club; and church services Nancy attends with her parents. Despite Nancy's having set up her own organizational development business, Harry continued to worry that she had not found what he considered a "permanent job."[15] Following a lunch with her in May 1979, he remarks in his diary that she has "boundless energy, which only needs to be hitched up to some great purpose";[16] in September he praises her "audacity and confidence" while continuing to "hope we can put her on the right track permanently."[17]

Her father did not live to see the path Nancy took as social justice crusader, feminist, philanthropist, and political activist—though it seems unlikely he would have judged it to be the "right track." Less than three months after his final diary entry about his daughter's future, in the early morning of November 22, 1979, Harry Jackman died in his sleep at the age of seventy-nine. Nancy recalls that she had been at a business meeting and just happened to stop by her parents' house late that morning to find her mother and brothers sitting around the dining room table. When her mother rose from the table and announced, "Your father is dead," Nancy's surprising first reaction was to laugh "because that guy wanted to live forever. And he hadn't made it. And somehow, you know, he was not going to be immortal, and I just thought, oh, Dad, you know, too bad. Good try." She goes on to say that, soon afterward, the reality of "Father's dead" kicked in and "the funeral was a bit horrendous."[18] But her initial laughter may have signalled both her intimate understanding of her father's steely drive for control and her own shock at seeing this powerful figure—both friend and foe throughout her life—brought down like any mortal.

In a monograph about Harry written by Mary Jackman for her children three years after his death, she says this about their father:

> Harry was very proud of our children's achievements, although he was not close to them. Wherein lay the estrangement? Although alienated from his own father, he expected the same obedience from his children that he had to give his father. When they were young, he enjoyed camping and playing games with them (the farm), but as they grew more restive and independent, he felt he was losing control, and tried to exert his authority by rewarding with money or withdrawing that support. The emphasis was on material goods, in lieu of understanding and emotional support.[19]

Mary offers a further insight about her late husband when she writes, "Harry was a loving person. He had so much love to give *to anyone that pleased him*."[20] Mary herself knew that, like her children, she had not always pleased Harry Jackman. In the words of the film made about her some years after her own death, she was "a person in her own right," and her marriage was marked by recurring conflict with her husband over their divergent interests and values.

And though the Jackmans had forged a truce for much of their marriage, its terms had worn thin in the year leading up to Harry's death. That fall, when Nancy asked her mother what plans the children should make for their parents' upcoming fiftieth wedding anniversary, her mother "banged her cup on the tabletop full force…and she said, 'I will not be there…. I have nothing, nothing to say thank you for in these 50 years, or to celebrate.'" According to Nancy, "It's the only time I ever saw her like this."[21]

Harry's diaries show him as someone who felt easily slighted when those close to him disagreed with him. He was a man who basked in the approval of others and he found that approval in several close friendships with women over the years. These friendships are faithfully recorded in his diary, where he refers often to his lifelong correspondence with Jean Anderson O'Neil, whom he had met during World War II when he was an MP and she was working at the American Embassy at Ottawa, and to whom he felt particularly close. The relationship was no secret to Mary and he realized that it made her unhappy but even so continued it until Jean's death in 1971. Nancy describes the Sunday after her father was buried, when she and her mother sat together in front of the fire in Mary's living room at 10 Cluny Drive, having retrieved from the basement two Bren gun chests full of letters that Harry had been sent by women friends over many years. Her mother "opened them and read them. And looked at them. And then we threw them into the fireplace. And at the end, this was done, almost in silence. I was sitting on the floor, handing her letters, and she was sitting on a chair. Of course, she was 75 at the time. And she said at the end of it…'at least there wasn't just one woman.' And there had, indeed, been letters from five women with photographs."[22]

When Mary Jackman was in her seventies, she confided to her daughter that Harry had asked her for a divorce in 1944, when Nancy was two years old, and that she had refused him.[23] Nevertheless, in her monograph about her husband, Mary asserts that one of Harry's virtues was that "he was very faithful and loyal to the institution of marriage and the support of his family."[24] Whatever dreams he may have had about spending his life with a woman who uncritically adored him, he seems to have honoured his marriage vows in the letter if not the spirit, as Mary had done. At his funeral Mary is reported to have said to her close friend and former bridesmaid, Alida Starr Martin, "We made it! We did it! We stayed together for 50 years! We made it to the end!"[25]

At his death, Harry Jackman's personal estate, aside from his corporate assets and the children's trusts, was valued at roughly twelve million dollars and, aside from specific legacies, was bequeathed to the Jackman Foundation. His will left Mary $600,000 and the house at 10 Cluny Drive, as well as a life interest in the remaining realty that Harry owned at the time of his death—West Wind Island and two farms—with the provision that if the properties were sold, she would receive the income from the investment proceeds during her lifetime and the investment would be divided among the children after her death. Hal, Eric, and Nancy each received $100,000, while Edward, in recognition of his having given up his "assigned share" of the King Vaughan Farms holdings, received $500,000.

Hal retained control of the business, while Eric and Nancy were entitled to the current value of the shares their father had assigned to them in King Vaughan Farms in 1956. Further, Harry's will included a clause that gave his executors and trustees—of whom Hal was one, along with Mary's cousin Henry Langford and the Victoria & Grey Trust Company, which Hal controlled—the power to purchase Eric's and Nancy's shares should either wish to cash in their portion of the King Vaughan Farms holdings.

Nancy did indeed want to cash in and gain control of her own funds and began moving to do so early in 1980. Hal writes in the Henry Rutherford Jackman diaries that the negotiations with Eric and Nancy "were not always free of acrimony." According to Harry's will, the price paid to Eric and Nancy was to be "fair market value, as determined by the trustees," yet the fact that Hal was not only one of those executors and trustees but also head of the family companies presented a possible conflict of interest.[26]

Although Hal records that he "tried desperately to stay out of the negotiations," in his view his siblings were suspicious of the other executors as well, seeing them as "simply Hal's agents." Both Nancy and Eric retained separate lawyers and investment advisors, and by March, according to Hal, the issue had become "not what was fair market value to the estate, but how much was it worth to Hal to get his two siblings, both of whom were threatening law suits, out of the picture." In late May, with Nancy and her lawyer pressing for closure, Hal decided that the estate executors would not be able to propose a price acceptable to her or to Eric and offered to purchase Nancy's shares through a family trust, TWIGMIE, at "net asset value as determined by the Price Waterhouse annual reports."[27] The net asset value calculated and offered to her on June 3, 1980, was $9,643,936.05 for all her shares, an offer she accepted on the same day. The deal was concluded in the Bank of Nova Scotia boardroom on the corner of Bay and King, at which time Nancy presented Hal with a five-cent piece in Perspex "for his trophy table, for having gotten rid of me."[28]

Interestingly, in the final stages of these negotiations, Hal dealt separately with his brother and sister, only informing Eric on the following day that Nancy had completed the sale of her shares. Hal comments that he found it surprising that they did not choose to act together in dealing with the estate but attributes their behaviour to the tension between them over ownership of the family's West Wind Island and cottage in Georgian Bay. As she aged, Mary Jackman couldn't manage the property any longer, so she asked Hal to offer it for sale to her children. In Nancy's words, although she and Eric both expressed an interest in buying it, her mother "favored Eric getting the cottage, as he had children." Nancy considered trying to overbid Eric in the sealed bid process controlled by Hal, but in the end "solved the infighting by moving on."[29]

Shortly after cashing in her shares Nancy made what was at that point the biggest purchase in her life, out-weighing by one hundredfold the cost of her Naramata Mercedes seven years earlier. Motivated by her loss of the family cottage and of Overdown, the farm that was sold to Edward Jackman, and by her desire to have a year-round residence with large wooded grounds, she bought her nine-thousand-square-foot house at 184 Roxborough Drive in north Rosedale for $800,000.[30] As she recalls, she went down to see Hal in his office to tell him she had bought the house. He "was sitting there with his feet on his desk and a cigar in his mouth. Down came the feet as he exclaimed, 'It's bigger than mine!'"[31] Even though she was now a wealthy woman, both the size and the expense of the house were stunning. But she lived there for sixteen years, gradually turning the spacious house into a centre for feminist activism and a haven for a diverse collection of groups and causes.

Not long after Nancy "got liquid," to use her words, she gave up her consulting work and initially focused on setting up a numbered company and investing her

newfound wealth in the stock market.[32] Within a year she also ended her relationship with Carol Gradenwitz, having by that time begun to develop a network of close friends among Toronto's second-wave feminist leaders.[33] The women's movement in Canada had been steadily gaining force throughout the 1960s and 1970s. Michele Landsberg describes this time as being "like a snowball rolling down a hill, gathering momentum, flinging new ideas into the air at reckless speed."[34] As Beth Atcheson and Lorna Marsden note in their prologue to *White Gloves Off*, a pivotal moment came in 1966, when thirty-two women's organizations across Canada joined together as the Committee for the Equality of Women in Canada (CEWC) and agreed to advocate for a royal commission on the status of women in Canada. The commission, established by the federal government in February 1967, submitted a final report in September 1970 that brought forward 167 far-reaching recommendations for legislative reform. Following the report's release, as Atcheson observes in her chapter "Equality is a Woman's Place: The Royal Commission on the Status of Women," "women organized themselves in ways that mirrored the way that jurisdiction works in Canada: dominantly federal or dominantly provincial, with overlaps or 'concurrent' activity."[35] Over the coming decade, Toronto became a hub of feminist activity, with many women in that city engaged as leaders within the movement at both the provincial and the federal levels.

Kay Macpherson was one of those leaders, a pacifist and a political activist with the New Democratic Party who had served in turn as president of the Association of Women Electors, the Voice of Women for Peace, and the

Left: Nancy Ruth purchased 184 Roxborough Drive and immediately made it into a "nuclear free zone," in Toronto, in 1980. The Women's Legal Education and Action Fund (LEAF) would be formally launched on April 15, 1985.

From L to R: Nancy Ruth, Kay Macpherson, Nancy Pocock, Ruth Brown, and Laura Sabia at Hart House, University of Toronto, March, 1985, for a speech on peace and disarmament.

National Action Committee on the Status of Women (NAC). Nancy had been an occasional donor to NAC while at Naramata and had used many of their materials in her work; following her father's death, she arranged for the Jackman Foundation to make a five-thousand-dollar gift to NAC. Kay visited her at Roxborough Drive to thank her for the donation and thus began what would be an important friendship.[36]

Following that first meeting, Kay invited Nancy to attend the December 1980 NAC Christmas party and she recounts in her memoir Nancy's belief that this invitation "launched her into the women's movement of the day." She goes on to describe her own response to this unorthodox new acquaintance:

I had first heard about Nancy while we were discussing the pros and cons of government funding. Someone mentioned this millionaire feminist who had returned to Toronto, bought a huge Rosedale mansion, and offered to match the contributions of all those present at a coffee party she had attended. So we invited her to the party, and she did offer to help with Friends of NAC. I had always been wary of people with lots of money; I think they made me feel inferior. And here was someone who was rich, who was given to awful language and questionable table manners, and yet she became one of my closest friends.[37]

The years 1980–1981 proved to be another watershed period for the Canadian women's movement, making the timing of Nancy's "launch" into the Ontario and national movement fortuitous. And she could not have had a better sponsor than Kay, who was both respected and beloved in the feminist community for her untiring advocacy on behalf of women's rights.

In early June 1980, Prime Minister Pierre Trudeau announced his government's plans to patriate the Canadian constitution, thus giving the country full sovereignty over its own affairs and ending the authority over Canada that the British Parliament had held through the British North America Act of 1867. A month later, Trudeau's government released more details on patriation along with a draft Charter of Rights and Freedoms that it proposed to entrench within the new constitution—that is, to make modifications to the document possible only by amendment to the constitution. Constitutional review and revision had been under consideration by the Canadian government since the centennial of Confederation in 1967, and there had been clear indications since late 1978 that matters were coming to a head—so much so that women's groups across the country had begun to mobilize.[38] In May 1980, for example, the Ontario Committee on the Status of Women wrote to Ontario Premier Bill Davis stating "that the special concerns of Ontario women must be represented during the upcoming constitutional negotiations" and urging that there be "strong positive guarantees for women's equality" under the proposed human rights code to be entrenched in the new constitution.[39]

Key among the women's groups who mobilized for action were the Canadian Advisory Council on the Status of Women (CACSW) and NAC. The CACSW had been established by the federal government in 1973 in response to a recommendation in the report tabled in 1970 by the Royal Commission on the Status of Women. Set up as an autonomous agency reporting to Parliament through the minister responsible for the status of women, it was charged with advising the federal government and educating the public about women's concerns. NAC was also an outgrowth of the Royal Commission but was established two years earlier than the CACSW by the same coalition of women's groups who had lobbied to make the commission a reality. As its name suggests, NAC was focused on direct action and grew steadily from a membership of thirty women's groups at its founding to more than seven hundred in its heyday, with about two hundred member groups at the time of the constitutional challenge.[40]

On June 15, 1980, NAC announced in a press release that "women's participation in constitutional reform" would be its priority for the coming year. Underscoring the importance NAC attached to the work ahead, NAC president Lynn McDonald was quoted in the release as saying, "When we look back at the birth of the Canadian constitution in 1867, we find the 'Fathers of Confederation' always in the forefront. But where were the 'Mothers of Confederation?' Women's special concerns and interests were not taken into account.... This time, women want to right the imbalance by participating fully in the process of redrafting the constitution."[41] The summer of 1980 saw intense activity on the part of NAC's contacts across the country. Women were not only interested in the issue of constitutional change but determined to see a positive outcome for women's equality embedded in the Charter of Rights and Freedoms.

The CACSW, in preparation for a planned conference on the constitution in September, commissioned thirteen research papers to set the stage for its deliberations.[42] These papers were distributed widely across the country and generated more than eight thousand letters in response, copies of which CACSW sent to the offices of the prime minister and Lloyd Axworthy, the minister responsible for the status of women.[43] Following the government's tabling of its proposed constitutional package on October 5—which ignored the recommendations in the CACSW research briefs—"CACSW issued a press release, made a public statement, and wrote to Lloyd Axworthy and the prime minister detailing the council's objections to the proposed wording" of the Charter. The council also followed up by sending out flyers across the country, asking recipients to mail a detachable coupon to the government communicating their "disapproval of the weak draft."[44] More than 17,000 coupons were returned by the following January.

In one of the CACSW-commissioned papers, Toronto lawyer Mary Eberts laid out in clear terms for non-experts what was at stake, ending with the exhortation,

It is up to us to make sure that we are included in the constitutional review process, and that the perspectives and goals of women are taken seriously. We have a special, historical relationship to the constitution, as we had to fight so hard for so long to be included in even its minimal provisions. Let us not stop now.[45]

Yet these resolute women were nearly stopped—or so it seemed at several critical junctures. The conference planned for September had to be postponed because of a threatened strike by government translators, whose demands included items that the CACSW endorsed, such as paid maternity leave. Crossing their picket line would have been unthinkable.[46] And NAC failed to secure funding from the federal government for its mid-year national meeting, scheduled for October and intended to focus on the constitution.

In place of its national meeting, NAC held an open session on October 18 at Toronto City Hall titled "Feminist visions: The mothers of Confederation," with sessions that dealt with "the many issues of relevance to women in the constitutional negotiations."[47] Nancy attended the meeting, where she met Mary Eberts and another Toronto lawyer, Beth Atcheson, both of whom would become close friends and colleagues and would play key roles in the women's constitutional lobbying that was steadily gaining steam.[48] That evening, Minister Axworthy addressed participants and made the first of what would be a series of mistakes in reading the intensity of women's concerns. He advised his audience simply to trust the government to improve the wording on equality rights in the draft Charter; most of those present were "outraged at being treated with such condescension."[49]

Fortunately, although national women's meetings planned for the fall of 1980 were postponed or cancelled, there were opportunities to give expert testimony before the Special Joint Committee of the Senate and the House of Commons that was established to hear feedback from Canadians about the constitutional proposal and report back to the government. Both the CACSW and NAC submitted written briefs to the Committee and on November 20 the Joint Committee heard over three hours of testimony from their representatives, including NAC's Lynn McDonald, CACSW president Doris Anderson, and legal experts such as Mary Eberts and Beverley Baines, who made use of the research they had done in preparing briefs for the postponed CACSW conference. Testimony centred on the Charter, especially the deficiencies in section 15, the so-called "non-discrimination clause," as well as on the section affecting Indigenous women's rights, and on the sections that held the threat of limiting enforcement of section 15. Further, there was strong objection to section 29, which stipulated a three-year moratorium on the implementation of section 15 to allow time for governments to revise laws in order to bring them into accord with the Charter. No other section of the Charter had such a moratorium.

On January 12, 1981, Justice Minister Jean Chrétien tabled a revised constitution and Charter that responded to some of the concerns that had been brought forward by women's groups. Nevertheless, there were still significant omissions: on analysis, "the feminist score-card showed thirteen areas where women could still slip through the cracks and be deprived of fundamental justice."[50] More action was clearly needed—but trouble was brewing again with regard to the CACSW conference on women and the constitution that had been postponed a few months earlier and was now scheduled to take place in Ottawa, in the West Block of the Parliament building, on February 14, Valentine's Day. Minister Axworthy opposed holding this national conference and, with the concurrence of the CACSW executive, cancelled it while president Doris Anderson was out of town. Anderson, a former editor of *Chatelaine*, the largest-selling magazine in Canada; a former Liberal party candidate for federal political office; and a powerful figure in the women's movement, was furious when she learned the news and insisted that the conference go ahead unless the executive's decision was upheld by majority vote of the full council. Unfortunately, the minister's decision held sway when council members voted seventeen to ten to cancel, upon which Anderson immediately resigned.

In her account of this conflict, future NAC president Chaviva Hošek comments that "It is difficult to understand what advantage the government might have gained from the cancellation. The Joint Committee had already publicized the process of constitution-making. The opposition parties and the provinces were so insistent on having a say in the process that a conference of women was not going to make things much worse." She concludes that "the political costs of cancelling the conference turned out to be high. The women's movement suddenly had a heroine [Anderson], a villain [Axworthy] and an event, all of which symbolized its exclusion from the constitutional process."[51] The event to which Hošek refers is the conference that ultimately took place on the same date and in the same location as originally planned—but without the official sanction of the CACSW and the government.

How that event came to be is now legendary in

Canadian feminist history—a story of David and Goliath proportions that has been referred to as "the biggest mass movement of women in Canadian history."[52] And it was on this battlefield that Nancy Jackman engaged for the first time as part of a community of female activists fiercely intent on political change. Very shortly after Anderson resigned, women started organizing to rescue their constitutional conference. An initial meeting chaired by Linda Palmer Nye was held at the Cow Café on John Street in Toronto; it was a gathering that one journalist called "obviously a council of war."[53] Kay Macpherson was in the thick of it and Nancy attended at Kay's invitation. Although she "didn't have much self-confidence" and only did "minor work in organizing the conference," Nancy was forging links to women and to a cause—equality of women before the law—that would inform her life for years to come.[54] As Beth Atcheson recalls it, "The Cow Café kicks off, and at that point Nancy Ruth is very much and clearly engaged in the circle."[55] While friend and fellow NAC member Madeleine Gilchrist observes that at this stage "Nancy was always behind the scenes," helping and supporting but "not imposing herself at all," her support and engagement would become central to the equality campaign.[56]

Out of the Cow Café meeting on January 27, 1981, arose what came to be known as the Ad Hoc Committee on the Constitution, a group of women mobilized by leaders such as Lynda Palmer Nye, Marilou McPhedran, and Pat Hacker. In just over two weeks, and with extensive enlistment of supporters and volunteers across the country and in the federal civil service, these women mounted an event that, to the astonishment of everyone involved, attracted 1,300 highly engaged participants to Ottawa for their "ad hoc conference." Several resolutions on the

Norma Scarborough, Pat Hacker, Kay Macpherson, and Doris Anderson singing together.

charter and on the constitutional patriation process were passed at the conference and on the following day at Ottawa mayor Marion Dewar's office in City Hall, and after its conclusion key participants remained in Ottawa to lobby Parliament on behalf of these resolutions. Further, as Chaviva Hošek recounts, in the days and weeks that followed, "women across the country contacted their MPs to make their support for the resolutions known." Just as importantly, "after initial resistance, the department of justice began to work with the Ad Hoc Committee members to draft what later became section 28: 'Notwithstanding anything in this Charter, the rights and freedoms referred to in it are guaranteed equally to male and female persons.'" This section was "passed unanimously in the House of Commons on April 23, 1981."[57]

One further crisis awaited the women's lobby in

November 1981, when first ministers announced that key provisions of the Charter would be subject to a clause that allowed "any level of government to 'override' Charter provisions promising legal, fundamental, and equality rights."[58] It was clear that this new provision applied to section 15, but it was not clear whether it applied to section 28. Women were outraged at this setback to guaranteed equality and further stunned when they were informed that to ensure that this override provision did not apply to section 28, they would need all ten provinces to agree. Ad Hoc Committee members then launched a furious campaign, as described by Penney Kome, "Women all across Canada were contacted and asked to send identical telegrams to the federal government and to their respective premiers. With the right address lists and enough phone contacts, Ad Hockers enlisted support that won over the federal government and turned the premiers around, one by one."[59] On November 24, after this brief but intense battle, the justice minister announced that section 28 would not be subject to being overridden.

Canada's new constitution with its entrenched Charter of Rights and Freedoms was signed into law on April 17, 1982. Most feminist analysis, with regard to what was lobbied for and what was gained, views the outcome as mixed. The three-year moratorium on section 15, for example, remained in effect despite a vigorous campaign against it, meaning that equality rights would not come into effect until April 17, 1985. And many changes proposed for section 15 were not incorporated in the final version. Mary Eberts, looking back more than thirty years later, comments that as far as women's aspirations for the Charter are concerned, "we must be disappointed with the result." Yet, she adds, "If we look at how much women accomplished in the face of indifference, resistance, or even hostility on the part of the government, the accomplishment is substantial."[60]

Eberts goes on to reflect that in her view, what women learned during this campaign, through reading papers, attending study sessions, and preparing briefs, "would inform significant post-patriation activities, like the conduct of statute audits to identify legislation that needed reform, educational activities to increase Charter literacy, the establishment of organizations to conduct Charter litigation, like the Women's Legal Education and Action Fund (LEAF), and a range of litigation and law reform activities undertaken by the women's movement after 1985."[61] Nancy Jackman was centrally involved in many of these post-entrenchment activities. She was now beginning to figure as a player in the Toronto feminist community and her Rosedale mansion became a popular meeting place for women intent on making change.

Decades later, as Nancy looks back on these years, she observes that "although the first big push, accelerated by the Ad Hoc Conference, was to get the best possible constitutional equality standard, there was very early recognition that we would have to do much more.... It was clear from the struggle to get the standard right that nothing could be taken for granted and that, in the present as in the past, nothing would be given with respect to women's equality. *It would have to be taken*."[62] And *take it* they set out to do—a cadre of women from across Canada who had been enraged, energized, and mobilized by the lessons learned from the constitutional battles. In May 1982, for example, two dozen women from across Canada held a workshop at Toronto City Hall aimed at "working toward a national strategy on using the Charter for Canadian women through legal writing, litigation and networking."[63] Among the strategic approaches agreed to at that workshop, such as a possible legal action fund; research and publication by experts on the Charter and women's equality; and conferences for Charter decision-makers, the one that engaged Nancy intensely over the years of the section 15 moratorium was the Charter of Rights Coalition, or CORC as it came to be known.

CORC evolved as a nationwide umbrella initiative for women and women's groups that, in Nancy's words, would work on maintaining "the learning, connections and mobilization of the 1980–1981 years...at least until section 15 of the Charter came into force on April 17, 1985."[64] Its mandate was two-fold: grassroots education about the Charter's importance to women and political advocacy to bring about change in discriminatory laws. In a 2010 essay, Nancy lists CORC as one of "five initiatives of which I am most proud." She goes on to say, "It was my first experience in managing a national lobby, and I had the time of my life. We produced slide shows complete with audio tapes, which we showed across the country. We spoke and spoke and spoke, in school auditoriums, in church basements, to annual meetings, to women's institutes, on the telephone, and over the fax machine. In short, we went anywhere a group of women was interested in hearing our message."[65]

Iris Nowell notes that these three years Nancy spent "'speechifying' on the Charter" across the country "established the beginnings of her national reputation." Her Rosedale mansion became a "bustling command centre" for CORC: "Six or eight women were always working. The phones rang all day. Nancy funded an education kit that was distributed nationally, and she contributed to the publication of *The Taking of Twenty-Eight: Women Challenge the Constitution* by Penney Kome." When Nowell asked her in an interview why she threw herself so intensely into the constitutional campaign, Nancy's response was a shrug and the terse reply, "I had enough money."[66] Nancy Jackman was now in possession of a fortune and a mansion of her own. Yet having resources at her disposal was only part of the story; she had at last found not only "stuff that mattered" but a network of women to work alongside. This convergence was a turning point, moving her onto the pathway she has followed throughout her life.

More than anything, Nancy sees that path as one dedicated to social justice. Describing her move from the church to feminist activism, she comments, "The God piece just sort of got dropped off and the feminist analysis got put on, but it was still about social justice."[67] In her view, social justice for women at this point in Canada's history hinged on educating them about their legal rights. Her friend and fellow Charter activist Beth Atcheson observes that Nancy "believed in the power of education, that education about women's rights would give them power in their own circumstances.... [T]his was a way to empower women in their own lives, if they could analyze their own situation. First of all, because you have to come to some knowledge about women and what's happening to women, and then if they had the tools, and tools of engagement, both personally and collectively. She really had that focus."[68] Mary Eberts agrees, noting Nancy's deep respect for the capacity of women who were not expert in the law to attain constitutional literacy. She had what Eberts describes as a "passion that women's common sense and ability to understand legal issues be recognized."[69]

In Atcheson's assessment, Nancy's contribution to this three-year Charter campaign was vital on a number of levels. "So what she brings is pushing us to do broader and different things to make this work effectively. We need the outreach. We need to educate. We need to mobilize. We need to build resources. And she probably wasn't alone in that, but boy, my memory is she was almost alone and way ahead." She was also, Atcheson recounts, a "very charismatic" public speaker: "women across the country were very hungry for knowledge about the Charter and what was happening. And Nancy Ruth was one of two or three people who really travelled across the country and did a huge amount of public speaking, from national conferences to church basements and everything in between."[70]

Having enough money—not simply Jackman money but a broad base of financial support—was another critical ingredient for the Charter campaign. Atcheson credits Nancy for her leadership in making their network of Charter activists understand the importance of securing adequate financial support for the undertaking. "She also had a focus on this issue of fuel and what we would need going forward. That there was a relationship between the work we needed to do and the money we needed to do it. She had an understanding about money that was much more layered and complex than any of us had…. [S]he constantly pushed us to think not just about the law and the standards of the law, but what we needed to fuel the work."[71]

Nancy's understanding of the need to "fuel the work" would come into play on a grand scale when attention turned to establishing LEAF—the Women's Legal Education and Action Fund that was central to the next phase of Charter activism. Mary Eberts recalls the "huge amount of fundraising for LEAF" that Nancy undertook and, like Atcheson, notes the importance of her "tremendous leadership ability, ability to bring people with her" as one key to LEAF's ultimate success.[72]

The idea for a women's legal action fund took shape quickly during the section 15 moratorium years. On June 17, 1981, for example, following the CACSW Conference on Women and the Constitution: The Next Five Years that had been held in Ottawa at the end of May, Mary Eberts sent out a letter to Nancy and others noting that many conference attendees had shown interest in establishing such a fund.[73] Over the next year the CACSW commissioned a substantial study of American legal defence funds and how a fund of this type would work in Canada. Completed and released in October 1984, the study concluded that a "legal action fund to concentrate on issues of sex-based discrimination is an essential component of an effective strategy to promote the interests of women in the Canadian legal system."[74] And the following spring, the day that the moratorium came to an end, April 17, 1985, saw the official founding of LEAF, whose purpose would be to "advance the equality of women in Canada through litigation, law reform and public education using the Canadian Charter of Rights and Freedoms."[75] Through Supreme Court of Canada test-case litigation that promised to have a substantive impact on women's and girls' equality, LEAF set out to turn Charter hopes into reality.

CORC sent out a press release a week prior to the momentous April date announcing that "In anticipation of the legal challenges which will bring about universal changes for Canadian women, the LEGAL EDUCATION AND ACTION FUND (LEAF) has been established as a legal defence fund for women challenging existing laws through the equality sections of the Charter. LEAF will use the Charter of Rights and Freedoms to win legal victories for women; do research on legal issues affecting women; and supply information to women, their lawyers, women's groups and the public."[76] Women across the country gathered on April 17 to celebrate and begin raising money for the work that lay ahead of them. In Toronto's St. Lawrence Hall, a "Feminist Fantasy of the Future" dinner and cabaret organized by Pat Hacker and her team included a "fundraising interlude" with Nancy Jackman taking centre stage as a tap-dancing tree—"A Tree for LEAF," as it was billed in the program.[77] In the years to come she donned her costume of green leaves and danced exuberantly for LEAF on many occasions, with hat or bucket in hand to welcome donations.

She also took on the hard slog of raising money through making personal appeals to donors and coaching her friends to do the same. Denise Arsenault, who served as treasurer for LEAF, recalls that "Nancy from the beginning was engaged in working out the fundraising strategy, not something that was in the zone of comfort for the lawyers who were in the group.... Nancy helped mastermind a lot of how the funding would happen."[78] Lawyer and Charter activist Marilou McPhedran recounts how she had been invited to Nancy's for tea and introduced to Susan McCutcheon, daughter of the late Senator Wallace McCutcheon. Nancy's blunt words to Marilou were, "This is Susan McCutcheon. A friend of mine. She's rich like me. I want you to tell Susan why she should give $50,000 to LEAF, and if Susan gives it to you, I will too."[79] Mary Eberts recalls as well that Nancy "used to take me along as her 'talking monkey' on fundraising calls" and goes on to note the financial cost of fundraising to someone like Nancy, who is expected by those whom she asks for donations to put her own money to the cause—and who does so without hesitation.[80]

Both Nancy and her mother made substantial gifts to LEAF, eventually seeding a foundation and an endowment

Some of the LEAF "mothers" gather at the McGill Club President's Dinner, Toronto, April, 1987. L to R: Susan Tanner, Beth Atcheson, Denise Arsenault, Susan Clark, Patricia Wouters, Barbara Hackett, Nancy Ruth, Marilou McPhedran.

that, up to the present day, helps underwrite LEAF's expenses. LEAF's accomplishments over the intervening years have been ground-breaking, with legal victories in such critical areas as violence against women, sexual harassment, rape shield laws, maternity benefits, unfair pensions, and reproductive freedom. A journalist writing six years after LEAF's founding marvelled that LEAF had in that short time "become a dominant force in fighting test cases protecting the rights of women, children and minorities."[81] LEAF's membership had by then grown to more than three thousand people from all provinces, with chapters, or "branches," from coast to coast and turnouts in the thousands for Persons Day breakfasts held as fundraisers for LEAF. The labour that Nancy and her colleagues devoted to giving LEAF breath, life, and a base of funding did indeed change the face of Canadian legislation and equality rights for women, and LEAF's advocacy continues to make a difference in Canada's current legal landscape.

In the early and heady days after LEAF got its start, however, Nancy found herself at odds with those she worked alongside, disappointed both in herself and in some of the directions they were taking. In the spring of 1986, she writes, "Woke up angry again. Got up for the 9 am LEAF meeting—I think I represent a different view point, but it's clear, I am not needed...or even wanted."[82] Most of the women in the forefront of LEAF were lawyers, intent on the legal challenges ahead of them, and their expertise could be intimidating to non-specialists like Nancy. Just as importantly, Nancy's own passion lay in the education part of LEAF's mission; she believed in the need to empower everyday women to take control of their lives by giving them knowledge of their rights under the new Charter. As early as 1981, when she received the letter from Mary Eberts about the interest at the CACSW conference in establishing a "Women's Legal Action Fund," she scrawled in the margin of the letter: "See—no 'education.'"[83] By the time LEAF was formally established, Nancy and others had ensured that education was part of its name and its mandate. She remembers sitting on her island in Georgian Bay with friend and special education teacher Libby Bradburne, struggling with the name "Legal Action Fund," whose acronym was LAF. Libby said, "Just put in an E for education and you'll get LEAF" and the altered name "suited everyone."[84] It was to be a new leaf in law. Nevertheless, in Nancy's view, "education has always been the weakest of LEAF's activities."[85]

Nancy was also dissatisfied with the contribution she was making to LEAF in its start-up phase; her colleagues relied heavily on her for her fundraising skills, but she did not feel she was making the headway that was needed. Looking back, she recounts that she was "sort of ashamed, so I stepped away in 1986."[86] Yet if she stepped away from LEAF, she also stepped into an unexpected opportunity: to try once again to find her vocation within the church. What she refers to as the "God piece" was not yet gone from her heart. A position was open at her lifelong church, Metropolitan United, and she made the decision to apply for it.

Footnotes for this chapter can be found online at: http://secondstorypress.ca/resources

Nancy Ruth, age 44 in
1986, about the time she
applied to be a full-time
associate minister at
Metropolitan United
Church, Toronto.

Chapter 6

METROPOLITAN UNITED CHURCH

We learned about God from Nancy Jackman.
　　　　　　　—The Very Reverend Bruce McLeod[1]

NANCY JACKMAN grew up in the Metropolitan United Church, where her family on her mother's side had been members for four generations. Mary Coyne Rowell was baptized at Metropolitan as an infant in 1904 and married Harry Jackman there on April 26, 1930. Harry, new to Metropolitan at the time of his marriage, became a church steward by the end of that same year. Both parents were active leaders in the congregation throughout the rest of their lives and Sunday attendance was a regular practice for the whole family while the children were growing up.[2]

Originally Toronto's "Methodist Cathedral," founded in 1818, Metropolitan acquired its current name in 1925 when the Methodist Church of Canada merged with the Congregationalists and two-thirds of Canada's Presbyterian churches to become The United Church of Canada. It has been at its present downtown Toronto location—on Queen Street East at the corner of Church Street—since 1872,

Mary Coyne Rowell Jackman, age 83, with Nancy Ruth
as "Muffin the Clown" at the 50th anniversary of the
Bond Street Nursery School, Toronto, in 1987.

although after a 1928 fire destroyed most of the building, the church itself was rebuilt on the same site, maintaining its original neo-Gothic design. Mary and Harry's wedding was the first formal wedding to take place in the new building after it was dedicated in 1929.[3]

Metropolitan was a good fit for Mary Jackman's lifelong commitment to social gospel principles. Its community service and outreach programs gave her scope to ensure that, in the words of the eulogy preached at her funeral, "what blessed her should bless others as well." She was a leader in many of Metropolitan's programs, including its war work, its cultural and artistic celebrations, and its Bible study classes. In his eulogy, the Very Reverend Bruce McLeod recounted the story of how Mary had started a nursery school at Metropolitan designed to serve the children of low-income working parents. During the Great Depression of the 1930s, seeing that there was nothing in the church's neighbourhood for little children, she said, "'Why not use the church?' She believed that these children should have the same access to education that her own children enjoyed, and thus began through her initiative the still thriving Bond Street Nursery School, the first inner city nursery school in Canada."[4] Throughout its history, Metropolitan has prided itself on its inclusiveness, its care for the poor, the homeless, and refugees, and its socially progressive values; Nancy, like her mother, felt at home there—at least for a time, until Christianity's patriarchal traditions, even within a liberal church, weighed too heavily on her spirit.

In 1986, however, the opening for a full-time associate minister at Metropolitan held a powerful attraction for Nancy.[5] Here was a chance to put her training and gifts to use in her home church. Among her papers is a list she drew up of the pros and cons of applying for the position. She recognized that taking on the job would require a "radical change in lifestyle," including "giving up the freedom to come and go—trips, cottage." She realized as well that "although you have the money to buy what is needed that this might not be acceptable to the people you work with." She understood that the position required discipline and commitment, including the discipline of "not blowing your cool when all about you are losing theirs." And she was well aware of how difficult it would be to effect the change she believed was needed within the church, wondering "how to go about accepting the present structure if others don't see the need for change" and asking how well she would do at "accepting the present style and contenting yourself with working slowly toward change."[6] She had trained, after all, to be a change agent, with a master's degree in organizational development and a love of the challenges that work entailed.

At the same time, she lists under the heading "The Other Side of the Coin" compelling reasons for taking on this risky venture:

1) This would give you a purpose in life.

2) You are young enough to commit three years or so.

3) Others feel you have the ability to do the job otherwise they wouldn't have asked you.

4) It would give you a new perspective on people, of economics.

5) It would enlarge upon your basic skills, deepen your understanding, strengthen and affirm a lot of your finer attributes.

6) Might teach you to find there are other ways of dealing with controversy than pulling the power bit.

7) Be rubbing shoulders with people you respect so you could bounce off each other.

8) Would probably lead to a whole new direction in life.[7]

Even after her years of intense involvement with the Charter of Rights Coalition and the Women's Legal Education and Action Fund (LEAF), and despite her growing stature as a leader within the feminist community, we can see that Nancy Jackman was still searching for direction, purpose, and validation of her worth. She also remained keen to gain new knowledge and skills as well as a greater understanding of her own dynamics and how to better manage them.

One further and very strong appeal of the position at Metropolitan was its new minister, Bruce McLeod, who urged Nancy to "come and work with me."[8] Bruce, a former—and the youngest—moderator of the United Church, had joined Metropolitan as its senior minister in October 1984, but recalls meeting Nancy many years earlier when he was invited to preach at Metropolitan in the mid-sixties: "I'm sure I met Nancy there that day. Probably her parents too, though I don't remember that. And I think she was probably dressed in an unexpected way; I think in jeans…." Nancy, then in her twenties, "stuck out from the usual churchgoer on a summer Sunday."[9] From the start, he saw in her a person who was making her own way, part of the congregation and yet set apart from her fellow worshippers by the choices she made.

Bruce also saw a young woman who "had a beautiful face…not necessarily the physical parts of it, but her spirit seems to flow out of her face. It was very warm. For people who are in that radius it's a very warm feeling to be talking with her. She really listens to you." He would continue to run into Nancy over the coming years and gradually "got to know her, and her unusual dress and sometimes her unusual language—which wasn't, again, what you'd usually find on a church summer Sunday…. She was well known for having a salty tongue."[10]

While Nancy doesn't remember that first meeting in the sixties, she does recall going to Bloor Street United Church to hear Bruce preach in the years that followed: he was "brilliant, charismatic," and she was drawn to him from the start.[11] Her regard for him, and his encouragement, were major reasons that she came down on the "pro" side, accepting Bruce's invitation for her to step in as associate minister on an interim basis at the beginning of March 1986, and subsequently apply for the permanent role. She was active and well-known within the Metropolitan community, having worked closely with Bruce over the past year, for example, as chair of the worship committee, a significant responsibility among the church laity.[12]

Still, there was an irony attached to Nancy's moving from a lay position to the professional ministry staff. It was standard practice for United Church clergy like Nancy, who did not have a congregation, to petition the Presbytery each year annually to be retained on its ministerial rolls; for the two years that she worked in London and Montreal, her Presbytery in British Columbia permitted her to remain on its rolls. Yet in 1980, her petition to her Toronto presbytery was unexpectedly denied. She was informed of this decision by a registered letter that told her that she had been removed from the rolls and would "not be recognized as a member of the order of ministry of The United Church of Canada or perform the functions of its ministry."[13] The story of this action by the church and her response to it is one that she has returned to frequently in her own accounts of her life, casting it as a turning point in her understanding of justice and fair play.

Nancy appealed the presbytery's and conference's actions on procedural grounds, pointing out to the judicial committee of the United Church—chaired by lawyer Bertha Wilson, who later became Canada's first woman Supreme Court justice—that she had responded as requested to a December 1979 letter from the presbytery, letting them know she wished to be retained on the rolls even though she was not currently employed within the church. In her submission of the required "Application by a Minister to be left without a pastoral charge or other appointment within The United Church of Canada," she had stated that her rationale for being retained was that "I consider my work related to the service of the Church, not only when I do consulting or teaching for Church groups, but also when I work with other organizations and spend a lot of time dealing with and calling out ethical & values questions.... I also work as a clown. I do clown worship services."[14] The Presbytery was clearly not persuaded by her argument and they recommended to Toronto Conference that Nancy be struck from the rolls. Without telling Nancy about the negative recommendation and giving her the opportunity to say why Presbytery was wrong, Toronto Conference accepted Presbytery's advice and Nancy was no longer a United Church minister.

The peremptory manner in which Nancy was informed of the church's decision denied her the chance to question the recommendation or to defend herself. As she wrote in her notice of appeal, "If I had known that my status on the roll of Presbytery was in jeopardy, I would have made additional submissions to the Presbytery Ministry Personnel and Education Committee and if I had known my case would be considered by Toronto Conference, I would have sought to make submissions to Toronto Conference.... [I]t is accordingly my position that I have been denied natural justice"—or in other words, she had not been given her day in court.[15] She won her appeal at the judicial committee and, along with ten others who had been removed at the same time, was reinstated on the Presbytery's rolls in the fall of 1980. Nevertheless, her sense of an injustice done to her by her church was profound. She sees this event as her first recognition of the power of legal action to protect human rights—a precursor to her lifelong campaign in support of the Charter and LEAF: "What I learned then was that if protections are not enshrined in the law, people don't have a hope in hell of getting justice. I was reinstated in the church but through such a painful process, what did it matter? But legal action can have a systemic effect."[16]

The following year, it was Nancy's turn to write to the presbytery asking that her name be removed from the rolls. The convenor of the ministry and personnel committee wrote back to say that, in light of her "strong feelings about this matter," he was surprised by her request, adding that "in view of the additional information which was brought forward concerning your involvement in various facets of the Church's work, I felt it was very likely your name would be retained on the Presbytery rolls."[17] Nancy replied, thanking him for the positive tone of his letter but explaining that her "decision was made on the basis of being tired of fighting and because the relationship, as I perceived it, with the United Church had been fraught with pain for so long. I simply was not willing to take that degree of pain any longer in my life." And she ended by telling him, "I think the act of removing myself from the roll was one of the most difficult things I have ever done."[18]

She had now been twice rejected by the church she longed to serve—when she first applied to be commissioned as a deaconess and when she tried to make the case that work such as her clown ministry was worthy of the church establishment's recognition. Both occasions caused her great pain, as she recalled years later, "I think the place where it hurt was [that] this was the community of love that was rejecting me. How could they?"[19] Yet even so, just a few years after she voluntarily removed herself from the presbytery roll, she once again dreamed of finding a place in church ministry. As matters stood when she became interim associate minister, she was in fact not eligible to hold such a position. She could have applied to be reinstated and the application likely would have been approved. Yet it seems the members of Metropolitan were unaware of her lack of standing, and her "boss," Bruce McLeod, felt it to be of little importance.[20] Given the twisting path of her journey with the church, it is somehow fitting that she should enter the doors of its ministry in this unsanctioned and unorthodox way.

Barbara Bouck, an outreach worker with the homeless at Metropolitan during Nancy's time there, recalls that "there was a real up and down about people who thought she would be OK" and felt that "she needs to be given a chance," while others thought, "no, never hire her, never hire her, never."[21] The church newsletter article announcing her appointment—"Nancy Jackman: Our Interim Minister till the end of June"—seemed designed both to provoke and assuage the fears of members of the congregation who might have wondered at the decision to hire her: "'Castrating witch' and 'feminist for God' are two of the names Nancy Jackman has been called," was the bold opening of the article, but then it added reassuringly, "Others say she is warm, compassionate, fun-loving, energetic, resourceful, competent, a free spirit, proven, safe, and creative. She follows in the tradition of her great-grandmother [Permilla Rich Langford], her grandmother [Nell Langford Rowell], and her mother who all believed that believing in Christ meant working for the Kingdom of God on earth."

The article went on to establish her bona fides—her academic degrees, her experience as an organizational consultant with the Archbishops of Canterbury and York, as well as her own lifelong commitment to Metropolitan and its people. And it included a tribute to what she had accomplished within the women's movement, ending with the statement that "Nancy sees her activities as fulfilling the prophetic tradition of her foremothers"[22] as captured in a poem by Adrienne Rich. The newsletter goes on to quote Rich's beautiful poem "Natural Resources" from her collection *Dream of a Common Language*.[23]

Here was a signal to church members that Nancy would be no ordinary minister but someone who would agitate, as her spiritual and biological foremothers had done, on behalf of a radical remaking of the world—and the church—to make it more just.

Nancy threw herself into her new responsibilities, which included participating in Sunday worship services—especially the prayers for which she became renowned;

Nancy Ruth, associate minister,
Metropolitan United Church, Toronto,
April 2, 1986.

coordinating and expediting committee work; assisting with home and hospital visits; and working with the outreach committee and its programs, including Homes First and Sojourn House, a refugee centre. Bruce McLeod recalls that she was always first in the office every morning. He also remembers her gift for pastoral care and cites one letter he received from a hospital patient "who wrote to the church thanking us for sending this wonderful woman whose name she had forgotten, or never knew, who had come into her room and just enveloped her with caring and compassion and warmth.... And that was Nancy, of course." Bruce goes on to comment that "To people who respond and react to her sometimes rougher exterior—intended sometimes to stir the waters—they would have been surprised to see that letter. Some at the Board meeting that read that letter were surprised, but moved and touched by it. They realized that there was maybe more to Nancy than they had thought."[24]

Church members may have been just as surprised at the rapport Nancy established with the homeless men who were supported by Metropolitan's outreach services. Barbara Bouck, who ran those services, recalls that Nancy regularly hired some of the men to do yard work at her home. She trusted them, treated them with respect, and gave them an opportunity to earn some much-needed money. Barbara likes to tell the story of the day that Nancy went to the Rosedale butcher and bought the men working in her yard steaks for their lunch. Later, she discovered the men in the kitchen trying to cut the steaks in half: "They thought they were too big or too thick or something. They weren't used to seeing meat like that," so Nancy had to say "No, don't cut them!"[25] She would cook the steaks herself and make sure that they each had a whole steak.

There may be a touch of Nancy as Lady Bountiful in this exchange—Rosedale privilege meets inner-city poverty—but as Barbara notes, "the street people, they loved her."[26] She played cards with them, smoked with them out in the yard, and tried to make sure that their bodies as well as their souls were fed.

Bruce recounts that Nancy's contribution to Sunday services, which she carried out "exceptionally well," may have been another surprise for those in the congregation who had witnessed her rough exterior but weren't aware of her deep spirituality:

> Her presence in a public service of worship is very evident and compelling. It lays itself upon the congregation and sort of commands their spirits to respond to her spirit. It is a spirit beyond her, I believe, that she is open to and that comes through her "performance," as people would say if it was the stage…. That resonates with people out in the congregation in a way very differently from some others who sort of just go through the words or read a book or a page out of here or something they got off the Internet or something and it just doesn't come from their heart. It always came from Nancy's heart, because she wasn't making it up. It wasn't fake in any way; it was out of the centre of her being.[27]

One of Nancy's key strengths as a minister was what Bruce calls her gift for prayer: "When she sets out to lead people in prayer…it just comes naturally. It is a flowing of that spirit through her words and her person, and it resonates. It touches the spirits of people who are there so they're not winding their watch or making notes on the calendar about what they have to do that afternoon. They're caught by it. She could do that. And not many ministers can, whether they've been defrocked or not!"[28] Nancy had hoped, when she considered taking the position at Metropolitan, that it would give her the chance to "affirm her finer attributes" and such was certainly the case as she embraced her ministerial role.

At the same time, she still worried about whether she would be able to content herself with working slowly toward change within the traditional structures of the church. Since the time of her religious awakening in Bali twenty years earlier, she had chafed at the patriarchal nature of Christianity. When he worked with Nancy, Bruce understood that "what troubled her most about the Church was the masculine and sexism and the insensitivity to women, the riding over and the war-like imagery and actions of the Church."[29] She was troubled as well by the tendency of Christians to turn inward, forgetting their broader ethical and social responsibility. Eleanor Wachtel comments in a 1989 article that Nancy "was an outspoken preacher, admonishing doctors for their greed in the overbilling wars. And she urged the congregation to look outside the walls of the church to the community around it."[30] She strongly felt the need for a different church and she struggled to find a way to bring that church into being.

In "Everyday a Damascus day," a sermon she preached in the second month of her appointment, Nancy found a perfect vehicle—one might say a parable—to speak with her congregation about her vision for change. The sermon begins, "When I opened the lectionary texts for the week, and saw that it was Saul's Damascus Rd. story…I couldn't believe it. Oh no, surely I didn't have to discipline myself to find the Good News in a story about this man, whose words have been used for centuries by the hierarchical church to cut out women's tongues, to tie our hands to the kitchen, whose words have been used to burn our bodies at the stake, and still, even today, the church using Paul's words breathes murderous threats against us, refuses to ordain us, still wants us to be silent and the Church continues to malign and oppress us…. Why should I, a woman… have to preach on Paul?" We can imagine some nervous people in the pews at this point, flinching at their brash minister's words and wondering what else they would have to endure before the sermon was over.

She quickly shifts tack, however, exclaiming, "But that's exactly it! That's what this story is about for women and men. Somehow we have to seek out, to be open to God's love in those we dislike and those who persecute us." She goes on to speak of Saul's experience on the road to Damascus, when suddenly "a light from heaven flashed about him and he heard a voice, Saul, Saul, why do you persecute me?" Saul, she explains, was not abandoned by God because of his persecution of Christians but was given the chance to change his behaviour, to become Paul, the Apostle of Christ. And by the same token, she calls on her fellow Church members to consider changing their mission and work, not because they have been unfaithful to God—Saul himself was a good Jew and faithful to God as he knew Him, before his conversion—but because "love needs to grow, it can't stay still, it is forever changing."[31]

Here she has introduced that fearsome word *change*. It is the launching point for the central message of her sermon:

The moment for us at Metropolitan is pregnant with changes. We must plan for our birthing process and our future…. We need to understand the challenge for Jesus on the Damascus Rd—in every time and place. A fantasy I have is that these brick walls and heavy leaded windows that block out the world when we worship, would ascend and leave us sitting and standing where we are allowing the world to look in. Those in the streetcars passing by, the sick in the hospital and those with desperate loneliness that makes people go to the pawn shops across the street, the street people, who might wander up and down the aisles, if all these people looking in said, "Do you love me? Why do you persecute me?" How do we respond? How else can we respond? At present, we spend something like 90% of our budget on ourselves, and when I know that, and know that Jesus asks, "Do you love me?" I know that I must move from my present understanding of faithfulness and this congregation must move too…. As Canadians and Christians we know we won't throw out our tradition. But that doesn't mean that all the old that we hang onto is useful now.[32]

In her final exhortation, she challenges her congregation to embrace change despite the fear it engenders, and to glory in its power for good:

I believe it is only when we are willing to move away from that status quo that we can be open to the possibility of Christ in our lives and in our congregation and in our families and in our work places…. We can be open to doing things another way…. We can change these systems that allow Dome stadiums to be built, when bag ladies freeze. We can change these systems that allow families to be split because of our selfish immigration laws. We can change our direction of spending 90% of our money on ourselves, and go through the pain and joy of a Damascus Rd. We too can be purified by fire like Isaiah, so that we can in all time and in all places say "here I am, send me." In our fear, remember always that God transforms and that God created us in her wisdom and said the comforting words: "Fear not, for I have redeemed you, I have summoned you by name, you are mine."[33]

Nancy's friend Marilou McPhedran, who had visited Metropolitan to hear Nancy guest-preach a year or two earlier, describes her as looking "majestic in her robes. You could tell she was having a great time walking down the aisle with her colored ribbons flying."[34] We can imagine her likewise in full flight on this day when she preached to her congregation about a Damascus Road conversion. She called on them to join her in "reconstituting the world," in Adrienne Rich's words, asking them to consider doing things another way. The principles about which she cared so deeply—social justice, systemic reform, a God who can be seen in female form, a church that is open and looks outward—are at the forefront of this powerful sermon. While she may have counselled herself to work quietly and patiently for change, she was now only six weeks into the job and was already using the pulpit to argue for radical transformation.

Nancy, as Bruce tells us, had her supporters in the congregation, including those who were pleasantly surprised to find how good she was at the full range of her duties. There were others, however, who likely found her disruptive, threatening, and too unorthodox for ministry in their church. When the decision was made to appoint a permanent associate minister, Nancy was not given the job, though she applied for it and held out hope she would be chosen.[35] The summer 1986 church newsletter announced that "Metropolitan's search for a diaconal minister is over. At a Congregational meeting on June 15, 1986, the Pastoral Relations Committee was directed to issue a call to Ann Gilbert, who is currently serving as diaconal minister at Forest Grove United Church, Willowdale. This call takes effect October 15, 1986." Nancy's disappointment was deep; a few months later she wrote to her ministerial friend from the 1960s, Shelley Finson, who ran the feminist movement within the United Church, "I adored working at Metropolitan—however, they chose Ann Gilbert so I was definitely not what they wanted."[36] Nevertheless, she not only fulfilled her interim appointment until the end of June, but agreed to come back in September, after the summer hiatus, to continue her duties until her successor arrived.

That July, however, an issue of the *Globe and Mail* magazine hit the stands with a smiling Nancy in her clerical robes emblazoned at the top of the page, Metropolitan's spire rising behind her, and a photo cutline that read, "Nancy Jackman and the male bastion of Metropolitan Church." The half-page article was clearly intended to shock. Nancy is cited as calling her church "an institution as unrepentantly male as a locker room" and her thoughts about the "male mystique" are summed up under a few headings. She accuses the worship service of lacking "roundness" and intimacy. The hymns are militaristic and use "such violent language" that it's "like putting the cruise missile in the church." But her comments on church architecture are the most provocative: "the church is laid out in the shape of a cross. To me, it looks like an inverted phallus, with the two pulpits on the crossbar as testicles."[37]

To say the least, the article stirred controversy at Metropolitan. In a letter from Kenneth Peel, the chair of Metropolitan's official board, to James Chisholm, the chair of the ministry and personnel committee, Peel refers to the "offense, pain or anxiety suffered by some in our congregation upon their learning of the article." While Peel had received only three letters from congregants about the matter, his view was that these letters "appear to reflect some wider response to the article," and he noted that "a range of views and concerns have been expressed to me."[38] Bruce McLeod, on the other hand, defended Nancy, writing to her mother soon after the article appeared, "Please don't worry about the Globe article. Most people have never seen it. Nancy's work in the last four months has been recognized by everyone as being outstanding. I just love working with her, and she has done a great deal for the church which she loves."[39]

Nancy herself decided to prepare a letter to the congregation in which she expresses her "deep concern that some people had been hurt by the Globe & Mail magazine's article, bearing my picture in front of Metropolitan." She laid out a number of extenuating circumstances behind the article's publication. The interview had taken place in early March, over the telephone, with a freelance journalist,

> a woman who I knew as a Metropolitanite. She was interested in doing an article on "sexism in the Church" and "women's experience in ministry" to commemorate the 50th anniversary of the ordination of women in The United Church of Canada. As I was a

member of The United Church's Toronto Conference, Women's Concerns Committee, it seemed reasonable and appropriate to respond to her request.

Nancy goes on to explain that she and the reporter spoke for one-and-a-half hours on a broad range of topics, including the history of women in the ministry, the significance of the Persons Case, architecture, music, language, polity, and practice in the context of women in the church and some of the issues being addressed by the Toronto Conference women's concerns committee. And, she concludes, "I was hurt and disturbed when I saw the printed article, and saw how distorted my interview had become. I can understand how members of our community have perceived this article to be an affront to Metropolitan. I certainly do! It does not reflect my love for Metropolitan nor my commitment to its people, its life and our future.... I am truly sorry the article had caused so much hurt, and accept responsibility in this."[40]

Nancy had in fact spoken truthfully to the reporter about many of her frustrations with the church, but she was taken aback by the way in which her words and photograph were sensationalized in their editing and presentation. We can see here a tension between her push to challenge the status quo and her longing to stay in the community and work from the inside for change. Interestingly, the interview took place before she learned she would not be given the permanent associate minister's position; the apology took place months after that and reflects her continuing desire to maintain a home within her church, even though they had chosen not to hire her as their minister.

The ministry and personnel committee met with Nancy on August 20 "to discuss the questions raised by publication of an article about Nancy Jackman." She reviewed with them the circumstances of the interview, pointing out that "references she had made were taken out of historical context, that others were run together and that others were incorrectly attributed to her." Her description of church architecture, for example, was taken from the American theologian Mary Daly. The committee's opinion after hearing her testimony was that "Nancy Jackman's comments were twisted and taken out of context in the article." Its report to the chair of the official board concluded, "The committee is of the view that the article has caused personal pain to Nancy Jackman, her family and the congregation. Because of this the committee feels it would serve no useful purpose to pursue the matter further."[41] Soon after this meeting, Nancy circulated her letter of apology to the congregation and in September stepped back into her duties until the new associate minister's arrival in mid-October.

On October 12, at her final worship service as interim minister, Nancy was recognized and thanked for her faithful service to Metropolitan. In "A Tribute to Nancy Jackman," published in the October newsletter, church member Julian Smith praised her as "a person of compassion with great social concerns," adding that "this has been evident both in and out of the pulpit, where she has demonstrated her particular interest in the welfare and equitable treatment for women." He went on to note her "sincerity and Christian dedication...reflected in her sermons and in the conducting of the worship part of the service. She has demonstrated her awareness of and concern for the people of this congregation, this city, this country, this world." And not surprisingly, given Nancy's gift for outreach, he thanked her for her assistance with "the pastoral work of the church.... She has provided personal counselling to those who have come to her with their problems, whether they were from this congregation or from the street."[42]

What is not mentioned, of course, is that Nancy would gladly have stayed on as minister at Metropolitan but was not given the chance to do so. In a diary entry for November 11, 1986, she writes about the pain both she and her mother felt at the recent "covenanting service" to induct the new minister into her role—"because it was not me. I felt a bit like the rejected bride as I sat in the congregation."[43] In a draft of a letter to Barbara Bouck early in the following year, Nancy expresses her disillusionment with Metropolitan, writing that

> There is nothing in our worship that tries to help those alienated & alone. We perpetuate the norm & do not push the extremity of community building and liturgical experimentation. For those of us, like myself, who are alienated from the norms of society, albeit for different reasons than the poor, to come to worship is to submit, like a battered wife, ever hoping that there'll be room for me, only to be battered again.[44]

Despite her alienation, Nancy accepted a seat on Metropolitan's board of trustees in December 1986—but only for a short time; she submitted her resignation in the spring of 1987. Fellow board member Ron McKinlay wrote to express his regret at her decision and to urge her to reconsider, telling her that "we need you and you need the Church."[45] In her reply, Nancy tells him that she is "profoundly moved" by his letter but not prepared to change her mind. She reminds him that "the Pastoral

Relations Committee had a choice around me to make last June. They made it. They decided that who I am, the kinds of things I think, and what I was willing to do, were not what they wanted." Though she has tried to make her peace with Metropolitan and to remain within its community, she cannot put the hurt and disappointment behind her.

Just as importantly, she was now reconsidering her relationship to Christianity. In her reply to Ron McKinlay, she goes on say,

> At the present moment I seem to have moved outside of what is normally called "the Church." I have been spending time reading about feminist spirituality issues, listening to the CBC Ideas programs on "The Goddess" and meeting with women who are trying to find some way to meet their spiritual needs. I think it's clear that if I was honest about what I was thinking in a group like Metropolitan, I would be perceived as a heretic and in other times would be burned as a witch. I am not willing to give my energies to fight battles with that group of people.[46]

Frank Brisbin, chair of Metropolitan's board and a former minister of the church who confirmed Nancy's baptismal vows in 1954 when she was twelve years old, also wrote to convey his regret at Nancy's resignation. Brisbin was particularly fond of Nancy and in his letter to her he expresses his sorrow that she has "given up on our church." He understands that she has been not only "deeply hurt" by the church but profoundly frustrated by the "male dominance deeply imbedded in its liturgy & structure." At the same time, he tries to persuade her that change, if slow, is coming, and asks, "I wonder how you can expect centuries of tradition and practice to give way in one lifetime." In defence of the Church, he writes "The United Church is trying to be more open, & is in turmoil because of that. To some we are too slow; to some we are too trendy; to some we are weirdly exhibiting an institutional death wish. I am distressed by all this, but choose to stick with my church & and help weather the continuing storms." His letter closes with the plea, "We could use your help, Nancy, & I pray that you will, sooner or later, decide to return, and that I will still be around & able to welcome you back."[47]

Nancy's reply to Frank Brisbin set out her position very clearly. She wanted him to understand that

> it is not that I "have given up" on "our" Church. It is not that I have "given up" on the United Church of Canada, or in fact, Christendom. It's not that I have "given up" but rather that I have "moved on." What I have "moved on" to is unclear and certainly my exploration relates to goddess religion at this time…. I need you to know that what has happened in my mind has created the greatest sense of freedom in my psyche and personhood. It is such a relief to no longer feel responsible for the sins of the past or the future of the Church. It's an absolutely glorious feeling to join with other women around the world in seeking out something new…. There truly is a big difference between having left or "given up" and having "moved on."[48]

Nancy's spiritual journey was not over, but she had abandoned her efforts to fit within a church whose spaces failed to accommodate her. Many at Metropolitan loved and respected her, not least Bruce McLeod, who would say of her time as minister that "we learned about God from Nancy Jackman." Yet the God Nancy sought to bring forth in her ministry was not a comfortable one. It was a God who challenged and prodded worshippers toward a Damascus Road transformation. Nancy dreamed of breaking open established customs and conventions, even imagining a church without walls where the homeless could walk down the aisles and feel at home. Such a church never came into being at Metropolitan. Catharine A. MacKinnon, a prominent American feminist lawyer and long-time friend of Nancy's, believes that spirituality has remained central in her friend's life and that "it's the Church's loss that it alienated her.... [T]his is somebody who really believes in grace and lives it, and they just did the wrong thing."[49]

In a 1990 speech at the University of Waterloo, Nancy told her audience that "she no longer describes herself as a Christian," and she has not turned back toward the established church since she left it.[50] Instead, she has sought meaning in other forms of spirituality as well as in the social justice mission she believes lies at the core of true Christianity. Janet Somerville—a writer, former producer of the CBC *Ideas* program on religion, and the first woman and first Roman Catholic to be appointed general secretary of the Canadian Council of Churches—says of Nancy, "I don't know what her idea of God is. I really don't know. But it's very clear to me that she has a commitment, like a rock-solid commitment...toward what Jesus stood for."[51]

Justice for women has of course figured largely in Nancy's personal commitments and in 1987 she was ready to throw herself back into generating support and raising funds for LEAF, taking on speaking engagements from coast to coast to coast over the next few years. She was also poised to consider a vocation very different from one within the church—a foray into the secular world of politics.

Footnotes for this chapter can be found online at:
http://secondstorypress.ca/resources

Chapter 7

"GO AFTER POWER,
AND MAKE NO APOLOGY FOR IT"[1]

HER DREAM of a church vocation now behind her, Nancy threw herself back into work on behalf of the Women's Legal Education and Action Fund (LEAF). One journalist tellingly described her as having "the aura of a 'born again'…only her religion is the women's Legal Education and Action Fund."[1] A high-octane and compelling speaker, she was in steady demand to give the keynote address at annual Persons Day breakfasts that had sprung up across the country to raise funds for LEAF. She also spoke at high schools, universities, teachers' federation meetings, and a raft of women's organizations. Still passionate about the educational part of LEAF's mission, she used these speaking opportunities to carry the message to women on the importance of the Charter as a tool to protect and expand women's rights. Her final exhortation at a speech in Charlottetown, for example, called on her audience to see themselves as "the continuation of the Alberta 5; we are those who will extend women's constitutional rights, and keep the living tree capable of growth and expansion. We are in the Cradle of Confederation. Well friends, let's rock it!"[2]

Fittingly, when the LEAF executive decided to hold a gala event in Nancy's honour and set up an award in her name, the award was designed to recognize not LEAF lawyers, volunteers, or board members, but "a grassroots woman who has chosen to take a case to the courts that will further benefit the equality rights of women." Given some of her differences with other members of the LEAF leadership, Nancy was surprised when friend and LEAF board member Marilou McPhedran visited to tell her that she was proposing a "Toast and Roast Dinner" to honour Nancy and to create this new award. In Nancy's diary account of Marilou's visit, she confessed to feeling strange at being "selected out and honoured" in this way when so many others have "put hours into doing this stuff too." At the same time, she felt gratified at Marilou's insistence that Nancy was one of the people "who kept the Charter issue alive for women in this country...as I criss-crossed the nation giving speeches...in women's groups from coast to coast and from the arctic to the border." Marilou is a lawyer and it still rankled with Nancy that "many of the lawyers have forgotten that I did that piece with all the grass roots women's groups in Canada. I must say I was proud of CORC, and I was proud of the work I did to help create LEAF."[3] Marilou's acknowledgement that Nancy had pulled away from LEAF a year earlier on "such a sad note" and her proposal that LEAF now highlight and honour her contributions went a long way toward healing those old wounds.

Marilou visited Nancy in the winter of 1987, and the gala, scheduled to be held in conjunction with the anniversary of LEAF's founding, took shape over the following year. On April 16, 1988, three hundred people gathered in the ballroom of Toronto's Sheraton Centre for what the evening's program called "A Tribute to Nancy Rowell Jackman." Sheila Shotton, who had travelled with Nancy in the south of France when they were in their twenties, wrote the story for the *Toronto Star*, calling it "a funny, oddball, eclectic, eye-rolling event" and adding that Nancy herself is a "funny, oddball, eclectic" who "has certainly been known to roll her eyes at many of the injustices toward women in this world." Of the photos that went with Shotton's story, one shows Nancy surrounded by her brothers, all of whom, along with their mother, were front and centre at the event. Hal, however, was the only one with a speaking part and he's the one Shotton singles out for a couple of "shocking" moments during his turn at the microphone. When he told the audience that his sister joined the women's movement because she had reached a time in her life when she was "dispossessed and disillusioned," Shotton describes the audience—most of them of course feminists—as "stunned." When he goes on to attempt an unfortunate play on the word LEAF, implying that the evening's event is a fundraiser for Dutch elm disease, Shotton relates that "there was a hush in the room at that crack that was even deader than Dutch elms."[4]

Another moment in Hal's speech, unmentioned in Shotton's article, was one that struck a happy note for Nancy. As he closed his remarks, Hal looked at his sister and said, "In our family, it isn't very difficult to be executive of a trust company or an insurance company. That's expected and very easy. Nancy is a little different. Nancy is one of the leaders of a great crusade to address social injustice. And I suspect if our father was with us today, of all his children, Nancy would be the one he'd be most proud of."[5] The camera recording the event cuts quickly to Nancy's table and we can see on her face how much this unexpected

Nancy Ruth and Claire L'Heureux-Dubé at Mary Lue Hind's home for dinner on the eve of the Sudbury LEAF Persons Day Breakfast, October 21, 2001. The Honourable Claire L'Heureux-Dubé was the second woman appointed to the Supreme Court of Canada. Both women were speakers at the LEAF Breakfast.

praise from her brother meant to her. All three brothers with whom she competed for their father's approval are in the room and the eldest, heir to their father's empire, has laid the mantle of victory on her—the youngest, the only girl, the sibling who has struggled hardest to find her purpose and place.

The speakers who followed Hal were chosen to chronicle successive stages of Nancy's life: Heather Hall, a classmate from Branksome, regaled the audience with teenage escapades such as the illicit trip to see Elvis while they were boarders; Donna Runnalls told stories about her year sharing an apartment with Nancy in Jerusalem; and Elaine Peacock spoke of what Nancy accomplished during her years at Naramata. Bruce McLeod, describing his six months of shared ministry with Nancy at Metropolitan, highlighted her rage against the church's failures but went on to say, "All her outrageousness never succeeded in hiding a heart that's as big or bigger than she is." Friend and lawyer Mary Eberts then paid tribute to Nancy's work on the constitutional lobby during the Charter years as well as her current focus on supporting equality rights through nurturing the work of LEAF. And to ensure that these achievements were placed within a broader context, emcee Susan McCutcheon closed by listing off a host of other organizations and causes that Nancy was currently supporting through her burgeoning philanthropy and her volunteer service, including feminist theatre, women's centres, women's health projects, a hospice for AIDS, and a house for pregnant teenagers.

It is noteworthy that, for this gala event, and not for the first time—her textbooks at the London School of Economics are inscribed in the same way—Nancy had dropped her given middle name Ruth and adopted her mother's maiden name Rowell. Nancy Ruth Jackman had morphed into Nancy Rowell Jackman as part of her continuing search for who she was and where she belonged. More than twenty-five years earlier she had sat alone in her London room and written in her diary, "I wish I could be something." Now, aged forty-six, she was surrounded by friends and family who assured her that she had indeed become something—somebody who must be reckoned with. This personage, furthermore, had a flair and flamboyance entirely her own, reflected in the evening's entertainment: the Clichettes, a trio of lip-synching feminists known for their satirical take-down of pop music's clichés about gender—a highlight was their performance in drag of "It's a Man's World"—and the night ended with one of Nancy's greatest sources of pleasure—dancing. Her love of a good time was famously on display throughout the evening, her enjoyment summed up in her own tongue-in-cheek closing remark: "Having lived most of my life in the shadow of my three brothers, I do appreciate the limelight."[6]

There was plenty of limelight for Nancy over the coming year; that same spring of 1988 saw her named a "Woman of Distinction" by the Toronto Young Women's Christian Association (YWCA), with the tribute going jointly to her, to her mother, and to her late grandmother and great-grandmother, in recognition of their "four generations of faith and purpose." The following spring she was awarded the first of four honorary doctorate degrees, this one from Mount Saint Vincent University. But the fall of 1988 brought a different kind of limelight, as she stepped for the first time into a campaign for political office.

For Nancy, her move into politics was a natural one: "I came from a political family. My grandfather and my father

Sheila Shotton with
Nancy Ruth at "A Tribute
to Nancy Rowell Jackman."
April 16, 1988.

*Shades of Paris
love
Sheila*

had both been members of Parliament, and two of my brothers had run. I had been a member of the [Progressive Conservative] Party...for decades." Bruce McLeod was also an influence; he himself had run unsuccessfully for the provincial Liberal party in 1981 and she recalls complaining to him about a provincial politician—Attorney General Ian Scott—and McLeod's telling her she needed to "get off the pot or shut up."[7] A remark Nancy made in a speech not long after her first political campaign also reveals her motives; she describes the fun she had working with LEAF but goes on to say "At my age, I am not going to become a lawyer so I reckon I'll become a politician. If I am not going to litigate, I'll legislate!"[8] The power in LEAF still lay with the lawyers; politics offered an alternative way of wielding power, of getting things done, that held a strong attraction for this ardent social activist.

For her maiden political voyage, Nancy chose to enter the race for the Progressive Conservative nomination in the federal riding of Rosedale. The seat had been vacated that summer when its popular incumbent, Progressive Conservative David Crombie, resigned as member of Parliament to accept a royal commission appointment. Crombie was seen as a "red Tory"—fiscally conservative and socially liberal—and the PC party leaders were anxious to find a strong left-of-centre candidate to replace him in the next federal election. Rosedale, while known for its mansions and old money in the north part of the riding— Nancy's neighbourhood—was also home to a substantial lower- and middle-income population living in housing developments and apartment complexes in its southern stretch. To have a chance of success, the PC candidate would need to appeal across these lines of class, money, and ideology.

With Nancy's deep roots in Rosedale, her commitment to social justice, and her experience working as a church minister at Metropolitan

The winners of the 1988 YWCA of Metropolitan Toronto Women of Distinction Award. From L to R: Margaret Atwood, Dr. Rose Sheinin, Meena Dhar, Mary Cornish, Julie Davis, Nancy Ruth, Mary Coyne Rowell Jackman, Jalynn Bennett.

United in inner-city Toronto, she might have seemed an ideal candidate. Yet she was not only untested in political office but well known for her independence and strength of mind, raising the same question that the church had raised about her when she applied to be commissioned as a deaconess: would she be willing to "toe the party line?" Jane Pepino, a real estate lawyer at the firm of Aird & Berlis and a member of the Metro Toronto Police Commission, observed to a reporter that, in her opinion, "the party has always looked at Nancy as a bit of a kook…. Nancy's that funny Jackman broad. She's been around at full volume for a long time. She's ruffled feathers and stepped on toes."[9]

Pepino herself supported Nancy's bid for the nomination, but the party's inner circle settled on David MacDonald as their choice and persuaded him to run. MacDonald—like Nancy, a United Church minister but also a former and long-time MP from Prince Edward Island, a former Cabinet member in Joe Clark's government, and Canada's current ambassador to Ethiopia—was seen as a safe bet; socially liberal and politically experienced. Although some people complained that he was a "parachute candidate" without strong ties to the riding, he was nevertheless judged to be both capable of winning the seat and qualified to serve as a Cabinet minister should the PCs win another majority in the next election.[10]

Undeterred by this lack of endorsement from the party's powerful, Nancy forged ahead with her campaign for the nomination, enlisting Marian Smith as her campaign manager and announcing her candidacy on August 8, 1988. A third candidate, Douglas McCutcheon, also entered the race; a businessman aligned firmly with the right wing of the PC party, he offered a distinct contrast to his opponents. Media coverage, however, tended to focus on the contest between the two "Red Tories," both of whom had colourful backgrounds that made for an exciting story. One journalist wrote, "Progressive Conservatives in Rosedale finally have the contest they wanted to replace former MP and Cabinet minister David Crombie," noting that there were now "two high-profile challengers for the downtown riding's Conservative nomination," either of whom would represent, as Crombie did, "the left wing of the governing party."

This journalist went on to say of Nancy that she "carries a wealthy and storied Rosedale family history into the nomination fight. Her father, Harry, held Rosedale for the Conservatives from 1940–1949. Her eldest brother, financier Hal Jackman, failed three times [to win the election] in Rosedale.... [She] is best known across the country as a feminist."[11] Another journalist describing the race called Nancy a "millionaire feminist" and "one of Canada's wealthiest and most opinionated women...best known for her commitment to women's issues."[12]

Nancy was at pains, however, to make it clear that she was not a "one-issue candidate." As she explained in an interview, "I'm as concerned about the environment as other things but the press usually picks up the feminist bit."[13] Her campaign literature highlighted her key concerns as not only protecting the environment but also providing affordable housing for all income groups; accessible childcare; equality of opportunity for all Canadians; and AIDS treatment and prevention. She also clearly signalled that she would support the Conservative's stand in favour of free trade—the 1988 federal election would come to be known as the "free trade election," culminating in the enactment of the Canada-US Free Trade Agreement in January 1989.[14]

Each of the candidates for nomination, of course, had to make the case that she or he was the most likely to be victorious against the other parties' candidates in the upcoming federal election. Nancy worked hard in her campaign to make it known that, despite being a multi-millionaire, she was a candidate "for all of Rosedale"—for the working-class south, where her campaign was organized by Barbara Bouck of Metropolitan Church, as well as for the affluent north. Her campaign newsletter urged people to consider that "80% of Rosedale voters live in the southern part of the riding. Nancy Jackman has worked for years with people in this area—they knew her long before she asked for their vote. Now they are coming forward to support her. Nancy is the only candidate in either major party who can and will pull solid support in the south."[15]

The Rosedale PC nomination was one of the most closely watched and hotly contested races that fall. In keeping with party nomination procedures, candidates signed up as many riding association members as possible so that these members could vote for them on the night of the contest. On the morning of the nomination vote, Dan Smith of the *Toronto Star* reported that "McDonald and McCutcheon, who has been strongly backed by Rosedale's Bay St. crowd, each sold roughly 1500 new memberships for tonight's meeting. Jackman trails with roughly 650, and another 400 eligible voters already belonged to the local riding association."[16] The riding association membership, in other words, had increased tenfold, from four hundred to more than four thousand, in preparation for the nomination battle.

Nancy had signed up the smallest share of this increase. In an opinion piece published a few days before the nomination meeting, one of Nancy's supporters, Sally Barnes, former press secretary to Premier William Davis, wrote of her frustration at the failure of women to endorse female candidates: "Nancy Jackman may win the Progressive Conservative nomination in the federal riding of Rosedale next Thursday. But if she does, it won't be because organized women's groups gave her the kind of help and support she has given them over many years." Barnes pointed to one of the tensions that was to plague Nancy throughout her political career: many of her natural allies—women who shared her feminism and commitment to social justice causes—were aligned with either the New Democratic Party (NDP) or the Liberal Party, and many of them would find it hard to reconcile Nancy's values with her Progressive Conservative political affiliation. Further, organizations such as inner-city groups and immigrant women's association, to whom Nancy had been "especially generous in her contribution of time and money," would not lend her their endorsement because their members "support the NDP or because they are opposed to the Tories' free trade policy."[17]

In the case of the Rosedale contest, Barnes found it particularly troubling that women "won't join a political party in order to qualify to vote at the nomination meetings. They insist they'll vote for women at election time—but they won't take the necessary step of party membership in order to help get the candidate to the election stage." In Barnes' judgement,

> Increasingly, especially in the urban areas where nominations are hotly contested, the only way to win is to deliver large blocks of votes. Ethnic groups have learned this. They might not agree with their candidate on every single issue, but they recognize it's to their advantage to get one of their own into a position of power and influence.... Women, however, still have much to learn about the political process. Until they accept the rules, they can't expect to win and women will continue to be underrepresented among those people who have the power and privilege of making our laws, deciding how our tax dollars will be spent, and how our society will unfold.[18]

Yet despite these challenges, Nancy took great delight in her first foray into electoral politics. A natural extrovert, she loved campaigning: "You lost twenty pounds. You did a lot of walking.... Running is fun, you know?"[19] She was also proud of the number of women and men from the feminist movement who worked on her behalf, contributed funds, and turned out for the nomination meeting, including dear friend and staunch NDP member Kay Macpherson. If, as Barnes suggests, the outcome could have been different had more women been willing to "play party politics," this campaign was nonetheless a beginning and an opportunity for Nancy to learn the rules of the game.

As expected, David MacDonald won the nomination. McCutcheon, who like Nancy was Rosedale born and bred and had pulled in substantial support from the well-heeled members of the riding, actually had the most votes on the first ballot: 595 to MacDonald's 590 and Nancy's 335. Fewer than half of those who had bought memberships actually showed up and voted at the meeting, but even so the combined numbers were so much larger than those for a typical riding association meeting that the association had to rent the Metro Convention Centre to accommodate them. Not surprisingly, after Nancy dropped out of the race, more of her supporters shifted their vote to MacDonald than to McCutcheon, and MacDonald carried the day—on what was still a "close second ballot."[20] He would go on to another narrow victory in the November federal election, defeating Liberal candidate Bill Graham by only eighty votes as PC leader Brian Mulroney retained his party's majority and his position as Canada's prime minister.

Looking back on the nomination meeting, Nancy is confident that even though she came in third she "spoke the best, thanks to the Church and all those speech therapy lessons my mother had given me as a stuttering child."[21] Drafts among her private papers show that she worked diligently on preparing her nomination speech, taking advice from colleagues and carefully rehearsing her delivery with her friend Mary Eberts in a boardroom at the legal firm of Tory Tory. She opened with a statement about why she wanted the nomination, telling her audience that "In the last 8 years, I've travelled this country from St. John's to Victoria, speaking about the Charter of Rights & Freedoms and constitutional law issues...and always urging women to accept the challenge of going as legislators to their provincial capitals, to Ottawa, so that our voice can be heard in the making of laws that affect us. Now is my season—to move from one form of public life, to the fulness of electoral politics."[22]

She positioned herself as someone with national experience and credibility in the public sphere, someone ready to take her place in governing her country. And she underscored a driving motive behind her run: the need to ensure that women were more equitably represented in the legislative process. After reviewing some key policy imperatives—for example, her support for free trade and her passion for environmental protection—she went on to say that she was "distressed that far too many still don't share in [Canada's] prosperity" and she was also "angry that so many women & members of minority groups are still not in the mainstream of political & economic life in Canada."[23] These themes remained constant over the years as she sought to become an elected politician; she continued to be an "outsider/insider," prosperous herself but a voice for those who were not; a member of Canada's establishment yet struggling to gain a foothold in the political mainstream; a member of the "second sex" under-represented to this day in the seats of power.

Finally, in the closing section of her nomination speech, Nancy confronted head-on the question of her "contrary" status within her chosen political party. Some of the intense

Nancy Ruth and Mary Eberts going off to the Supreme Court of Canada, Ottawa, in early October 1987, where Mary would appear as co-counsel for the Women's Legal Education and Action Fund in *Andrews v. Law Society of British Columbia*. *Andrews* was the first case interpreting section 15 of the Canadian Charter of Rights and Freedoms to be decided by the Supreme Court of Canada.

media coverage the contest attracted included speculation about her well-known independent streak and the likely fear among party leaders that she would be difficult to rein in. To that speculation, Nancy responded,

> You have been reading in the Globe that I am at odds with our party on some issues, that I will resist party discipline. I'm certain that each & every member in the room has at times differed from the party's position on some issues. In fact, my reading of our party is—that it has been made stronger and better by those who were not afraid to take a stand & express their own hearts and minds—and those of their constituents. The special strength of our party is that it provides means for discussing different points of view, & coming to consensus. For these reasons—I understand the necessity of party discipline. I understand & accept the rules of the game because I know that only by working within the process can I achieve those things that are dear to my heart.[24]

Such a resolution for someone as outspoken and strong-willed as Nancy could not have been an easy one to reach. Looking back thirty years later, she confides that she probably delayed her entry into politics because "I was not sure I would ever submit to Party discipline," and that "It was only when I believed I could submit, and eat the shit, so to speak, that I actually ran."[25] In subsequent campaigns for provincial office and during her twelve years in the Senate, Nancy faced again and again the need to calibrate the point at which she would be prepared to compromise her values—to "eat the shit"—in order to stay within her party's fold.

Nancy Ruth with the Right Honourable Brian Mulroney at the American Express Reception for the *Je suis le cahier: The Sketchbooks of Picasso* exhibition, Art Gallery of Ontario, July 30, 1988–October 2, 1988.

Linda McQuaig, reporting on Nancy's speech the following day for the *Globe and Mail*, observed that while Nancy "fought the image" of being too independent, she "also tried to use it to her advantage. In a speech that no doubt sent shivers through those who feared she might not toe the party line, Ms. Jackman told the nomination meeting that 'the party is made stronger and better by those not afraid to express their own minds.'"[26] A few days later, Laura Sabia—who herself had run twice under the PC banner and lost—took exception in the *Toronto Sun* to characterizing Nancy's "independence" as a deficit: "Since when have brains and honest forthrightness been a detriment to achieving political office?" In hot defence of the candidate she went on to say, "I know of no one who has done more for the needy, for the battered and bruised, for legal rights for women, etc., than Nancy" and ended with the exhortation "Seize the next opportunity to run, Nancy. We need spirited, bold, independent people like yourself."[27]

On September 14 Nancy wrote to thank her team of volunteers, telling them, "What a wonderful thing we all did. To have achieved the amount of credit I now have with the party is quite an accomplishment. I intend to build on the strengths we have. Be assured that the base you helped me create is moving on up the mountain. I'll be back, and I hope you will be too."[28] With hard-won experience under her belt and her appetite whetted for success in electoral politics, Nancy was more than ready to seize the next opportunity to run and it was to provincial politics that she now turned her attention.

In September 1987, after more than forty years of Progressive Conservative rule, the Ontario Liberal Party won a majority of seats in the provincial legislature. The election two years earlier had ended the PC dynasty; the Conservatives won the most seats but not enough to form a majority government and, with the NDP's support, the Liberals put together a minority government that held until 1987. Now firmly in control of government, the Liberals under Premier David Peterson were not expected to go back to the polls for at least another four years, perhaps five, in 1991 or 1992. Even so, Nancy knew the strategic importance of being ready well ahead of an election call. In 1989, she and Marian Smith began looking for the most promising riding in which to seek the PC provincial nomination.

In her own riding of St. George-St. David—at that time, federal and provincial electoral boundaries differed in Ontario—the sitting member was Liberal Ian Scott, who had served as Ontario's attorney general and a member of Cabinet since June 1985. He was a highly respected and effective politician and Nancy knew that even if she won the PC nomination, she "couldn't have defeated his machine" in the next election. In deciding which other riding looked most promising, she believed her prospects were strongest in the neighbouring riding of St. Andrew–St. Patrick (now the riding of St. Paul's); it had been held by the Conservatives for decades until the 1987 upset, when the incumbent Larry Grossman was defeated by Liberal Ron Kanter.[29] In November 1989, she approached the executive of the St. Andrew–St. Patrick PC riding association to let them know she was interested in being their future candidate, only to be shown a distinctly cold shoulder.

Despite this chilly response, over the coming months Nancy worked to sign up members, raise her profile within the riding, and signal her desire to run as its candidate in the next election. She also tried to build ties within the riding association, asking, for example, to be included in its activities, but her attempts met with little success. With a growing sense that "no matter what she did, she wouldn't be accepted into this small closely knit group,"[30] she decided to put into play some lessons learned from her former nomination contest: "Read the party constitution, know it by heart. Know the rules. Make sure you have a loyal team."[31] Diplomacy had failed, so she would master the rules of engagement and call in her troops to do battle.

The association's annual general meeting (AGM) was scheduled for April 5, 1990, and in early February Nancy set about signing up new association members. Since the riding's existing constitution stipulated that members did not have to live in the riding but could come from anywhere within the city, or indeed even in the province, she recruited members accordingly; out of four hundred people she signed up, about two-thirds lived inside the riding and the balance came from outside. In March, however, she got wind of a move by the executive committee

Nancy Ruth campaigning for the Progressive Conservative
nomination in the federal riding of Rosedale, Toronto,
early fall 1988.

Campaigning,
Toronto, early
fall 1988.

to propose at the AGM revisions to the constitution that would restrict membership to those who lived within the riding. She herself believed that such a restriction was appropriate but sought to negotiate with the executive a "grandmothering" clause to cover any out-of-riding members who had joined before the constitution was changed. Those negotiations, led by lawyer David Merner, Nancy's prime political operative, went nowhere.[32]

On the night of April 5, in what Nancy refers to as the "1990 takeover," her loyal supporters turned out in full force for the AGM.[33] In place of the existing executive committee that had been proposed for re-election, a whole new slate, supportive of Nancy, was nominated from the floor—and won. Further, the constitutional amendment had to be withdrawn because members had not received the required notice of the proposed change in advance of the meeting. Even though Nancy tried to hold out an olive branch to the former executive, inviting them into positions on the new executive committee, most of them immediately resigned.[34] The most virulent of her opponents followed up by filing a protest with the executive committee of the Progressive Conservative Party of Ontario, but on June 19 a tribunal of that executive unanimously ruled against the protesters, and on June 21, the books, records, and funds were at last turned over to the new riding executive.[35]

This resolution finally cleared the way for the riding to hold a nomination meeting and select its candidate for what was now rumoured to be a provincial election just around the corner. During the interim period, as columnist Doris Anderson noted, Nancy had been "pounding the pavement, knocking on doors and trying to drum up votes" but had been "handicapped by not being able to call a nomination meeting and be officially nominated."

She had also been denied access to "the membership lists, the computer software and the riding funds—all frozen by the former executive" and all vital to a successful campaign.[36] The nomination meeting was held at Forest Hill Collegiate on July 18 and Nancy, with the endorsement of her executive and with no opposition, was acclaimed as the St. Andrew-St. Patrick candidate for the PC party. There were few people in that large auditorium, but as always Mary Jackman was there to support her daughter. Having won the nomination battle against an entrenched and unwelcoming riding association, Nancy now began in earnest her first run for political office.

The official nomination had come none too soon since the Liberals dropped the writ less than two weeks later, on July 30, calling a snap election for September 6, 1990. Both the Green Party and the Libertarians fielded candidates in St. Andrew-St. Patrick, but the two mainstream party opponents Nancy faced were Liberal Ron Kanter, running for re-election, and NDP Zanana Akande, an elementary school principal running for the first time. Campaigning on issues similar to those of her 1988 federal nomination race—the environment, childcare, affordable housing—Nancy presented herself as a social activist who was at the same time experienced in business and philanthropy, someone who could "balance social issues with fiscal responsibility."[37] The list of boards on which she served had continued to grow and now included the Economic Council of Canada, the Canadian Centre for Arms Control and Disarmament, the Canadian Women's Foundation, and the International Institute of Concern for Public Health. Here was someone deeply engaged in the causes that mattered to her and poised to make a difference should she gain a seat in government.

Nancy Ruth's 1990 campaign photograph. She ran in the Ontario provincial election on September 6, 1990, as the Progressive Conservative candidate in St. Andrew-St. Patrick, Toronto.

Those endorsing her candidacy included an impressive array of figures well known in the Toronto community. Prominent author Margaret Atwood was quoted in campaign brochures as saying, "Nancy Jackman knows how to ask the difficult questions. If the Emperor has no clothes on, she will be among the first to say so."[38] Nobel Prize chemist John C. Polanyi also weighed in: "There is no mistaking Nancy Jackman's deep concern for environmental issues—and when Nancy is committed things get done."[39] Toronto journalist and social justice icon June Callwood said, "Nancy Jackman is an able and committed woman whose generosity, compassion and concern for principles have made her a legend in the community."[40] Lawyer John Tory, future mayor of Toronto, went on record saying, "Nancy makes me proud to be a Progressive Conservative. She has a social conscience but she also knows we depend on a strong private sector to generate the money needed to run our social programs."[41]

Premier Peterson and his Liberals enjoyed a substantial lead in the polls before the election was called, despite a lingering scandal (the Patti Starr affair) connected to party fundraising. That lead quickly eroded during the hot summer days of campaigning, and one major cause was anger at the timing of the election. As one journalist reported, "Canvassers for both the Tories and the New Democrats say they are surprised at the depth of voter anger over the fact that the election was called two years before the end of the Liberal government's term."[42] The Liberals held a comfortable majority—ninety-five out of one hundred thirty seats—and this election marked the third time Ontario voters had been sent to the polls in five years. The election was seen as manipulative—an attempt to take advantage of the Liberals' popularity and lock in

Celebrating at Doris Anderson's 80th birthday bash, held at the Royal York Hotel, Toronto, in 2001. L to R: Barbara Hall (61st mayor of Toronto); NDP leader Alexa McDonough (1st woman to lead a major, recognized political party in Canada); Nancy Ruth; and opera singer and comedian, Mary Lou Fallis.

another five years of power—as well as a waste of public funds.

The outcome of that election has been called "one of the most stunning reversals of fortune in Canadian political history."[43] The New Democratic Party, for the first time, won a majority in Ontario, leaping from nineteen to seventy-four seats; the PCs made a slight gain, from seventeen to twenty seats; and the Liberals dropped precipitously to only thirty-six seats. Unexpectedly and to the Liberals' great chagrin, Premier Peterson lost his own seat and immediately stepped down as party leader.

Not a single PC candidate won in Toronto's nine ridings, a bastion of Tory power for much of the twentieth century; six of those ridings went to the NDP and three to the Liberals. In St. Andrew-St. Patrick, Nancy ran one of the election's closest races, losing by only one thousand votes to the NDP candidate. She was in fact the second-highest Tory vote-getter in Toronto's ridings. And given the value she placed on inclusion, she found some comfort in the fact that the person who defeated her, Zanana Akande, was not only another woman but the first Black woman ever elected as a member of the legislative assembly in Ontario and subsequently the first Black woman Cabinet minister in Canada.

Speaking about women in politics to University of Waterloo students a couple of months later, Nancy told her audience of her "immense satisfaction [at] seeing the only male candidate, who was the incumbent, finish third." She went on to say, "I lost to Zanana Akande, the minister of community and social affairs. She's an excellent woman and although I hate to lose it's easier when it is to another feminist who will have I believe a major impact on our current government at Queen's Park."[44] Although Akande was her opponent in this instance and of course represented a competing political party, Nancy consistently endorsed female candidates across party lines. In her words: "To help women gain political power, I support women…of all political parties."[45] For the balance of power to be shifted, for women to gain leadership roles in equitable numbers, she believed that such solidarity was essential.

In her Waterloo speech, Nancy left a strong impression that, even after two electoral defeats, she would still look for further opportunities to run for office. She urged her audience not to distrust power but to learn to embrace it as a means of making change on behalf of social justice: "We do not have the luxury of saying we won't play that grubby little game of power. If we refuse to accept our share of it, others will snap it up and use it for their own ends…. Go after power, and make no apology for it." Her words are a riff on one of her favourite Nellie McClung quotations: "Never explain, never retract, never apologize. Just get the thing done and let them howl!" Turning the spotlight on herself, she confided, "So here I am at 48, wanting to make good, just and fair law. Law that respects people and moves this province, country and planet towards equality for women and survival of all species."[46] She is convinced that women need to gain political power in order to champion laws that will not only benefit women but will advance the cause of equality and justice. And she remains unabashed in sharing her personal dream of winning office so that she can play a part in this necessary work.

It was a provincial by-election in her home riding of St. George-St. David (now Toronto Centre) that offered Nancy another chance for political office. During the period 1990–1992, she remained busy advocating and fundraising for LEAF, serving on numerous boards, and running her

own foundation—all occupations that mattered greatly to
her. Yet she had not given up her
hope that she "could help make
laws that are just and good."[47]

Nellie McClung, one of the "Famous 5" who initiated the Persons Case, as depicted in the Women are Persons! monument by sculptor Barbara Paterson, which sits outside the Senate of Canada. There is also a version of the monument in Calgary's Olympic Square.

In September 1992, Liberal MPP Ian Scott, who had been narrowly re-elected in St. George-St. David in the 1990 NDP sweep, resigned from provincial parliament—not surprisingly, since he had gone from being attorney general to being a member of a party that no longer held power. In December, Nancy announced that she would seek the riding's PC nomination in advance of a spring by-election to fill the vacancy left by this resignation. She was acclaimed for the nomination in the packed hall of St. Paul's Anglican Church on Bloor Street: "my eighty-nine-year-old mother came, as she had to all my other nominations," and the party leader, Mike Harris was there. "I had an uncontested nomination, with Mike and me on the stage."[48] But if the nomination itself was a cakewalk, the election would turn out to be the toughest she had fought.

The key opponents Nancy faced ahead of the April 1, 1993, by-election were George Lamony of the NDP, Tim Murphy of the Liberals, and their respective machines. The NDP had fallen into such disfavour with the public since their 1990 victory that Lamony's chances looked very slim. At the outset, however, it seemed that Murphy, a thirty-three-year-old lawyer, would have no difficulty hanging on to the seat for the Liberals—that is, until Nancy's entry made it clear there was going to be "a fierce two-way race" for election.[49] She was not only well known in the riding but was by now an experienced and savvy campaigner, eager to engage with her constituents and offer them "a strong voice and a better future."[50] As in the past, her messages centred on social issues, such as adequate and affordable housing and daycare as well as other government interventions needed for a just and equal society. And in light of the financial downturn that had plagued the province for much of the time the NDP had been in office, she stressed jobs and the economy, underscoring her own experience in the business world and stressing her party's commitment to fiscal accountability.

St. George-St. David, like its federal counterpart Rosedale, where Nancy had sought the nomination in 1988, was a riding of great divisions and diversity, spanning "established midtown neighbourhoods, the mansions of Rosedale, the housing projects of Regent Park and the vibrant gay ghetto around Church and Wellesley streets."[51] In some ways, the riding offered an ideal campaigning ground for a red Tory who could speak to her fiscal conservatism in the wealthier neighbourhoods north of Bloor Street and stress her liberal social agenda in the diverse

Nancy Ruth in her campaign office for the
April 1, 1993 by-election in the Toronto riding
of St. George-St. David.

enclaves south of Bloor. Yet Nancy's wealth could also be a source of vulnerability in this riding; Tim Murphy saw it as such and proceeded to exploit it using classic "negative campaign" tactics.

Drawing on an article about Nancy published in the *Financial Post* in 1989, Murphy's campaign team prepared a flyer—"authorized by the St. George-St. David Liberal Association"—that pilloried Nancy for her wealth and privilege. In the *Financial Post* article, she had spoken freely and with characteristic humour about her upbringing, her family's money, and her own financial peccadilloes. The flyer excerpted out of context some of her more outrageous escapades, for example, that "She went into a nearby town to run a few errands and came back with a white Mercedes" and twisted the knife further with tag lines such as "Would you like caviar with your Cheerios?" The reverse side of the flyer featured a picture of her nine-thousand-square-foot house with the question underneath, "Who needs rent controls?" And the flyer's key message, in bold type, read: "How Could She Understand the Needs of Our Community? On April 1st, DON'T BE FOOLED!"[52] The flyer was, not surprisingly, distributed exclusively in the southern part of the riding where it could do the most damage.

It was also rumoured that, in the northern part of the riding, Murphy intended to spread the word that Nancy was a lesbian in hopes that this revelation would undermine her support among conservative voters. As Nancy recalls, "It was a nasty election because he decided to out me, which meant I had to out myself. I had to control the message."[53] She chose to make her statement at the last all-candidates meeting, where a bill, then before provincial parliament, to extend spousal benefits to same-sex partners was under debate. Dropping the casual phrase "as a lesbian" into the conversation as she expressed her support for the bill, she pre-empted any disclosure that Murphy might make.[54] When this news hit the front page of the *Globe and Mail*, she remembers lawn signs in support of her candidacy "came down in the north end of the riding."[55]

Nancy was apparently the first "out" lesbian to run for political office in Canada, but she believes that "the media had known I was a lesbian for years, but for whatever reason they chose not to write about it until then."[56] Her objection to publicizing her sexual preference was two-fold: first of all, she felt this aspect of her identity had "nothing to do with a person's ability to serve or relate to people or work with the community."[57] And secondly, she was adamant in saying that "I dislike being known as a lesbian first and foremost. It's not why I've done what I've done. My sense of social justice as a child had nothing to do with my sexual preference."[58] Nevertheless, once her sexual identity was a public part of the campaign, she could be heard in Church Street and Wellesley coffee shops urging voters to "put a tough dyke in for tough times."[59]

Many journalists did choose to write about Nancy's lesbianism after she came out and a number were quite supportive of her candidacy. Jim Coyle, writing in the *Ottawa Citizen*, noted that Nancy was "very rich" and "openly gay" and went on to say, "No one with mischief in their soul would think twice about who to back in the Ontario byelection Thursday in St. George-St. David. In what may be the most interesting constituency in the province, Conservative contender Nancy Jackman is a certifiable eccentric who, if elected, could be a one-woman dose of parliamentary reform and as much a trial to her friends as her enemies."[60]

On April 1, don't just send a message to Bob Rae...

Campaign literature for Nancy Ruth's run as a Progressive Conservative in the April 1, 1993, by-election in the Toronto riding of St. George-St. David.

N A N C Y
JACKMAN

Send Nancy Jackman to Queen's Park for a strong voice

N A

.JAC

N A N C Y
JACKMAN

Jobs and education: "we can do better"

What people are saying about **Nancy Jackman**...

"Nancy's compassion is matched only by her integrity. We have all benefitted from her work on behalf of the Gay and Lesbian community. She has earned our support."

June Callwood

"Nancy Jackman has done more to support policy measures concerning AIDS , same-sex spousal benefits and equity issues than any member of the Liberal-NDP Governments of the past eight years. I look forward to her continued ..."

N C Y

KMAN

Nancy Jackman Campaign HQ

625 Church St. (at Charles St. East)
Phone 920-5118

Authorized by the C.F.O. for the Nancy Jackman Campaign   Printed on Recycled Paper

The *Toronto Sun*, a conservative tabloid, published its endorsement of Nancy a few days before the election. Like Coyle's, it had a touch of "mischief in the soul," referring to St. George-St. David as "the wacky world…where gay rights is the hot issue and everyone seems to swing in all directions at once, so to speak." After announcing the paper's support for Nancy, the editorial writer went on to say,

> After all, why should all of the outrageous lesbian militant feminists be on the government side of the house? Okay, that was a joke. What is not a joke is this Rosedale philanthropist's huge heart and her long and proven record of community and public service…she will also have a huge impact on Queen's Park and help the PCs counter the NDP-fed perception that Tories are all heartless white males incapable of appealing to a broad coalition of interests.[61]

Haroon Siddiqui, the editorial page editor of the *Toronto Star*, predicted the outcome in Nancy's favour—incorrectly as it turned out. She came in second, Murphy defeating her by about 2,300 votes. After the election, Hal Jackman bought and gave to his sister the cartoon that Siddiqui had had prepared for his editorial section, with the following note from the editor attached: "Ms. Jackman: Too bad you lost, and I lost a good cartoon for my page. Terry Mosher had done it on the strength of my fearless prediction that you were sure to win."[62] The cartoon showed a smiling and pearl-festooned Nancy towering over a stone-faced Mike Harris, leader of the provincial PCs. Both her arms are held high, each hand flashing a V for victory, with one hand clasping Harris' hand and

It was anticipated that Nancy Ruth would win the 1993 provincial by-election in St. George-St. David. If she did win, and joined Mike Harris' Progressive Conservative caucus, it was assumed that this red Tory would pull Harris up. *Toronto Star* cartoonist, Aislin (Terry Mosher), drew this cartoon to celebrate her victory. Unfortunately, she lost, and the cartoon was never printed.

hoisting it over his head. It's a celebratory moment for her, less clearly so for the party leader.

Mike Harris had been elected Ontario PC party leader in 1990 and had established a reputation for being not only fiscally but socially conservative. He did support Nancy's 1993 campaign, providing an endorsement for her literature, turning out for several of her events, and lending his staff to help with campaign work. Yet the two of them were worlds apart on many policy issues. Had Nancy been elected in the by-election of 1993—and re-elected in 1995, when the PCs won a majority government under Harris—the question of her adherence to party discipline would surely have come into play. Looking back, she recognizes that being part of the Harris-era cuts to social welfare and environmental programs in Ontario would have been difficult—the experience "would not have sat well with me."[63]

While the election outcome was disappointing for Nancy, Tim Murphy's underhanded campaign tactics were even more so, leaving her disillusioned at what she saw as a fundamental lack of fair play. And she was equally disturbed by the failure of his party leader, Lyn McLeod, to intervene and challenge his campaign's behaviour. In the days following the election she wrote to McLeod, expressing her "very deep regrets" at the way Murphy conducted himself and her "profound dismay that you as leader sanctioned this kind of campaign." In particular, given her personal commitment to philanthropy, she was stung by Murphy's allegation that her wealth "left me unable to understand or even sympathize with those who have not been nearly as fortunate in life as I have.... I deeply resent the lies and malicious distortion that Mr. Murphy distributed and that makes it appear I have been frivolous and irresponsible in the face of the needs of others."

If we might wonder at Nancy's expectation that the leader of a rival party should protect a political opponent's interests, her letter to McLeod makes her reasoning clear. She had supported McLeod's bid for the Liberal party leadership with a ten-thousand-dollar donation, as she had supported so many women across party lines, "because I have spent my life trying to ensure that women have a chance to go as far as their talent will take them…. The fact that you are a Liberal and I a Tory was of little concern to me; what I believed I saw in you was a woman who would bring substantial change to the political process."

She concludes her letter, "the saddest part, the most regrettable aspect, is not that I lost…but that you as party leader did not feel comfortable enough to challenge [Murphy] and his tactics. That is what rankles me the most; I had hoped women who finally reached leadership positions would begin to change the way we have been carrying on politically in the country for the last three decades but obviously I was wrong."[64] In 2019, speaking to undergraduates at Queen's University, Nancy would continue to promote this vision of feminist solidarity: "We can only have power if women support & work for other women, and see the problems not as personal but as systemic. Sisterhood is all-important." She would also urge these undergraduates—students in a women and politics course—to consider playing a direct part in changing the political system: "We need women to run & when I say this, I mean right-thinking women. Lady patriarchs are not the goal; feminists are."[65] In Nancy's view, Lyn McLeod, acting in the fashion of a "lady patriarch," had condoned politics as usual rather than using her power to change the game.

The 1993 by-election was Nancy's last foray into electoral politics. By the following year, when candidates were starting to stake their nomination claims for the 1995 provincial election, her mother's health had seriously declined and she "made a decision to be with her until she died.... This meant I couldn't campaign for the 1994 nomination."[66] In the long run—twelve years down the road—she finally had a chance to play a role in government when she was appointed to Canada's Senate. In one of those ironies of history, it was none other than Tim Murphy who would have approved Nancy's name on a future list of proposed Senate appointments. Murphy, who returned to practising law after losing his seat in the 1995 election, remained active in the Liberal party and became Prime Minister Paul Martin's chief of staff in 2003; Martin appointed Nancy to Senate in 2005.

But for now, Nancy turned her attention to caring for her mother, nurturing what she had come to see as one of the most important relationships of her life.

Footnotes for this chapter can be found online at:
http://secondstorypress.ca/resources

Chapter 8

A DAUGHTER'S JOURNEY

*Now I can see that, on some level,
I'm trying to redeem my mother's life.*[1]

DESCRIBING THE COMPLEX and tangled bond between mothers and daughters, Adrienne Rich writes, "Many of us were mothered in ways we cannot yet even perceive; we only know that our mothers were in some incalculable way on our side."[2] Nancy's understanding of what it meant to have her mother on her side grew steadily throughout her life. She came to see how her mother had repeatedly defended her against her father's temper, "patiently, and probably with a great deal of pain."[3] She also recognized how many doors her mother had opened for her, introducing her to art and theatre; showing her by example the importance of service to others; sharing with her the beauty of Georgian Bay; connecting her with the World Council of Churches (WCC) work camps in Greece and Bali; and persuading the Reverend Dr. Harriet Christie, principal of Covenant College, to admit her without the required high school marks.[4] As protector, mentor,

Mary Coyne Rowell Jackman at Overdown, the family farm, in front of the sour cherry trees, 1953.

and advocate, Nancy's mother played an enormous role in shaping her daughter's life.

Mary Jackman figures prominently in Nancy's childhood memories. Nancy recalls as a small child stroking the foxtails in the stole around her mother's neck.[5] She also recounts how her mother would attach a harness to her, dress her in a tweed coat—adding leggings and hat and gloves if it were cold—and take her on shopping expeditions or errands at the bank. Coming home from these outings, passing the Shell station on the curve of Church Street, just east of Park Road, Nancy vividly remembers how she loved the smell of gasoline from the station's pumps. When she grew older, the shopping trips included visits to Mary's dressmaker and to Ada Mackenzie's sports shop where Mary bought her daughter "beautiful clothes...tweed skirts & coats, Liberty blouses and Shetland sweaters."[6] Nancy and her mother shared a love of fashion and Mary fought with her husband to make sure that Nancy had her own clothing allowance for everyday items by the time she was twelve. When Nancy was a teenager her mother went on to teach her how to budget her funds for coats and boots.

Mary also introduced Nancy to "all sorts of interesting

artistic friends, like Ann MacIntosh Duff, Douglas Duncan, Will Ogilvie, A.Y. Jackson…, Paraskeva Clark, Sophia Buckingham (whom I adored), Jack Nichols, etc."[7] It was her mother who arranged for her to take pottery lessons with ceramic artist Illy Gepe at the Women's Art Association and who "dragged me around to Douglas Duncan's picture loan society and Roberts Gallery. And of course the Studio Building at the bottom of Rosedale Road hill."[8] Nancy's love for art grew from these shared experiences with her mother: "I still hang many of her paintings such as the Marthe Rakine of a teenage girl she thought looked like me, and some of her Ogilvies, Ann MacIntosh Duffs and [A.Y.] Jacksons," as well as "a water lily by Helen Lucas, which she loved."[9]

Nancy's interest in sculpture was inspired by Mary's gift to Victoria University of an Alexander Calder mobile that Nancy saw installed over the piano in the student union building. Years later, in keeping with her mother's belief in the value of public art, Nancy donated to the same university the Maryon Kantaroff sculpture *Anadyomene* that had been on her lawn at 184 Roxborough Drive.[10] The plaque on the sculpture notes that it was given by "Senator Nancy Ruth in honour of the women who walk here." Nancy's lifelong love of the theatre and dance was also instilled by Mary, who would take her and Edward as small children to the Christmas pantomime at the Royal Alexander Theatre. As her daughter grew older, Mary often took her to the ballet and on trips to the Shakespeare Festival in Stratford, Ontario, and when the family travelled to London, "we always went to plays." Those London trips included visits to bookstores to look at first editions of Virginia Woolf, where Nancy was bored but remembers enjoying the artwork on the book endpages and covers.[11]

It was Mary Jackman who organized the myriad activities of Nancy's girlhood: "She made sure I had lessons for riding, piano, ballet, fencing, etc." She drove her daughter to the Pony Club for her beloved riding lessons, helped her with her piano practice, and played endless games of cards with her. She was not only faithful in advocating for her daughter when she had difficulties at school but she attended all her school events, going to every concert and graduation ceremony even though "she knew she was the oldest mum around, but she came anyhow to support me."[12] And Mary was also patient and loving with Nancy, forgiving her for stealing twenty dollars from her purse, coming into her bedroom and rubbing her back when she had trouble getting to sleep.

Mary's constant support of Nancy when she had conflicts with her father is another source of Nancy's gratitude to her mother: "I knew when I heard my parents fighting that mom was taking my side." One clash in particular, when she was about eleven years old, has seared itself into her memory. The Jackmans were at the cottage and Nancy had been told to wash the dishes but kept on reading the comics instead of doing her chores. Her father became so enraged at her delay that "he picked me up out of my chair, threw me on the floor, got on top of me and started to choke me." Mary "came running from the kitchen when she heard my screaming, and hauled him off. I was very frightened. I thought Dad was going to kill me."[13] Although Harry was the dominant personality in their marriage, Mary was resolute in standing up to him in defence of her daughter.

Yet as a teenager and young adult, Nancy fought bitterly with her mother and identified with her father's power: "It was he that I modelled myself after, and in some ways put down my mum just like he did. Oh she and I had yelling matches. She would walk away from me when I started to yell, and it made me furious. I had nothing to push back at."[14] It was only when she had her feminist awakening in Finland in 1968 that twenty-six-year-old Nancy realized for the first time "how unfair I'd been to myself and to my Mom."[15] Her anger at watching her mother give in to the men in her life had been mistakenly directed at her mother rather than at the root cause of the problem: the patriarchal structures that oppressed them both. She had scorned her mother for knuckling under to male power, failing to understand that such behaviour was typical of her mother's era, upbringing, and social class.

She did not know who her mother was, Nancy recalls, because "her life was never highlighted at the dining room table or anywhere within the family. Dad usually criticized her. It's amazing that my mom kept her 'outside' life going in spite of the battery at home. That life was her salvation."[16] Not long after her eye-opening encounter with feminism, Nancy wrote to her mother expressing her hope that the two of them could arrive at "some greater understanding of each other." While acknowledging that there was much in their lives that they would never share with the other, she confessed that she longed nevertheless to know "who my mother is." She told her mother that many details of their life together stood out in her memory—"your love, your protection, your concern"—but she was still left wondering, "who are you and what are you?"[17] In the ensuing years, both women sought answers to these questions about each other and Nancy continued her quest for understanding long after her mother's death.

Mary's own appreciation of her daughter's character is wonderfully captured in a letter she wrote to Nancy when she completed her master's degree in 1977. The letter accompanied a graduation gift, *The Lions of Delos*, a painting by Will Ogilvie, a Canadian watercolourist and close friend of Mary's. In the letter, Mary writes, "'The Lions of Delos' remind[s] me that in you—the strength and fearlessness of your father are combined with the thoughtfulness and gentleness of your mother. Even as the lion and the lamb lie down in peace together, may your inherited qualities blend and harmonize, so that your life may become less stressful and you achieve a happy resolution for your future."[18] It is a mark of Mary's love for her daughter that she frames Nancy's often volatile nature in such positive terms, as the outcome of inherited traits that, if "harmonized," could give rise to a future in which she resolves her inner conflicts and finds peace within herself.

Nancy felt very fortunate that "mom and I were largely reconciled" by the time she moved back to Toronto permanently in late 1978.[19] Reconciliation between an adult child and her parent can be a hard-won achievement, calling as it does for understanding, respect, and generous love—sometimes between individuals who are wildly different. It is to the credit of both women that they claimed this gift together.

In the decade after Harry Jackman's death, Nancy and Mary found the space to nurture and deepen their relationship. Nancy accompanied her mother to art galleries and openings as Mary continued her active engagement with the Toronto arts community. In May 1980, Mary was awarded an honorary doctorate from her alma mater, Victoria University, founded in 1836 and federated with the University of Toronto in 1890. It is comprised of Victoria College, an arts and science college from which Mary, her mother, Nell Langford Rowell, her aunt Mary

Coyne Rowell, and her sons Hal and Edward received their degrees; and Emmanuel College, where Nancy took classes in the 1970s. Professor Doris Dyke's honorary degree citation lauded Mary for her "life long commitment to Canadian Art" both in her art collection and in her "friendship and encouragement of Canadian painters."[20] Nancy was very proud of her mother on that day and grateful for the influence that had led to her own knowledge and appreciation of art.[21]

Mary continued to pursue the passion for collecting first editions of Virginia Woolf and related Hogarth Press and Bloomsbury materials that was originally sparked by her mother Nell's engagement gift to her of a first edition of *A Room of One's Own*. Her donation of her Virginia Woolf first editions and Hogarth Press publications to Wymilwood, the women's residence library at Victoria College, formed the nucleus of the very fine special collection now housed in Victoria's E.J. Pratt Library. Bruce McLeod recalls how important Virginia Woolf was to Mary and, through her teaching and precept, to her daughter, who "was taught by her mother that it's right to have a room of your own, a space that is yours and nobody can take that from you or intrude on it."[22] Only a couple of years after Harry's death, perhaps as part of her own newly found "space that was hers," Mary flew to London for a Bloomsbury symposium. The trip was a gift from Nancy and Mary writes after her first day there to thank her daughter for "giving me such a wonderful holiday." She also describes the symposium's opening events, assuring Nancy that "you would have been as thrilled as I was."

Among the symposium speakers was Nigel Nicolson, who spoke about Woolf's novel *Orlando* and about his mother Vita Sackville-West's relationship with Woolf.

According to Mary, Nicolson told his audience that *Orlando* was "written as a lark and for a gift to the person she loved [Vita] so she made [the character Orlando] androgynous." Mary bought a copy of the novel for Nancy and writes that "I do hope you will enjoy reading it."[23] In light of the well-known love affair between Vita and Virginia, Mary was surely signalling through this gift her understanding and acceptance of her daughter's sexual orientation. Nancy remembers with gratitude that "Mom always welcomed my lovers.... She said she loved me and therefore would love those I loved."[24] One cannot help but think that Mary herself would have liked to be treated in the same way.

Both mother and daughter, as well as Hal Jackman, pulled out their portions of the Jackman Foundation in the 1980s to pursue their own charitable interests. After Harry's death, the foundation, whose directors were Mary Jackman and her four children, had holdings of thirty million dollars. Because the charitable interests of these trustees were widely divergent and often difficult to reconcile, the five of them verbally agreed to divide the foundation's annual income, which was intended for disbursements, into sixths, with one sixth assigned to each family member.[25] The exception was Edward, who had been allotted two-sixths because his 25 per cent share of King Vaughan Farms shares had been signed over as the initial capital base of the foundation when he became a Catholic priest. This nominal division meant that instead of arguing or horse-trading over the foundation's donations, each director could make decisions about his or her own share of those donations.

This attempt at compromise unfortunately proved inadequate to bridge all the differences that flared up among family members. After Mary, the original board chair, resigned, Hal discussed with Nancy whether she wanted to take the chair. She declined, so they agreed to give the position to Eric, a decision that Nancy later regretted.[26] Eric was adamant that the foundation's capital should be preserved and donations made only from annual investment earnings. Nancy argued that she should be entitled to spend her sixth of the capital before her death should she choose to do so, given that, unlike Hal and Eric, she had no children to continue as trustees in the future.[27] The trustees also disagreed about matters such as investment policy—for example, "the tension between maximizing the income and making socially responsible investments"—and both Nancy and Hal chafed at Eric's exercise of power as the chair.[28] Meetings became increasingly acrimonious and by the spring of 1987, Mary Jackman, who found the whole situation "too exhausting for me," wrote to her four children to ask if she "might receive my share [i.e., five million dollars] of all the Foundation's capital."[29]

For Nancy, Mary's letter opened the door for her finally to follow suit and move her five million dollar portion to her own NaRuth Foundation, which she had set up in 1984 in hopes of such an outcome. Nancy was angry to discover that Hal, suspecting Mary of acting under Nancy's influence, had interrogated their eighty-three-year-old mother three times to make sure the withdrawal was her idea, denying "his mother's own agency and her own voice, certainly a Virginia Woolf principle." Nevertheless, she and Hal joined forces long enough to make the stock transfers of fifteen million dollars happen while Eric was out of town. Hal's companies bought the shareholdings so that Nancy and her mother each received five million in cash rather than family shares and shortly after the disbursement, Mary, Nancy, and Hal resigned as trustees of the Jackman Foundation. Nancy and Hal encouraged Edward to follow suit but after much discussion Edward chose to leave his two-thirds portion in the foundation and remain as a director. Nancy notes that Edward had never signed the original papers transferring his stock to the foundation from King Vaughan Farms and therefore the transfer itself was questionable, but when he chose to leave his holdings in the foundation, his inheritance from his father remained there.[30]

In her letter to her children, Mary Jackman made it clear that she wanted to donate her five million dollars soon after receiving it and planned to make sizeable gifts to her alma mater, Victoria College; to science programs at the University of Toronto; and to Toronto's ballet and opera. Her one-million-dollar gift in support of science led to a chair in chemistry named after Nobel laureate John C. Polanyi, while her donation to Victoria supported the building of a new residence there. She wanted to have the building named in honour of her aunt Mary Coyne Rowell, who had taught modern languages at Victoria College as the institution's first female professor, as well as her parents, who had sat on many committees and boards at the university, and her brothers Langford and Frederic Rowell. But, according to Nancy, Mary was pressured to "include the name Jackman, who made the wealth she gave," and "Mary gave in."[31] The residence was named Rowell Jackman Hall. When Nancy discovered, however, that the cornerstone for the building highlighted the Jackman family story at the expense of the Rowells, she paid five thousand dollars to replace it so that it would reflect her mother's wish to commemorate her birth family.

Mary had also grown interested in two of Nancy's major initiatives: the creation of the Canadian Women's Foundation and the establishment of a foundation in support of women's equality initiatives, such as the Women's Legal Education and Action Fund (LEAF). With their newly liberated funds, she and her daughter each made gifts of $500,000 to those staunchly feminist organizations. While Mary might not have described herself as a feminist—"She still subscribed to a view of the world where men were heads of families, heads of corporations"[32]—she had learned from her daughter the importance of investing in feminist causes. The Canadian Women's Foundation would aim at creating systemic change to improve women's economic and social conditions, while LEAF focused on legal challenges and remedies to discrimination against women. Both organizations were clearly aligned with Mary Jackman's vision of a fair and just society.

If Mary followed Nancy's lead in her support for feminist projects, Nancy learned from her mother's example the value of service to others. In the words of friend Diane Goudie, Nancy "is absolutely impelled to help anyone that she thinks needs help.... If you're sick you have to put a barrier up at the door if you don't want soup. It comes from her mother, and that tie with her mother is very strong."[33] For both women, service to others encompassed not only personal acts of kindness, but the broader ideals reflected in the social gospel. It was through her mother that Nancy came to her love for the church and, in particular, a vision of the church as open, embracing the poor and the hungry, a church without walls. Recalling her mother's years at Metropolitan United, Nancy spoke admiringly of Mary's successful campaign "for the right of street people to wander in and out, sing out of tune, call out in the middle of a service," adding, "Oh my mother loved the music, the space, the memories of her parents, but she loved the social gospel more!"[34] Bruce McLeod, in his eulogy at Mary's funeral, noted that there were two books on her bedside a few days before she died: Virginia Woolf's diary and a critical study of poverty and destitution in Canada.[35]

Mary spoke of her devotion to the tenets of the social gospel when, in 1992, at the age of eighty-eight, she was awarded an honorary doctorate from the University of Toronto. Although her health was failing by then, she gave an address to the graduates that prompted two standing ovations, a rare event at university convocations. She told her audience about the passions central to her life: her love of art; her belief in the importance of women's education; the inspiration she had taken from Virginia Woolf; and her keen interest in

Mary Coyne Rowell Jackman, BA, LLD, age 88, with her children on the occasion of being awarded an honorary Doctor of Laws for Public Affairs in June, 1992, by the University of Toronto.

international affairs. She urged graduates to "have the courage to care deeply about such matters as social justice" and to join her in seeking "a community, a nation, a world where life is fair for everyone, where children are fed and treasured, where there is safety and clean air and no war. None of you should be satisfied with less!"[36]

Then, in words aimed directly at her daughter, Mary Jackman described herself as standing at the midpoint of three generations of women who "have cared deeply about what was called sixty years ago 'the social gospel,'" which saw religion not as "a private vision of God but a message about responsibility and concern for others." Mary explained that her mother, Nell Langford Rowell, had been a woman who "was vigorous in political life" and had been one of the founders of the Ontario Women's Liberal Association, which pushed for the abolishment of child labour. Nell had also been active in women's movements such as temperance and the Young Women's Christian Association (YWCA), where she served as national president. Just as Nell had gone before her and paved the way for her daughter's work, Mary in turn had handed the torch on to "my daughter, Nancy," who was following her grandmother and mother by devoting "the same vitality to her efforts in such organizations as LEAF, which carries women's equality issues into the courts."[37] For Nancy, this ceremony recognizing her mother's accomplishments — along with Mary's public affirmation of the bond between the two of them — was a moment of deep emotion. Nancy knew that her mother had practiced her speech over and over, and when she heard it, "I wept. She delivered her speech well. She meant every word of it."

Nancy found it especially poignant that Mary had turned away from her audience before the second standing ovation and had started to walk back to her seat. Rob Prichard, the university president, had to take her by the shoulders and turn her to face the students so she could witness the strength of their tribute.[38] Near the end of her remarks she had said to them, "Life is an adventure. I can testify to that with every fibre of my eighty-eight-year-old self." The graduates must have been inspired not only by Mary Jackman's example of a life lived richly and by her testimony to the importance of creating a world that "is fair for everyone," but also by her gallantry in the face of advancing frailty and age. The day was a remarkable one for both mother and daughter.

Mary's health declined quite rapidly in the ensuing two years. She had taken medication for heart problems since the 1960s and had suffered a number of small strokes in the 1980s. By 1993, her health was very poor and it was at this point that Nancy decided to give up her ambitions to run for political office so she could assume responsibility for Mary's care.[39] She tended to her mother's needs lovingly over the coming months, helping ensure that Mary was able to stay at home until the day before her death. On July 11, 1994, Mary Jackman died at Women's College Hospital, where fifty years earlier she had given birth to her beloved son Edward and two years after that, to her beloved and only daughter. At her bedside were Nancy and other family members as well as her faithful caregivers Rosario Onand and Diana MacLean. Mary's estate at her death was roughly three million dollars; in her will she left small legacies to family and friends, but the bulk of the estate went to her residual beneficiary, the Toronto Foundation, to support the community programs for women and girls in which she so deeply believed.

In her Christmas letter a few months later, Nancy

Mary Coyne Rowell Jackman with her
daughter, Nancy Ruth, Christmas, 1992.

explains that "my life since the Provincial by-election in April 1993 was a commitment to see my Mother daily until her death. It was a rewarding time, and one in which much reconciliation happened on both our parts." Although she had commented elsewhere that the two of them were "largely reconciled" when she moved back to Toronto fifteen years earlier, Nancy's words here suggest that the work of mutual acceptance between child and parent is never a finished task.

One source of friction between Mary and her children, for example, was the children's ongoing conflict over money. Bruce McLeod recalls that it broke Mary's heart "that she couldn't have all her children for dinner at once because they were all suing each other.... She didn't reject them for that reason, or reject Nancy ever. But it hurt her a lot, I know."[40] In a letter written to her daughter in the spring of 1989, Mary lamented Nancy's angry outbursts, saying "I love you—my daughter, Nancy, and also my three sons—I can't bear hearing you talking such hateful language about your brothers."[41] Mary had spent much of her life placating an overbearing and sometimes abusive husband and trying to keep peace among her strong-willed children. Nancy, by contrast, had learned to vent her emotions openly, for good or ill. As different as they were, however, neither woman gave up on her commitment to understand and cherish the other.

Nancy's 1994 Christmas letter goes on to record some major changes in her life since her mother's death. While she has no regrets about her choice to care for her mother, she confides that she is "somewhat sad" to have given up the opportunity to run for the provincial PC nomination in the riding of St. Andrew–St. Patrick—Mike Harris's PC party went on to win a majority in the 1995 election—and then to have lost her mother so soon after. Nancy adds that because of the demands on her time in caring for her mother, she had also resigned from most of the boards on which she had served, meaning that she would now have to look about her for "new possibilities." As she explains, "I seem to be driven by my Methodism, and at times only feel of worth when I am doing something for others!—so I'd better get busy again—or—learn to be at peace with myself."

Being busy was never far from Nancy's agenda and her letter gives some indication as to important projects in her future: "Part of the thought process I went through in cleaning out Mother's papers and house, is the need for a women's museum." Her initial impulse was born from her desire to find a place to donate her mother's exquisite 1920s wedding dress, which ended up going to the fashion division at Seneca College. But her vision soon expanded to the idea of a women's museum "that integrates class, race & society. Perhaps it should be an international museum that uses the latest technology & satellite distribution for wandering through the exhibits. In this day and age do we need a building for a museum?" In time, this fledgling idea comes to fruition as CoolWomen.ca, a website and virtual museum chronicling Canadian women's accomplishments, and eventually archived at https://archive-it. org/home/nancyruth.

Another project that occupies Nancy over the coming two years is the move from 184 Roxborough to a renovated 10 Cluny Drive. She and Sirje Sellers, her partner since 1990, bought her mother's house from the estate and, after completing extensive renovations, made it their new home together. Nancy recalls that when her mother was dying in Women's College Hospital, she "asked Sirje to look after me"; she and Sirje stayed together until 1999.[42] After their separation, Nancy bought out Sirje's share of the house, vowing to remain at 10 Cluny Drive in Rosedale as the "4th generation of [Langford Rowell] women to walk these blocks to my death."[43]

But perhaps the most momentous event following her mother's death was Nancy's decision to change her name. "The evening Mother died, after I'd packed up the hospital room, I found myself at home, sipping wine with some friends [Pat Hacker, Linda Nye, and Sirje] & saying, 'Thank goodness I don't have to be a Jackman anymore.' So I have applied for a legal change of name to 'Nancy Ruth,' the two names both my parents gave me.... It all takes a bit of getting used to though, but after dithering for 30 years with a variety of names from Rowell Jackman to Nancy Toronto—why not?"[44] Why not indeed? Although it is her father's surname she has dropped, it is also the name Mary Rowell assumed when she married, so Nancy waited until her choice no longer had the power to wound her mother. Like women she admires—such as Judy Chicago, Cher, Venus, Diana the Huntress, or Cleopatra—she "did not want to be known by any man's name." She saw this change as "a move from the dominant, patriarchal, exclusionary tribe to a women-centred inclusionary tribe, where I could speak my values and language and be understood."[45] She would now stand singular and apart from the Jackman patriarchy.

The change did not take legal effect until December 11, 1994, but Nancy asked to have her honorary doctorate from York University awarded under the name "Nancy Ruth" on November 5 of that year. From then on, she used both names together with the stipulation that "Ruth" should never be used as a surname. She fashioned a unique identity for herself, asking to be dealt with on her own terms outside the naming conventions used by most others in her society.

In Nancy Ruth's convocation address she told the graduates that, just as the day was a special one for them, it was equally special for her because "I have named myself. This is the first occasion on which my chosen name has been used in public. And it gives me great joy to hear it." Her act signalled, in her words, that "as an individual & especially as a woman, I can direct my own life & choose my own path."[46] Her friend Beth Atcheson speculates that, even though she felt the loss keenly, "her mother's death freed her up in a way…when the prior generation goes there's nobody holding you to another standard. You now can hold yourself to your own standard."[47] Naming herself was without doubt a moment of deep significance in the former Nancy Jackman's life, marking a critical step on her path to autonomous selfhood.

Perhaps not surprisingly, after Mary Jackman's death Nancy Ruth began to explore ways of naming her mother, of telling the story of a woman who should be recognized as an individual in her own right and not simply as wife and mother within the Jackman family. In 1999, she engaged Christine Donald to write Mary's biography, a project that she saw as "trying to redeem my mother's life." Her mother, in Nancy Ruth's view, was "invisible in the family…. We were all so absorbed by the money & the dominance of Dad."[48] Nancy Ruth knew that Mary Jackman, Harry's wife for almost fifty years, had been a key partner in building the family's fortune; as she writes in her 2004 email Christmas letter, she felt driven to "somehow let my family know that Mother is partly responsible for them being rich."[49] Yet Nancy also knew that Mary Jackman represented a set of values profoundly different from those of her husband. While Nancy Ruth had identified in her youth with her father's drive for wealth and power, she came to realize that in many ways she was more like her mother than her father, "since the objective of my life's work has never been to make money." She also believed that "Mother's tradition of public service was far more radical than Father's. I manage assets and dabble here and there in projects, but my gut is for social justice, not money."[50]

In order to "redeem" her mother's life, Nancy Ruth proposed to tell the story of that life in a way that both revealed its significance and affirmed its value. The project would serve as an act of reclamation, bringing her mother out of the shadows into her rightful place of honour. It might also be an act of expiation—few children are without guilt for those things left undone when a parent dies and Nancy Ruth was no exception. She had regrets, for example, that during the 1980s when her mother wanted her companionship, she was busy with the Charter equality work and would not go to spend two weeks with her in Bermuda: "I feel guilty to this day."[51] Exploring those questions she had posed to her mother so many years ago—"Who are you and what are you?"—might yield both a tribute to Mary and a balm to her daughter's spirit.

When the biography Nancy Ruth envisioned fell through because Christine Donald was not able to finish the book, she hit on the idea of producing a film using the research Donald had done for the proposed biography and engaged Laura Sky to produce and direct the film through Laura's company, Skyworks Documentaries.[52] Laura's prospectus for the film reflects extensive conversations with Nancy Ruth about what the film should accomplish:

Our goal in this film about Mary Coyne Rowell Jackman will be not only to document and recreate significant events and memories in her life, but also to explore the historical, cultural and political context that informed Mary's times. Our plan is to document her life in a manner that links her strengths, her vulnerabilities, her disappointments and her accomplishments to the lives of other women. This documentary will create a framework and a map that will help our audiences to develop a deeper understanding and appreciation of the role of our mothers, grandmothers and those women who came before us. The film will encourage viewers to link our lives to hers, and to learn from her struggles, her passions and her integrity.[53]

Mary's life was to be placed firmly within the context of twentieth-century Canadian history, culture, Methodism, and politics. Nancy Ruth was by now well steeped in the principles of second-wave feminism, including an insistence that the personal is political. She wanted the film to show clearly the broad arc of her mother's life, the ways in which her personal choices were shaped by the constraints of sexist and oppressive social structures. Further, it was vital for the film to underscore that these constraints affected not just Mary, but the lives of other women as well.

Most of the work to produce the film was done in 2004, with final editing in the spring of 2005, and a public launch later that year at Victoria University's Isabel Bader Theatre. Conflict erupted from time to time between Nancy Ruth and Laura Sky during the film's creation. Nancy Ruth's strong interventions—her practice of what Laura called "commanding rather than discussing changes"[54]—evoked protests from the filmmaker. Laura is a highly respected documentary artist and a consummate professional, while Nancy Ruth is a headstrong daughter on a mission to make "more obvious" what her mother stood for.[55] Laura wrote to reassure Nancy Ruth that as part of her test-screening and editing process, she and her team were already rebuilding the first section of the film, "entirely highlighting historical context" and "focussing on issues that are related to international, national issues and the reality for women at that historical period."[56] In other words, she fully intended to create the film that Nancy Ruth envisioned.

At the same time, Laura cautioned Nancy Ruth not to "damage the film because of your anger. Your stream-of-consciousness response—your rage and mistrust—may be the way you handle your other relationships, but it cannot be the way you handle this one." Nancy Ruth's response to this "calling out" from Laura was to express her "regret that what you hear is anger and distrust—I am forceful, and I am impatient, and you are definitely hearing both of those. We are both intelligent and thoughtful people, although we are also very different."[57] Nancy Ruth's approach in this instance was part of a recurring pattern in her interactions with other people: what she saw as forcefulness and impatience others sometimes experienced as an immoderate display of temper that bordered on bullying—the "lion" in her nature devouring the peaceable lamb.

Looking back many years after the film was completed, Laura observed that "although the process with Nancy could be difficult—flurries of late-night emails, each of us standing our ground and finally coming to a number of negotiated settlements, she provided me with an amazing opportunity to learn, to grow my craft and to represent the person who was and is the most important in her life—her mother. For that I am grateful." She also acknowledged that the "intensity of my own creative force and particular personality" contributed to the working dynamic between the two women: "Here we were, Nancy and I, two control freaks, engaged in a mutual endeavour. More than that—a shared imperative." Laura is confident that in the end they met that imperative, creating "a nuanced portrait of a remarkable woman together."[58] Nancy Ruth also judged the project to be a success, helping to ensure that her mother would not "remain invisible" but be entered into the public record. And it was equally important to her daughter that Mary Jackman's story should be known to her family, bearing witness to what she had contributed to their inheritance not only financially but in less tangible ways.[59] As her brother Eric describes this legacy when interviewed for the film, "Mother gave us the best of ourselves, our humanity."

Mary Coyne Rowell Jackman: A Person in Her Own Right, 1904-1994, made in 2005, directed by Laura Sky and produced by Nancy's Very Own Foundation—the film and accompanying educational materials can be accessed at https://archive-it.org/home/nancyruth—is a sensitive portrayal of a woman constrained by the conventions of her time and yet quietly persistent in adhering to her own strong values. The account of Mary's girlhood and young womanhood places her in a lineage of women committed to the social gospel, seeking a world where "life is fair for everyone." Her struggles for fulfillment after having a miscarriage and then bearing two sons in five years of marriage are underscored in a 1935 letter to her husband that is quoted in the film: "There is part of me that must have some self-expression that can't be found in children or a house.... I must somehow find myself." She complains that Harry has so entirely dominated her that she

Mary Coyne Rowell Jackman, age 48 (1952), with
"McGinty" on West Wind Island, Georgian Bay.

has been "crushed to try to find an outlet" and goes on to argue that "we must each lead our own lives." The film documents the myriad ways in which Mary Jackman did indeed go on to shape a life that was true to her core self through, for example, starting the women's branch of the Canadian Institute of International Affairs (CIIA) at a time when women were excluded from the University of Toronto's Hart House, where the CIIA held its meetings. She also found fulfillment in her volunteer service; her church work—including organizing the church's war service unit during World War II and starting the Bond Street Nursery School for children from economically disadvantaged families; as well as her ongoing engagement with art—wanting to become an art critic, she returned to university to take art history courses in her late forties; her devotion to Virginia Woolf and the Bloomsbury circle; her philanthropy, and her compassion for the poor and marginalized. She was a woman who believed deeply in the cause of social justice—her politically conservative family members enjoyed telling the story of her once voting for Tim Buck, the communist candidate in a Toronto municipal election.

At a feminist event held at Metropolitan United Church on Mother's Day a few years after Mary's death, Nancy Ruth told those in attendance,

I am pleased to be here to talk about my mom. Why?

Because the last time my mother was talked about from this pulpit was four years ago, when Mom died and the brass memorial plaque on the back wall was installed.

The minister said briefly how wonderful Mom was, and then he proceeded to talk at length about the famous men in her life: her father, her husband, her eldest son [who was at that time lieutenant governor of Ontario].

I was livid.

So, thank you for giving me the chance to say now some of what I would have said then about my mom, Mary Coyne Rowell Jackman.[60]

Her film about her mother, completed seven years after this speech, fulfilled at least in part Nancy Ruth's mission to reveal to current and future generations the significance of Mary Jackman's life. Although Mary's deeds had frequently been eclipsed by the more public achievements of the men around her—as has been the case with women throughout recorded history—hers was a life of accomplishment, a life that mattered. Her daughter's own journey to maturity was marked by a growing understanding of how and why this was so.

Nancy Ruth has continued to experience deep regrets on behalf of her late mother—sorrow for her years in an unhappy and abusive marriage, for the opportunities she missed as a woman of her generation, for the way in which her children and husband discounted her worth: "I think of her every day now, and only occasionally of my Dad.... I ache for her lots, still do to this day."[61] One place where she remembers Mary most keenly is Georgian Bay, where throughout her childhood and until her father's death she spent summers at West Wind, the family cottage that Mary Jackman had persuaded Harry to purchase in 1949. The cottage was "the only stable home in my life between boarding school, camps, and my parents moving houses," and it was "the place where I had the best times with my mother."[62]

In her Mother's Day speech, Nancy Ruth describes the memorial banners hanging beside an arch that frames the chancel at Metropolitan United. Her mother had joined Canadian artist Doris McCarthy's sewing group that made the banners, for her contribution stitching a panel of a mother, a little girl, a dog, and a pine tree. Nancy Ruth tells her audience, "It's her, me, and our spaniel McGinty having a picnic by a pine tree in our beloved Georgian Bay, where she would walk me around the island and teach me about the tiny orchids, the jack-in-the-pulpits, the lichen. Every time I come here and look at those banners, my heart breaks a little—that Mom made that panel of her and me."

In 1982, a few years after her father's death, Nancy Ruth built her own cottage on her own island in Georgian Bay. She had bought a group of islands on the outskirts of Go Home Bay from King Vaughan Farms and chose one on which to create a retreat that figured prominently as her spiritual home over the years to come.

As June Callwood observed in a television interview, "People who know you will say that you are a different person at your cottage. Being there is something that matters a lot to you."[63] But Nancy Ruth is clear that it is not the cottage itself that draws her but "the landscape, the setting, the rocks, the quartz and granite, the water, the storms, the sunsets, the stars, the west-bent pines, the lichens between one's toes, the tiny orchids, the spider webs in the glistening crevices"—all those elements her mother once taught her to observe and to treasure during their rambles together.[64] On Georgian Bay she is most herself, and it is there she feels closest to her late mother.

Footnotes for this chapter can be found online at: http://secondstorypress.ca/resources

Nancy Ruth's first cottage
on Georgian Bay, Ontario.

Chapter 9

GEORGIAN BAY

Up there is her soul.

—William Berinati[1]

NANCY RUTH'S FRIENDS describe Georgian Bay as the place where she's happiest, where she blossoms, where her abundant playfulness is on full display. With its multitude of granite islands dotted with white pine forests, this northeastern arm of Lake Huron, about a two-and-a-half hour drive from Toronto, is an iconic part of the Canadian landscape. Carolyn Bennett, Mary Jackman's physician and later an MP and Cabinet member in three Liberal governments, says that "I'm not sure it's possible to experience the view from Nancy's island and not be captured in the spell of the Georgian Bay and the majesty of the Canadian Shield." She calls the region "the most beautiful place in Canada and possibly the world."[2]

Mary Eberts suggests that Nancy Ruth's time at the family cottage as a child was perhaps the one part of her childhood that wasn't full of suffering, giving Georgian Bay added importance as a place for her to return to in her

Nancy Ruth with Elizabeth Riddell-Dixon in
the Arctic outside of Iqaluit, Nunavut.

adult life.[3] Nancy Ruth's partner, Elizabeth Riddell-Dixon agrees, seeing Georgian Bay as the place where she had the "happiest memories" growing up.[4] Nancy Ruth recalls that, in her youth, the Bay—as she calls it—was "a place where I knew my mother loved me and she defended me against my father."[5] Her decision after her father's death to buy the group of twenty-nine outer islands in Go Home Bay—many of them hardly more than rocks jutting out of the bay—gave her the chance to create a retreat of her own, apart from the family cottage yet within the same beloved locale.

The Jackman cottage, of course, was where Nancy Ruth escaped to spend time alone with her first great love, Trudy van Asperen—an interlude she describes in her diaries as perhaps the only "honeymoon" they would ever have. When she built her own cottage in 1982, she constructed it to be at the same angle from which she and Trudy had watched the sunset together a decade earlier.[6] Pat Hacker describes that cottage as simple and comfortable with one notable exception—the lack of an indoor toilet.[7] Its bedrooms were furnished with chamber pots and guests could also repair to a nearby outhouse, whimsically papered with pictures of the queen and photos of Nancy Ruth's parents taken on their tour of the Far East many years earlier. Snakes—including poisonous rattlesnakes—were a constant presence, however, discouraging nighttime visits to the outhouse. The one sink with running water was in the kitchen; water came cold from the lake and had to be boiled for drinking.

Nancy Ruth relished the simplicity of life in this first cottage, which offered her the chance to live close to the land and do the kind of maintenance jobs she thrived on. Each spring, for example, her guests would watch her dive into the water to connect a pipe to the water pump and

Nancy Ruth and friend, Olga Strashun, dancing on the "Goddess Rock" on Nancy Ruth's island, Georgian Bay, Ontario, circa 2010.

start the flow of water into the kitchen. Her canoe and kayak dock was made of rusty bedsprings pulled up on the rocks. Much of what was in use at the cottage came from furnishings her mother had given her from West Wind Island or from Overdown, the family farm, and some of it was fashioned from items salvaged as she cruised around Rosedale on garbage pickup day.[8] She is well known among her circle of friends for her "dumpster-diving" ways—seen as an endearing eccentricity but also as a trait in line with her frugality and her belief, honestly come by, that nothing should go to waste. She remembers her Granny Rowell winding butcher string around her finger to put in the string bag and her father's family breadboard emblazoned with the words, "Waste Not, Want Not." Her use of repurposed and recycled materials at the cottage led to her island's being christened by Go Home Bay friend Kitten Graham, as "Flotsam and Jackman."[9]

Even though Georgian Bay has remained a place where Nancy Ruth could "test my physical and psychological strength," as she and her friends grew older, she found herself ready to embrace greater comfort and convenience—an indoor toilet, a shower, hot water. She knew that the building rules of Georgian Bay township were about to change so she applied in advance of the changes to build a new cottage a short walk from the original one. Even so, neighbours on other islands took her to the planning board three times and each time she was required to alter her design, ending up in 2010 with a new cottage half the size of the one that should have been allowed according to previous regulations, but one equipped with a bathroom, dishwasher, and washing machine, and oriented so the living room would catch a breeze on even the hottest of days.[10]

Neighbours Tuan Nguyen
and Richard Bingham by their
cottage feast, Georgian Bay,
Ontario, 2012.

This greater luxury, however, hasn't kept Nancy Ruth from the manual labour that defines her cottage experience. As Elizabeth Riddell-Dixon describes it, "She loves doing what she would call puttery chores. Getting out and finding the right little stones to fit in the right little crack in the rock so it's smoother walking.... She has lots of projects she can do and she feels healthier because she's getting outside and doing things."[11] At her seventy-fifth birthday party, Georgian Bay friend and neighbour Richard Bingham described watching her the previous summer "move several dozens of rocks, small, medium and large, by hand, in buckets, on upright dollies, and in carts as she determinedly shored up the edges of some 400 feet of crushed-paved roadway on her island. She grew in vigour and strength day by day as the task progressed, and to my amazement, as Nancy always seems to amaze, the road was completed before the end of summer."[12]

The island isn't only a place of labour, however, but also where Nancy Ruth and her friends have had many "wild adventures" together.[13] Kay Macpherson describes watching Nancy Ruth strip to her black lace bra and scarlet panties and dive into the bay to retrieve a missing part from her boat's motor so that they could make the crossing to her island before nightfall: "Thus clad, and roaring and squeaking mightily, our heroine waded into the freezing water up to her shoulders. Then, feeling around with her toes, she miraculously found the part and brought it to the surface, enthusiastically applauded by her audience. After a brisk towelling, she donned her clothes and proceeded to help Ralph [King] improvise a connection with a piece of wire. Luckily the motor started and didn't stop."[14]

Kay's story is characteristic of the adventures—and misadventures—of life on Nancy Ruth's island. A fair number of tales recounted by her friends involve mishaps with boats and it's not unusual for Nancy Ruth to show up naked or near-naked at some point in the account. Pat Hacker remembers, "We all had so much fun there. One year, as you piloted the Boston Whaler full of feminists from dock to cottage, we all shucked off our shirts and travelled bare-breasted and noisy across the lake."[15] Of a trip to the original 1982 cottage in the 1990s, Iris Nowell writes that "She had not exaggerated its plainness. No larger than a two-car garage with an add-on, the grey [cedar] structure reposes starkly atop Nancy's private island, essentially a [two-acre] rock."

At Nancy Ruth's suggestion, she, Iris, and three other guests—Sirje Sellers, Diane Simard Broadfoot, and Jane Cooney, all of whom worked on her 1990 campaign—set off by boat for a picnic on South Wooded Pine Island, one of the sites made famous by the Group of Seven painters

After a spaghetti food fight amongst close friends: Dot Graham, Nancy Ruth, Gwyneth Graham, Caspar Sinnige, and Oliver Graham.

who helped immortalize the Georgian Bay landscape. After a ramble around the island, the women returned to where their boat had been tied to discover that it had gone adrift and was floating half a mile from shore. With no cottages on the surrounding islands and no other boat in sight, they found themselves "truly marooned." Without hesitation, Nancy Ruth "stripped off her clothes and headed naked into the water; she would swim out to get the boat." And retrieve it she did: "It was a vision of wonderment and horror. She swam strongly, occasionally flipping on her back, waving to us and hollering, and a moment later our collective hearts would skip a beat as her body disappeared in a swell of waves. The swimming figure grew smaller and smaller. Finally she reached the boat and at the sound of the motor kicking over, we on [South Wooded] Pine Island cheered mightily." Iris ends her story by recalling with glee that, shortly

after Nancy Ruth returned to shore, a fishing boat motored by. "Little did those two fishermen know that they had just missed the sight of a large, naked lady in a boat."[16]

Nancy Ruth building a deck at her cottage, Georgian Bay, Ontario, circa 1990.

The myriad friends who have spent time on Nancy Ruth's island over the past decades have not only shared adventures but have watched her throw herself—and her visitors—into countless projects. Over the years she has built and anchored docks, erected flagpoles in stony ground, repaired boat motors, painted, pruned, sawed, laid and mended pipes: her island has been the only place "where I get to dress how I want to, do jobs I like."[17] One friend observes that he sometimes wishes "she would just sit down occasionally…and just *be*, you know? It's hard for her."[18] Another speaks of Nancy Ruth's need for control, recounting an incident when she was helping load some wood scrounged from Rosedale's garbage into Nancy Ruth's boat for delivery to the island. After being told several times to rearrange the wood in the boat, and after displaying a flash of irritation, the friend was soundly admonished: "Look it. Nancy's boat, Nancy's island, Nancy's rules."[19]

Yet if Georgian Bay is a place where she can both exert her authority and stay endlessly busy, it's also where Nancy Ruth confronts what Carolyn Bennett calls "a place we can't try to control.... Wind, waves, fog exert their power [and] even control-freaks like Nancy Ruth and I have to succumb."[20] This paradox of domination and surrender may be a key to understanding why Nancy Ruth calls her island retreat the one place "where I am at home."[21] It is a place where the contrasting traits in her own nature can have full play. There she can ride the storms, test herself against the elements, and at the same time, in Carolyn Bennett's words, give in to forces that are "bigger than we are."[22] Her friend William Berinati believes that "up there is her soul"—on her island she is able to tune in to the rocks, the air, the water, the "spirit energy" all around her.[23] Other friends comment in a similar vein. "Nancy's spiritual home is in Georgian Bay. That is where she is most herself. Most at home. Most at peace," they have said.[24] "When she's there that is giving her something in her spirit, I think more than perhaps anywhere else on earth."[25] And, "Oh, it's her favourite place in the world. Georgian Bay."[26]

"She's always communed with the water," reflects Richard Bingham. "With the rocks. I think she likes big things, and rocks are big.... I think she feels very comfortable communing with the harshness. But she's also very focussed on the intricacies of the miniscule, like looking at the different colours of the lichen…inside this what could appear to be quite a cold, brutal landscape, there's a lot of subtlety."[27] Georgian Bay offers grandeur counterbalanced with quiet, intricate beauty—and no understanding of Nancy Ruth is possible without this glimpse of its anchoring role within her life.

Nancy Ruth herself recognizes the island as "my spiritual home."[28] Georgian Bay has helped fill a void left after she finally stepped away from her dream of a vocation within the Christian church in the mid-1980s. She spoke then of her attraction to the goddess religion and her island boasts its own "Goddess Rock" near the second cottage.[29] The Bay is also a place where her spirit has been fed by the love she has received there—from Trudy, from other lovers,

A quiet moment on Georgian Bay.

partners and friends over the years, and importantly, from her mother. "It's always where I remember my mum."[30] It's a place both of solitude and of communal celebration, of madcap escapades and industrious labour, of control and abandon.

The years between the time she built her first cottage in 1982 and the present day have seen Nancy Ruth become a woman of purpose and influence, joining forces with Canadian feminists to fight for justice for women and girls in Canada's constitution and laws. They have seen her as a woman of political ambition who ran twice for a seat in provincial parliament and who was ultimately appointed to Canada's Senate. They have seen her as a loving and then grieving daughter, determined to chronicle her mother's life. Through all these years, from the time she first claimed her financial inheritance after her father's death, Nancy Ruth has emerged as one of Canada's leading feminist philanthropists. She has, with increasing intention and deliberation, used her inheritance to support initiatives aimed at producing systemic change on behalf of women and girls in the name of social justice. Her efforts, as we shall see in the next chapter, have had a significant impact on Canada's social fabric and legal framework.

Footnotes for this chapter can be found online at:
http://secondstorypress.ca/resources

Chapter 10

CHARITY THAT CAUSES CHANGE

*She is the patron saint of worthy
unfunded righteous feminist causes.*

—Gail Asper[1]

NANCY RUTH'S 1980 gift to the National Action Committee on the Status of Women (NAC) had given her a taste of what her money could do. Although it was only five thousand dollars, it was the largest private donation NAC had ever received and it drew her into the sisterhood of women who would mount a fierce campaign for women's equality in the Charter of Rights and Freedoms. But the money was granted through the Jackman Foundation and every donation from that foundation to one of her chosen causes had to be negotiated with her brothers and weighed against their interests. She believes that this experience "sowed the seeds" of her feminist philanthropy: "As we awarded our grants, I began to notice that most of the funding—about 90 per cent—was going to groups that benefited men and boys or male-controlled institutions. I'd suggest giving money to organizations like the Elizabeth

Fry Society and my brothers would vote it down." This experience increased her determination to "get her full share of the capital" so that she could devote her philanthropy to the causes in which she believed.[2]

In 1987, when she transferred funds from the Jackman Foundation and placed them in her own NaRuth Foundation, Nancy Ruth could begin to do things differently, but what exactly would that difference be? Over time, she would come to be known and widely respected as a passionate feminist philanthropist. She confesses, however, that "When I started, I didn't know I was involved with feminist philanthropy.... I simply knew the distribution from the Jackman Foundation was unfair. My brothers gave most of it to their sex for things that helped to maintain the status quo and continued the oppression of women. I also saw this pattern on the public records of other foundations.... Charities, like the rest of society, are hugely discriminatory."[3] A few years later she confessed that, during her early experience with philanthropy, she only "slowly...realized that if women and girls were to be supported in Canada and not the victims of...economic violence, then I had to change my giving patterns to donate almost all my extra dollars and all of my extra time to women and girls."[4]

She did know from the outset of her charitable giving that she wanted to spare other women the abuse her mother had gone through as a woman in a male-dominated household; that desire was one of her central motivations. "Watching my mother 'give in' to her husband and her sons made me very angry. When my dad died and I inherited some of his wealth, I wanted to use that money so that no woman would have to go through the shame and pain my mother experienced."[5] Her engagement with the national work of the Charter of Rights Coalition (CORC) in the mid-1980s can be seen in the same context. While she contributed more time than money to CORC, her volunteer leadership was one critical component in educating women across Canada about the importance of the Charter to their future legal rights as well as in reducing the inequitable structures under which her mother had suffered.

Engagement through both volunteer service and financial support has been a hallmark of Nancy Ruth's philanthropy. Elizabeth Riddell-Dixon observes that "she gives her money, which is very significant because there are very few in the position to do what she's been able to do, but also she gives of herself. She gives her time. She gives her energy. Really puts her heart into trying to make these things go."[6] Mary Eberts, in a similar vein, praises her friend for being

> one of the few lives in our century that has brought about a considerable amount of social change while freelancing, while not attached to a big unit of the Establishment. I guess the biggest unit of the Establishment she was attached to was her family and her family's wealth. But she wasn't a writer or an artist or a dancer or anything. She was a kind of freelance social agitator.... She has brought about a tremendous amount of social change while being almost entirely a volunteer.[7]

Nancy Ruth herself comments on what it felt like to be "freelance" after she came into her fortune: "Okay, so once I cashed in my chips I didn't have to earn a living. But the down side is you don't have a place in society any more, you don't have a community. What are you going

Catharine A. MacKinnon, on the right,
greets Nancy Ruth at her 75th birthday party
on January 6, 2017.

to do if you live off the stock market? Get up at 11 a.m. and do nothing?" She saw this way of living as "anathema" to the generations of Methodists from which she came. Instead, she realized, she would "have to create. All of us have to create structures when you choose to leave the normal strictures of the job. You have to do more than have fundraisers once a month. You'd go nuts."[8] Through the years, Nancy Ruth has shown herself to be a person driven to belong to a community as well as someone with a strong need for vocation. Her alliance with feminism gave her the community she yearned for. And now, after her many forays into possible careers—as a jewellery-maker, a human resource consultant, a clown, a United Church minister—she can begin to forge a meaningful vocation for herself as a philanthropist focused on social change.

Beth Atcheson, who has worked very closely with Nancy Ruth over the years, has noted an evolution in her approach to philanthropy. "Initially, I don't know that her giving out of the foundation was strategic, but her thinking about feminist philanthropy grows as she does more of that herself, actually is a practitioner…. She's getting more practical experience about especially large gifts. Who can give them? Who are they giving to? How do you influence them? So, I think there's a trajectory here. I don't remember her coming to the NaRuth Foundation with a kind of fully formed view. Part of it, she's gaining experience as she does all these things and as she raises money and as she becomes a donor."[9] Nancy Ruth will come to see her vocation as not simply giving money away but as persuading others to join her and do the same. She has served as donor, advocate, and fundraiser for all the major initiatives she has undertaken—in Elizabeth Riddell-Dixon's words, "putting her heart into trying to make these things go."

As mentioned previously, when the Jackman Foundation funds were divided up among family members' charities or foundations in 1987, Nancy Ruth and her mother each made gifts of $500,000 to the Women's Legal Education and Action Fund (LEAF). The three-year moratorium on Section 15's coming into force had been lifted in April 1985, and LEAF, now proving to be a powerful tool for challenging discriminatory laws, was launched that same day. While Nancy Ruth had stepped away from LEAF for a time to take a position at Metropolitan United Church, she never lost her belief in the importance of its work. Whether tap-dancing with a donation bucket in hand as a "Tree for LEAF," or challenging attendees at a Persons Day breakfast in Sudbury by offering to match all their donations to LEAF, she maintained her commitment to LEAF's success.[10] Over the years, as Catharine A. MacKinnon observes, Nancy Ruth's support for LEAF "has been monumental."[11]

Denise Arsenault, LEAF's first treasurer, remembering the financial stresses of LEAF's early days, tells the following story about Nancy Ruth in her role as chair of fundraising:

> We may have been a year into our life as a charity. We had a board meeting [in the Pauline McGibbon Centre] and we needed to raise funds. We could not cover expenses without more money coming in the door. It's Nancy's job to inspire these non-fundraisers and I thought, how the heck are you going to do this? She came in using all her pastoral skills, let me say, and she gave—I wish that speech had been taped because it's a classic.... Instead of doing a direct—I'll say using the whip—she found a way of creating the

most beautiful carrot for people. Talking about LEAF and how we had planted this seed and needed for its roots to take so that it could do the work. I remember that part of the analogy that she used. You know how well Nancy can carry a phrase; she was at her best. She took many people into a commitment to fundraise who were working seriously against their natural inclination, desire, comfort, whatever you want to say…. We made our numbers and in fact were able to have a small surplus that gave us a bit of a reserve. And I sincerely believe that would never have happened without Nancy.[12]

When the LEAF Foundation was set up a couple of years later, Nancy Ruth served as its first president and by 1990, estimated that she had personally given LEAF about $1.5 million. Speaking at a Persons Day breakfast sponsored by the Toronto chapter of LEAF that year, she told the two thousand people in attendance that LEAF was Canada's most effective weapon against "systemic discrimination," adding that "Most organizations—even those for battered women and children, or children who are incest victims—support the status quo…. They don't have the capacity or the how-to to change the society. Law is a way to change the rules of how society works."[13] And transforming how society works would indeed become the hallmark of her labours over the coming years. As Nancy Ruth herself says, "I'm interested in charity that causes change."[14] This sentiment is echoed by Denise Arsenault: "…systemic change is what I think jazzes her the most. Which is why LEAF was so important, and the Canadian Women's Foundation as well."[15]

After her founding support for LEAF, Nancy Ruth's

The Canadian Women's Foundation opened its first
office at 214 Merton Street, Toronto, in May, 1991.
L to R: Beverley Wybrow (CEO), Geetha Sriharan
(Assistant), and Nancy Ruth and Julie White
(founding mothers and directors).

next major effort went toward setting up the Canadian Women's Foundation (CWF). "My mother gave $500,000 to get it going and I gave half a million as a matching pledge." Although she was aware that the idea for a women's foundation had been kicking around for years, she was spurred to take action after the death of Margaret Horan, an Irish immigrant who had worked as a downstairs maid for her mother. Nancy Ruth helped care for Margaret in her old age and held her power of attorney before she died. It came as a shock when she discovered that Margaret had left forty thousand dollars—"a phenomenal sum of money for someone in domestic service"—to the Scarboro Foreign Mission Society, a Roman Catholic organization that sent priests abroad to evangelize for the Church. "I was upset. All her money was going to men! She might have left it to an organization like INTERCEDE, which works on behalf of female domestic workers like her."[16] A women's foundation could accomplish multiple important goals: it could, for example, serve as an estate beneficiary to which women like Margaret could direct their funds; it could catalyze and fund projects to enable women's economic independence; and it could provide guidance to other foundations that were interested in supporting causes of benefit to women.

Susan Woods, credited along with Nancy Ruth as one of the founding mothers of the CWF, tells the story of how the two of them first hatched the idea for the foundation. Susan, a grade-school friend of Nancy Ruth's and former president of the Young Women's Christian Association (YWCA) board of directors, visited her on an early spring morning in 1986 to pitch her suitability for an administrative role in the Jackman Foundation. Susan recalls that,

Hospitable as she is, Nancy Ruth invited me to have lunch with her, which she thought would be more enjoyable if consumed outside in the pale sunshine of that March day. So we hauled two dusty lawn chairs from her garage, set them in a south-facing corner of her driveway and began to talk about what was really needed, namely a foundation for women. It was a natural and easy progression on that hopeful spring morning to bring to life a new idea, one which held such promise for women across Canada.[17]

Nancy Ruth would of course leave her family foundation the next year and make a gift to the CWF that helped seed its work. Following their lunch, rather than hiring Susan to work for the Jackman Foundation, she hired her to develop the concept of the Canadian Women's Foundation. Susan had extensive contacts within the YWCA volunteer network, comparable to Nancy Ruth's connections within LEAF, and between the two of them they were able to generate significant enthusiasm for their project to establish Canada's first foundation focused exclusively on creating broad-based social change that would benefit women.[18]

In the spring of 1989, an article in the *Toronto Star*, reporting on a meeting in Toronto of the US-based National Network of Women's Funds, noted that "The only Canadian philanthropist attending the conference was feminist Nancy Jackman, who is currently incorporating the Canadian Women's Foundation."[19] By 1990, work on establishing the CWF was well underway with Nancy Ruth in her usual role of stumping, speaking, and advocating. That year, she joined with Susan Woods and others to hold focus groups across the country in rural and urban settings, and with individuals, national women's groups, community organizations, and funders, to seek advice on what directions the foundation should take.

Speaking to the Canadian Association of Women Executives and Entrepreneurs in May 1991, Nancy Ruth explained that from every corner during these consultations the CWF was urged to target its programs on "helping women & girls achieve their full potential" through supporting "economic development projects that encourage self-determination, self-reliance and independence." Further, they were advised to give priority to programs designed to support women and girls who are economically disadvantaged or at risk. As Nancy Ruth told her audience, "the common thread throughout these stories was the need for women to have economic control over their lives."[20]

Michele Landsberg, chronicling the CWF's progress, tells her *Toronto Star* readers, "Maybe you'll recall that I wrote about the brand-new Canadian Women's Foundation last year. It's the first and the only charitable foundation in Canada specifically designed to meet the needs of women, and it's not afraid to challenge the outworn social structures that keep women at a disadvantage. For the past year, as it energetically got itself on its feet, the foundation has shown that it deserves to be taken seriously, supported and celebrated." In her column, Landsberg lauds the foundation for its commitment to being "a real instrument of change" and notes that in its first year of operation it has already granted $88,000 to a diversity of projects across the country and has raised $1.5 million toward a $5 million fundraising goal. "If you're thinking of supporting the foundation," she concludes, "consider the Nancy Jackman challenge. Jackman, probably the leading individual benefactor of women in Canada, was the prime mover behind

Rosemary Brown, Nancy Ruth, and Julie White,
Canadian Women's Foundation founding mothers,
blow out candles on the CWF 5th anniversary cake.
The party was held at St. Lawrence Hall, Toronto.

the foundation and, with her mother, Mary Jackman, is a major donor. Nancy will match your donation, dollar for dollar. Over $1,000, she'll double your gift; over $5,000, she'll *triple* it. Quite a deal."[21]

Nancy Ruth was under full steam as she contributed her resources, both time and money, and her leadership skills on behalf of an initiative in which she passionately believes. Like LEAF, the CWF met her baseline criterion by being an agent for systemic change for girls and women in Canadian society. Its initial grants, as detailed by Landsberg, had gone to self-help employment projects in Montreal, Collingwood, Halifax, Toronto, Vancouver, and Edmonton; to support for training math and science teachers in Halifax so they could encourage junior high girls to explore careers in science and engineering; to a BC housing society constructing non-profit housing for single-parent families; and to a Winnipeg drop-in centre for Indigenous women to help its clients market their handmade crafts.

By 1997, when the CWF celebrated the successes of its first phase of operation, the foundation had raised more than six million dollars in donations and pledges and had attracted twenty-six major corporate and foundation partners and sponsors. Two hundred and fifty people gathered at St. Lawrence Hall in Toronto on March 5 to toast this success and honour CWF's eight "founding mothers"— Nancy Ruth, Susan Woods, Rosemary Brown, Mary Eberts, Dawn Elliot, Kay Sigurjonsson, Elizabeth Stewart, and Julie White, all strong feminist leaders who had helped make the dream a reality. In addition to its focus on economic development, the foundation had also by that time developed a grants program aimed at the prevention of violence against girls and women. That spring it awarded almost a quarter of a million dollars to violence prevention projects across the country.[22] Nancy Ruth's vision—that no woman, whether wealthy or poor, should be treated as her mother had been—was now imbedded in the foundation's core mandate.

Nancy Ruth continued to work closely with the CWF for many years, serving on its board and giving volunteer leadership to its fundraising. In the mid-1990s her foundation—by then renamed Nancy's Very Own Foundation—became part of the Women and Economic Development Consortium administered by the CWF and made up of corporate, foundation, and cooperative sector partners. The consortium offered money and technical support to model projects across the country that gave low-income women and girls a chance to start their own businesses.[23] In the late 1990s, she and CWF's executive director, Beverley Wybrow, undertook a campaign to establish the Women's Future Fund, conceived of as a workplace/payroll donation system similar to that of the United Way but dedicated to supporting national women's organizations such as LEAF, the CWF, NAC, the Elizabeth Fry Society, and the National Congress of Black Women.[24] While the concept in the end failed to take root, the fund was another bold idea for redressing gender inequity in charitable giving.

Unlike the Women's Future Fund, however, the Canadian Women's Foundation has both survived and thrived. Since its inception it has raised more than eighty million dollars and funded programs in more than fifteen hundred communities across Canada. Its current giving programs still focus on the prevention of violence against girls and women and the promotion of women's economic independence, but it has also added grant streams for the empowerment of girls and for inclusive leadership. Nancy Ruth's determination to do something that would bring about systemic change for girls and women helped give birth to two of Canada's most important feminist initiatives, LEAF and the CWF, and both organizations to this day continue to have a powerful impact on women's equality within Canada.

> Author: "Would you have been a different person if you had gone to The Linden School?"

> Nancy Ruth: "Yes. I wouldn't have needed to be angry for so long. I would have been legitimized much earlier, have been given voice."[25]

Nancy Ruth met Diane Goudie and Eleanor Moore when they were both on the staff of St. Clement's, a private girls' school in Toronto; Diane was acting principal and Eleanor was vice-principal. At the time, Diane was preparing herself to compete for St. Clement's permanent principalship, a position she landed in 1990. Eleanor was working on her master's degree at the Ontario Institute for Studies in Education (OISE), where her research focused on the difficulty girls faced in finding their voices and being heard. Publications that had appeared over the previous decade, such as Carol Gilligan's *In a Different Voice: Psychological Theory and Women's Development*, had posited key differences between the ways in which girls and boys learned as well as suggesting that girls were disadvantaged when their education did not take these differences into account.[26]

Diane recalls that, when she had asked the then-principal what the expectations were for her in her role as vice-principal at St. Clement's, she had been told, "Watch what UCC [Upper Canada College, an elite boys' school] does and we do it just like that." And she remembers thinking at the time, "Hang on, have you noticed that these are girls and those are boys and, at the risk of stretching the point, there may be a slight difference in how they learn and what they learn and how they are brought up?" Eleanor also recognized, not just through her master's research but from her many conversations with the girls of St. Clement's, that even these "privileged young women" often felt themselves silenced and were unable to understand why.[27] Visits both to Emma Willard School in upstate New York and to Wellesley College in Massachusetts added to their growing conviction that education for girls needed a fundamental re-thinking.

Fired up by what they were learning, Diane and Eleanor hatched the idea of transforming St. Clement's by putting feminist principles to work in its curriculum and pedagogy. They shared their vision with Nancy Ruth in several conversations, and one weekend, not long after Diane was appointed principal, her phone rang. Nancy Ruth, in her "high-energy, brusque mode, exclaimed, 'Did you mean what you said?' and I said, 'Of course.' She said, 'Well then, I will give you a quarter of a million dollars to make this happen at St. Clement's.'"[28] In her keynote speech earlier that year at the Woman of the Year banquet in Hamilton, Ontario, Nancy Ruth had told her audience, "My money enables me to do what I want to do." St. Clement's seemed to offer a perfect match between her wealth and an opportunity to create a school unlike the ones where she had struggled as a girl and young woman. She had the foresight, however, to make her gift to St. Clement's contingent on her friend's remaining principal;

less than a year later, the board of governors, unnerved by the changes she was introducing at the school, fired Diane Goudie. Very little of the gift had been spent by that time and the balance was returned to the donor.[29]

Unwilling to let go of the vision even after the disappointment at St. Clement's, in June 1991 Nancy Ruth invited Diane and Eleanor to a meeting at Roxborough Drive. In her typical role of catalyst and connector, she had called together "people she knew"—a couple of women who had started a private elementary school in Oakville, Ontario; Romily Perry, a mother who had planned to send her daughter to St. Clement's but withdrew her after she learned that the proposed reforms weren't going to happen; and friends of Romily Perry who were also interested in an alternative model of education for their daughters. The meeting was a brainstorming session and Eleanor recalls Nancy Ruth "disappearing into the woodwork" after putting the group together. "I don't remember her saying really anything except making it happen and being very warm and greeting everybody, but then kind of just backing right out and letting it sort of flow." Even though Nancy Ruth stayed in the background, Eleanor and Diane nonetheless view her as pivotal in the creation of the new school they would open just eighteen months later. In Eleanor's words, "without her that would not have happened, that group, and it was the beginning of The Linden School."[30]

Before the school could open, of course, its founders needed to raise start-up money. Business plan in hand, they went out to "beg"—Diane says, "You are interviewing two of the best beggars you ever heard in your life"—and on one of their sorties ended up back at Roxborough Drive. In light of Nancy Ruth's former and unsolicited gift to St.

Nancy Ruth's friends celebrate her Governor General's Award in Commemoration of the Persons Case on October 20, 1997 (under the portrait of the Right Honourable Jeanne Sauvé). Standing L to R: Eleanor Moore, Dr. Carolyn Bennett, Kashmeel McKöena, Nancy Ruth, Marie Frye, Sirje Sellers, Chaviva Hošek, Pat Hacker. Seated L to R: Pat Baxter, Kat Chuba, Diane Goudie, Beth Atcheson.

Clement's, they hoped she would offer them seed funding for The Linden School. To their surprise she at first refused. Nancy Ruth wanted them to make the school stand on its own feet financially, as the Oakville school had done, not to be dependent on charity because "being dependent on donations can be a killer."[31] She challenged them by saying, "You can't do it. You just can't do it. It'll never work. You cannot do it." When Diane retorted in a flash of anger that they would "either do it with you or we'll do it without you," Nancy Ruth stomped off into her study where they heard her tell her secretary, "Jean, they've got a fucking dream."[32] At that moment, they knew the gift was theirs. Not only did she make a donation, Nancy Ruth helped them put together a group of other women who could assist with fundraising and pitched in on mundane tasks such as putting together the school's first newsletter. Diane sums up her contributions by saying, "So that's how Nancy wove into the very early days and really is a founding mother of the school."[33] She has also continued to be a generous donor over the years, contributing almost one million dollars to the school.[34]

True to its founding vision, The Linden School has fully integrated girl-centred education and feminist theory into all its operations, even down to the organization of classrooms and the meeting procedures of its board. The school opened its doors in 1993 to thirty-seven students in grades 4 through 9 and now enrolls more than 130 girls from pre-kindergarten through Grade 12. In 2007, when she and Eleanor were awarded honorary doctorates at York University, Diane told York's graduates, "When we founded Linden, girls told us that they had felt silenced in their schools. We know that for each of us being able to speak, being heard and taken seriously is very important.

Therefore, enabling our students to have a voice is an essential tenet at Linden, as it is in all quests for equity, liberation, and change. In our curriculum and structures, we teach our students to ask, Who speaks? Who is heard? Who is missing? And who decides who has the voice at any given time and in any place?"[35]

In an article written seventeen years after The Linden School opened its doors, Nancy Ruth praises its achievement as a place "dedicated to training young feminist leaders." The school is noteworthy, she observes, because it

> teaches all its subjects through the eyes of women. When studying English or French literature, the students read women authors. The curriculum includes the great women scientists, mathematicians, and healers, and explores their remarkable contributions. History is taught through the eyes of the women who lived it. Courses on imperialism focus on the experiences of the women who were exploited. Aboriginal history in Canada is seen from the perspectives of Indigenous women.[36]

Had she attended such a school when she was a girl, Nancy Ruth believes she might have found her authentic voice sooner and spared herself years of confusion and rage.

Although the number of girls Linden educates each year is relatively small, the education they receive opens up enormous opportunities for those girls to lead and advocate for positive social change. At Linden's June 2005 graduation ceremony, Nancy Ruth told the students,

I stand before you—bursting with pride. What a fine group of young women you are! Your intelligence, your talent, your confidence are obvious to me every time I come to Linden for a festival or an event. And now you are graduating…! Where do you go from here? Anywhere you want to go. The Linden School has given you plenty of tools. Tools to use—in any situation that might arise in your lives. Tools such as honesty, sisterhood, intellectual curiosity, and a feminist perspective…. Your school, The Linden School, happened because a group of women and men chose "to engage" with the educational process. They sat down together and made your school happen. It continues to happen because the teachers, principals, the wonderful volunteers and you, the students, put your shoulders to the wheel and make it happen. And that's the way the world works.[37]

Her message here is about efficacy, about what is possible when people are given the right tools, share a passion, and work together on behalf of a common cause. She is confident that the tools that Linden provides to its graduates will help ensure that they can become activists on behalf of a more just and equitable world.

Nancy Ruth lists The Linden School, the Canadian Women's Foundation, LEAF, and the Charter of Rights Coalition as four of the five initiatives of which she is most proud. The fifth, as mentioned earlier, is her project to create a women's history museum.[38] The idea for the project arose when Nancy Ruth was faced with the task of deciding what to do with her mother's remaining possessions, most particularly her wedding dress, after her death. Beth Atcheson explains that, for Nancy Ruth, from a napkin to a very valuable painting it all has to be used, used properly and a home found for it. I mean, this is just a very big trope in her life…so Nancy has all these things, and of course she goes looking for homes for them. She also wants her mother's story told, so it's not just, "where do I put my mother's wedding dress?" I think she went through life with an intuitive understanding of the systemic, but by the time we've gone through all the Charter analysis, man, she gets the systemic and the substantive in a very big way. So it's not just where does Mother's wedding dress go, it's why are institutions not taking these things. Why are they not telling stories about women's lives in their fullness…? [I]t seems to be about the practical: where do I put this?—which is part of Nancy Ruth and her life. I never want to waste a single thing and it all has to go somewhere—that kind of compulsive side that she has. But there's also a bigger thing: Why are they not interested? Where are the women's stories? Why is it not visible?[39]

Nancy Ruth called together a diverse group of women—historians, journalists, visual artists, fundraisers—to sit down with her and hammer out a strategy for making women visible by telling their stories. She convened the first planning meeting in early January 1995, just a few months after her mother's death. Over the following year, the group met twice a month to canvass opinions and explore possibilities, ranging from a stand-alone "Historia Femina/women's museum" through story boxes for schoolchildren to a "virtual" museum that would tap into the emerging power of the Internet and the World Wide Web.[40] Although Nancy Ruth was intrigued by the

The Honourable Barbara McDougall, MP, and Nancy Ruth meet campaigning during the 1988 federal election. McDougall inscribed the photograph, "Nancy, keep on keeping on!"

prospect of an "up in the sky" or Internet-based approach, she initially argued that it should be combined with an "on the ground museum." But women at the first meeting quickly agreed that before any decision could be made, they needed to learn a great deal more about the technology and capabilities of the Internet.[41]

Another key question was the project's scope: should the women featured in the museum be drawn from around the world or should the project focus exclusively on Canadian women? Discussion at the early meetings assumed an international orientation and the capabilities of the World Wide Web seemed to support this approach.[42] Yet as the planners grappled with both the magnitude of their project and their vision of its central purpose, they recognized the need to continue sharpening their focus. A valid approach, they came to agree, would be to "seek the international perspectives of women who have immigrated to Canada...and begin to map out the diversity of the women who are based in Canada."[43]

By the time the project launched in a downtown Internet café in November 1996, Nancy Ruth explained to those assembled that "Over the past year, a group of us have met over endless lasagna to talk about what we wanted to create...stories of women and girls, readily accessible, & about how women & girls have participated in making Canada the nation it is. In fact, we wanted to do this in every country on the planet! Then we realized that women/girls in Canada reach out to every country and they will do this 'reaching' for [us]. For, when we talk about our foremothers, we are telling women's stories from every country."[44] In other words, Canada's own multiculturalism would itself be the source of the project's international reach.

The record of almost two years of planning also demonstrates a growing interest in the project's potential to inspire activism, in keeping with Nancy Ruth's continuing drive to catalyze systemic change. Cataloguing women's history would be a means, not an end. As Sirje Sellers, Nancy Ruth's partner at the time and a member of the planning committee, emphasized, "It's not the data you present that's important, it's the thought you provoke."[45] On March 15, 1995, under a discussion of "Preliminary Direction for Museum," there is consensus that "Our project needs a decided feminist bent; we need to create a body of data that will spur up feminist activists all over the world." The May 11, 1995, minutes record the fact that "There is very little available which emphasizes how important it is for women to be visible and to take power for themselves," followed by the question, "How can we demonstrate our history to become a visible tool for living now?"[46]

One significant evolution in the planners' thinking was the ultimate decision to address the project primarily to an audience of girls and young women. The April 12, 1995, meeting minutes identify a desire to reach and educate those who are "up and coming," and by October of that year there are plans to hold focus groups on the project with girls at local high schools. The following summer, a "Draft short description of project" attached to the minutes of June 19, 1996, states that "In September 1996, Nancy's Very Own Foundation will go on-line by launching a World Wide Web site for young women on women in Canada. We will tell stories of girls and women from our past and from the present, making connections and supporting critical thinking about how society is organized and how this impacts our lives." Nancy Ruth and her co-planners "shared a view that women's history was largely invisible in our society and that, as a result, each generation of girls growing into women had to learn to challenge their place and treatment in society without the experiences, insights, ideas and support of the women who had gone before." Through reaching and educating girls and young women, they aimed to inspire "collective action for women in Canada and around the world."[47] Nancy Ruth was twenty-six when she had her own feminist awakening; she wanted future generations of girls to fare better than she had.

Ideas for a "museum on the ground" fell by the wayside as excitement grew about the potential of the Web. Catharine Devlin, a former member of the NAC executive and a member of Nancy Ruth's planning committee, owned Devlin Multimedia, a digital communications company, and was able to provide expert guidance on website development. On October 18, 1995, she presented the group with a proposal to develop a site to be called *CoolWomen*, and the following day that domain name was secured. It took just over a year for the website to launch, but with decisions about scope, audience, and medium now made, Nancy Ruth and her colleagues could turn their minds to more specific questions about content and design.

Because they aimed to reach a youthful audience, the planners knew that, above all, the site had to be interactive and engaging. As draft content was reviewed, there were recurring cries of "this is too academic!" and "this is still boring!" Nancy Ruth had now adopted the Internet address of "webmom"—which she in fact kept for many years—and with her high need for control and low tolerance for stuffy prose, she made it clear that all content would be reviewed by "webmom" in advance of being uploaded.[48] To increase the sense of immediacy and encourage engagement, the design would incorporate an online café populated by "café regulars," fictional young women of diverse ethnic backgrounds who carried on conversations about featured articles on the site. The planners also agreed to include a chat line; a bulletin board with news of feminist publications and relevant upcoming events; articles about topics of current interest; a "fe-mail" section inviting comments from site users; and a guest book for visitors to sign.

The highlight of *CoolWomen*, as the name suggests, would be weekly profiles of individual women, with diversity of background and accomplishment a key criterion for their selection. Over the years, for example, they would include African Nova Scotian Rose Fortune, who in the early nineteenth century set herself up in business as a carter moving baggage by wheelbarrow from arriving ships to hotels and homes, a business that remained in her family for 125 years; Mrs. Kwong Lee, the first Chinese woman to arrive in British Columbia in an era of rampant discrimination against Chinese; Nellie McClung, leading first-wave feminist and women's rights activist; Joy Kogawa, writer and activist for Japanese Canadians; Rosemary Brown, the first Black Canadian woman to be elected to a provincial legislature; and Nancy Meek Pocock, jeweller, feminist, and peace activist.[49]

At the *CoolWomen* launch, Nancy Ruth stressed the work that had been done to make the site accessible and interactive. The "café regulars," she explained, were imaginary characters drawn from a variety of cultures and ethnic backgrounds so that they could offer diverse perspectives on the topics being featured. She encouraged visitors to the site to send emails directly to these café characters to "find out why they think the way they do & to give their own perspectives." The introduction on the site's

CoolWomen.org illustration
by Martha Newbigging.

homepage read, "If you or your classmates or your organization have an idea about an historical or contemporary girl or woman, or group, share it with us. Even better, be a guest contributor; prepare a feature and we will work with you to publish it on the site."⁵⁰ In her remarks, Nancy Ruth noted with pride that *CoolWomen* was one of the first sites, along with *Chatelaine*, to offer its readers the chance to submit their own material and have it published online.⁵¹

In February 1997, following a campaign to promote awareness of the site in schools and among the general public, *CoolWomen* had almost 100,000 "site hits" or visitors. Over the following years it averaged more than forty thousand hits a month. Nancy Ruth and her team continued to meet, though not as frequently as in the start-up phase, to revise and refine the site's design and content. Although they considered applying for grants to support their work, in the end the costs of feature writers, design, site maintenance, and an editor were covered by Nancy's Very Own Foundation.⁵² By 2001, its creators could take pride in knowing that *CoolWomen* had become the "largest women's history site in Canada."⁵³

In 2008, Nancy Ruth agreed to a proposal to redesign the site and change its name. With exploding activity on the Internet, a search for the phrase "cool women" now yielded a multiplicity of sites, some of them pornographic. The site editor who had been hired to enhance interactivity, Jude MacDonald, chose the name *Section15.ca* in honour of the historic equality section in the Charter of Rights and Freedoms. But by then, working with the schools to encourage girls' use of the site had become increasingly difficult. Teachers wanted lesson plans, which called for additional investment in staff and money; according to Nancy Ruth, "We did a few plans but needed a huge marketing effort to sell it…. It wasn't being used by the schools as we had hoped [and] it was using up a lot of resources of the foundation."[54] Nancy Ruth had also become fully immersed in her Senate responsibilities, as had Beth Atcheson, who had worked diligently supporting the project but was now engaged as Nancy Ruth's director of parliamentary affairs. About a year after the name change, the group made a decision to cease maintaining the site altogether, letting it become "static" on the web. Nancy Ruth's executive assistant, Martha Grantham, "managed what needed to be managed on section15.ca" until it was finally archived in 2019.[55]

As an initiative aimed at creating systemic change, *CoolWomen* satisfied Nancy Ruth's basic criterion for philanthropic engagement. Telling the stories of diverse women—making their achievements visible—was meant to inspire future generations to act on behalf of women's equality and social justice. And she found further satisfaction in the means by which this project came to fruition. She relished the process of building the "virtual women's history museum"—the camaraderie of those endless lasagna lunches, the pleasure of working alongside women who shared her vision and passion, the sheer fun of the work—along with the site's practical outcome.

While *CoolWomen* did not fulfill all the hopes that Nancy Ruth and her team had for the project—"Our goal was to influence every child in Canada. We did not accomplish that"—it nevertheless remains one of the initiatives in which she takes the most pride. "It was a first. Women's history. Our staff meetings were awesome, lots of ideas, every story was exciting. Our launch was successful, putting it all together, expanding when we hired Judy, to make it an interactive site. Many women contributed to it, and we brought many women to the spotlight, as they had been unknown before." Nancy Ruth, working with a small team of dedicated friends and her two colleagues, Beth Atcheson and Martha Grantham, had moved from frustration about an "orphaned" wedding dress through the prospect of an "on the ground" women's museum to the creation of an interactive women's history website. And even though the site is no longer active, "the information will always be accessible, as a database" (https://archive-it. org/home/nancyruth).[56] The journey was a circuitous one, but Mary Jackman's wedding dress, at least in spirit, had found a home.

Not all of Nancy Ruth's major gifts were to projects that engaged her as closely as did LEAF, the CWF, The Linden School, and *CoolWomen*, but all of them were intended to catalyze change and remediate women's inequality or social injustice. As Pat Hacker has said, "She was always opening something, doing something, supporting something."[57] In 1998, she donated $500,000 to Mount Saint Vincent University to match a challenge grant from the federal government and endow the first chair in women's studies in Atlantic Canada. In 2006, a gift of the same size helped to save the childhood home of Japanese Canadian novelist Joy Kogawa from demolition. The house figures in Kogawa's novel *Obasan*, which chronicles the persecution of Canada's Japanese population during World War II, and following its purchase it was turned into a writers' retreat.

In recognition of the Canadian Museum for Human Rights' mission to enhance public understanding of the importance of human rights, Nancy Ruth gave a one-million-dollar gift to the museum the following year. When she was given the choice of a space to be named in her honour, Nancy Ruth "claimed" the board room—so

The Honourable Hilary Weston presents
the 1998 Ontario Human Rights Award to
Nancy Ruth at Queen's Park, Toronto.

that "nobody was going to get in there and make decisions without having to see my face, understand systemic discrimination against women and girls, and do a gender-based analysis of every Board decision they make."[58] Another gift of one million dollars to the Toronto YWCA in 2012 supported its creation of Elm Centre, a residential community that offers apartment housing to low-income women and their families, women with addiction or mental health problems, and families of Indigenous ancestry. And over a thirty-year period, Nancy Ruth has donated almost three million dollars to Toronto's Women's College Hospital, whose mission focuses both on women's health and health equity.

The gifts to the Women's College Hospital have come almost equally from Nancy's Very Own Foundation and from her private wealth. Indeed, her philanthropy over the past thirty years has been split between those two sources, with several larger gifts, totalling almost nine million dollars since 1984, coming from stock shares in her personal portfolio.[59] Her giving, of course, hasn't been restricted to large gifts; the foundation has donated over fifteen million dollars to more than seven hundred organizations since its inception, with gifts ranging from three to seven figures.[60]

Her financial support has not always been directed to institutions and organizations. Those in her close circle are aware of the gifts she has made to friends over the years. Mary Martin, a friend from childhood days in Georgian Bay, observes that Nancy Ruth's "generosity is unparalleled."[61] Catharine A. MacKinnon, noting that "she's helped out some few individuals who she believes in," observes that in many cases her personal philanthropy "has made a major difference."[62] And these personal gifts have been quiet, unheralded. James Cowan, a Halifax lawyer who was appointed to the Senate at the same time as Nancy Ruth and served beside her for twelve years, says that "she's not one to talk about these things, but my sense would be that there are a lot of causes and a lot of individuals she's helped just without telling anybody that she was doing it and without looking for any kind of recognition."[63]

In her 1991 curriculum vitae, Nancy Ruth offers a list of organizations and institutions to which she has donated under multiple categories that reflect her diversity of interests and causes. The first category, "Economic Development," lists only one organization, the Canadian Women's Foundation. Under "Cultural" the list is wide-ranging and includes theatres, art galleries, music performances, and museums. The "Education and Community" category consists of literacy programs and religious organizations, while "International" lists the Canadian Institute of International Affairs and MATCH International Women's Fund. The section on "Health and Environment" shows that she has donated to organizations such as Planned Parenthood in provinces across Canada, Casey House AIDS Hospice, Sister Rosalie Bertell's International Institute of Concern for Public Health, the Canadian Coalition on Acid Rain, and Greenpeace. Donations to "Peace and Disarmament" include Voice of Women for Peace, the Centre for Arms Control, the University of Toronto's Chair for Peace Research, Conscience Canada, and Project Ploughshares. Finally, her entry under "Women's Organizations" simply says "Many white, native, and immigrant women's academic, legal, literary, cultural, and service organizations across Canada."

Nancy Ruth's philanthropy in the ensuing decades has followed a similar pattern. Peace, the environment, and economic and social justice for girls and women have remained her major concerns. In addition, she has been a faithful patron and supporter of the arts, an abiding love since her childhood. Yet in many cases, what look like gifts to conventional arts organizations have in fact gone to encourage the inclusion of women artists and feminist issues. As Iris Nowell has observed,

> Nancy makes donations of from $100 to $5,000 to "arts and culture," but while the donations indicate mainstream philanthropy on paper, all have a feminist component. For example, she donated $2,500 to Vision TV for a television series about women clergy. She gives to the Danny Grossman Dance Company to support its feminist programs, and to the Nightwood Theatre because it is a feminist theatre company.[64]

Nancy Ruth notes that she made a personal investment of a quarter of a million dollars in "Barbara Barde's group to get a CRTC license to establish a women's TV station." They got the license and "made a million $ on this one." By contrast, her foundation invested $150,000 in Linda Rankin's WETV application to get a CRTC license for an environmental station and "lost money on this one."[65]

Nancy Ruth's commitment of time during these decades has also been substantial. She has served on numerous boards to support the causes she believes in. In addition to LEAF and the Canadian Women's Foundation, she has been a board member or honorary director of organizations such as the Arms Control Centre, the Canadian Abortion Rights Action League, the National Forum on Climate Change, the Canada/US Fulbright Foundation, Womynly Way Productions, Canadians for Choice, the Canadian Association for Community Living, the

The Right Honourable Roméo Leblanc invests
Nancy Ruth as a Member of the Order of Canada
at Rideau Hall, Ottawa, May 3, 1995.

Sculptors' Society of Canada, and the National Roundtable on the Environment and the Economy.

Nancy Ruth travelled widely during these years as well, going, for example, to the United Nations Conference on Women in Nairobi in 1985. And, thanks to minister of foreign affairs for Canada Barbara McDougall, who was impressed by Nancy Ruth's strong character and speaking abilities when she ran for the federal PC nomination in 1988, she was sent with two MPs to Cambodia as a UN Observer of elections in 1993.[66] She has also been in wide demand as a speaker, giving dozens of talks across the country to the Federation of University Women's Clubs, Rotary Clubs, university classes, Persons Day breakfasts, business and professional women's clubs, and other women's groups. Her advocacy work earned her the Order of Canada in 1994 at the age of fifty-two; the Governor General's Award in Commemoration of the Persons Case in 1997; the Government of Ontario Award for Outstanding Achievement in Human Rights in 1998; and the South African Women for Women Friendship Award in 2004.

Speaking to a group of women university students in 1990, Nancy Ruth told them, "We need wealthy and not-so-wealthy women to support feminist charities, like LEAF and the Canadian Women's Foundation that are using the system to change the system. We need women to support women.... We know, or ought to know, that no one is going to help us but ourselves."[67] In 2018, she cited her inability to galvanize "a pool of feminist philanthropists" as one of her life's failures.[68] But her rallying cry for women to support women has never abated—nor has her own commitment to the cause of feminist philanthropy.

In 2005, Nancy Ruth was given a new outlet for her campaign on behalf of women's rights and human rights when she received a call to ask if she would consider accepting an appointment to the Senate of Canada. She was then sixty-three years old and beginning to wonder if the time had come to retire, and, if so, wondering what retirement would look like for someone in her "freelance" position. Instead, she was at last given entry into Canada's political establishment—her opportunity to find out what she could achieve by moving from the margins to the centre of the legislative process.

Footnotes for this chapter can be found online at:
http://secondstorypress.ca/resources

Chapter 11

SENATOR NANCY RUTH

She brought a voice that wasn't there.

—Denise Arsenault[1]

UNTIL SHE WAS alerted in March 2005 by her friend Caspar Sinnige that she was "on a list" and should keep her phone handy, Nancy Ruth had no idea that she might be appointed to the Senate of Canada and become a parliamentarian. She heard this news while in Vancouver visiting Lois Campbell, an old friend from Naramata who was in palliative care. When the call came from Prime Minister Paul Martin a few days later, she held the phone to Lois' ear so her dying friend could share vicariously in the moment's excitement. As she recalls, "The news certainly got Lois out of bed, and we shuffled down the hall to the nursing station where she told the world of the PM's call. It was a great day, as Lois was so happy for me and that made me happy."[2]

Shortly after the prime minister's call, Nancy Ruth wrote to a friend, "It is terribly exciting for me.... How did my boat come in so well. I am so lucky. It's a perfect

Nancy Ruth on the occasion of her swearing-in.
She was the 73rd woman to serve in the Senate
since the Persons Case decision on October 18,
1929. There have been 833 men appointed since
Confederation. Behind Nancy Ruth are her
guests Captain Kashmeel McKöena, Sirje Sellers,
Father Edward Jackman, Diane Goudie, and
Eleanor Moore. April 12, 2005.

job for me."[3] The potential for action seemed boundless. After years of agitating for social change, she would be at the centre of power—a lawmaker, a person of consequence with the tools to make change happen. In the words of her speech to students graduating from The Linden School that June, she had "been handed a gift, of influence and privilege."[4] At long last her ship had come in.

Yet her initial euphoria was soon dampened by a series of frustrations, some mundane, others more far-reaching. Soon after her swearing-in on April 12, 2005, she wrote to her friend Mary Eberts that she was already exhausted. Orientation for new senators was sparse—"I don't even understand the order paper...there is no time to read or think"—and she had not managed to find a permanent place to live in Ottawa but was camping out in her Senate office. "I came home (i.e., the office) from the politics and pen dinner the other night, washed out my stockings, and hung them on the office windows to dry. Only I forgot to take them down the next day...and then my lunch guest walked in and noticed them; oh my goodness."[5] She felt keenly the gap between her newly exalted status and her sense of personal insecurity. In August, she wrote to a friend from her United Church days, "It's rather fun having the security guards salute you, being called Senator, having The Hon. in front of your name, and all the while you are still the wee one, just struggling through life." She had also begun to experience the sense of isolation from her familiar circle of companions that would be a hallmark of the next twelve years, lamenting that "Ottawa takes you far away from your normal patterns and associations, so I have found even within these 4 months that I am quickly losing contact with my colleagues and friends."[6]

This isolation was compounded by her role as an

independent member of the Senate. She had been a long-term member of the Progressive Conservative Party, which no longer existed as a registered federal party since it had been replaced at the federal level by the Conservative Party of Canada (CPC) in 2003. Nancy Ruth did not like the merger of the Progressive Conservative Party with the much more conservative Reform Party that had resulted in the formation of the CPC. From her early days—growing up with a father and brothers who were Progressive Conservatives and working actively as a teenager for the Young Progressive Conservatives—she had felt at home within the PC "tent." Although she had many friends and allies who were social democrats—members of the New Democratic Party—as well as many who were Liberal Party members, she continued to believe that "there are only certain things you should go into debt for" and that social progress could be achieved in the context of fiscal responsibility. She thus strongly identified as a "red Tory," that is, fiscally conservative but socially progressive.[7]

In her new position as a senator, then, Nancy Ruth faced a difficult choice. The Conservative party under Stephen Harper's leadership was often to the right of her own political leanings. Yet senators who were not in the caucus of a registered party had to sit as independents—with no access to a caucus and therefore no access to appointments as a formal member or officer of a committee—and much of the Senate's work is done in committees. Independent members could take part in a committee meeting only with the consent of that committee. An intensely social person, Nancy Ruth found her position "a little boring and lonely" and missed not only committee work but "the natural community of a party caucus."[8]

When Paul Martin's Liberal minority government fell

and was replaced in early 2006 by a Conservative minority government headed by Harper as prime minister, the time had come for her to make a move. Until then, she recounts, "I had nine months of not being part of anything.... I'm a person who likes to be part of a group, and being part of the Independents was like nowhere, no how. It just didn't work for me."[9] She began signalling her interest in joining the governing party caucus, telling Marjory LeBreton, leader of the government in the Senate, that as a condition of her move she wanted to become a member of the Senate standing committee on national finance. She well understood the importance of "following the money" when political decisions were made. Further, and more audaciously, she asked that core funding for women's groups be reinstated with an allocation of twenty million dollars.[10]

Senator LeBreton's response was positive as to the first request but otherwise circumspect: "I am aware of your interest in serving on the Finance Committee and could certainly support this. With regard to core funding for women's groups, I will choose not to comment because these are matters that would have to be decided by Cabinet and the government." She then added a pointed piece of advice to her junior colleague, "Suffice it to say that the only way to promote and support such initiatives is to be part of a Caucus."[11] And on March 28, 2006, the deal was done; Senator Nancy Ruth officially became part of the Conservative caucus. She had chosen to align herself with power.

In a speech she made to the Voice of Women for Peace AGM at the end of that March, she admitted that her decision had shocked many of her friends because "the Conservatives have many social conservatives in the ranks in the House of Commons—and very few women—just

In 2006, Nancy Ruth was the highest bidder for an auction item at a fundraising dinner for NDP MP Olivia Chow. The auctioneer was the late Jack Layton. The item was a "date" with Chow's assistant, Helen Kennedy. Nancy Ruth paid $650 for Kennedy to take her to dinner and give her a ride on Kennedy's motorcycle.

11% in the House. This hardly seems to be the kind of environment for a women's activist." At the same time, she argued that if anyone needs to hear more feminist voices, "it is a government where there are too few [women]."[12] And as she had explained to a reporter in the weeks leading up to the formal announcement of her move, "I expect to join the Conservative caucus because that's the best way to get access to Cabinet ministers and others," including the prime minister. "You've got to get something for your vote. If you're going to vote for things you don't like, you better get something in return."[13] For the rest of her time as a senator, she would not only make her voice heard as a feminist but would devote herself to securing something in return for her service, most particularly action that would advance women's equality.

Nancy Ruth's first statement as a new senator signalled her interest in the empowerment of girls and women but otherwise gave little indication of the role she would later assume as an *agent provocateur* on behalf of women's concerns. On June 8, 2005, she rose from her seat to commend the Girl Guides of Canada on their recent celebration of their ninety-fifth anniversary, noting "the valuable role that the organization plays in building self-esteem in women and fostering their belief that they are capable of achieving their dreams."[14] These words were mild in comparison with what would come in the years to follow, especially in her committee work. As one journalist commented three years into Nancy Ruth's term, she had become known by then as a "particularly colourful questioner."[15]

On March 5, 2008, for example, in a meeting of the veterans' affairs (VA) subcommittee of the standing Senate committee on national security and defence, she pressed a committee witness, the Honourable Greg Thompson, minister of veterans' affairs, about whether VA staff were "being trained to be gender sensitive to women soldiers returning from Afghanistan." His reply—"I know that this is a question you put to officials the last time they met"—indicates that members of government were now primed to anticipate certain kinds of questions from Nancy Ruth in her committees, although they seldom came prepared to answer those questions.[16]

The ensuing exchange between Nancy Ruth and Minister Thompson shows her tenacity in resisting glib or formulaic answers from committee witnesses, even those who were members of her own government. When the minister held forth on the "beauties of the New Veterans Charter," applauding its emphasis on the family, Nancy Ruth shot back with what will become her hallmark emphasis on results and accountability. If there was no attention to possible gender issues in the treatment of veterans and their families, she asked, who will be "watching for complaints…so if there needs to be a correction it will happen." She then went on to sharpen her questioning, reminding him that "there may be members of the Armed Forces who are homosexual" and therefore staff who offer counselling should be trained to deal with "whatever kind of family they have."[17] What type of counselling, she wondered, would be given to non-traditional military families, whether headed by a same-sex couple or by a woman.

Minister Thompson, repeating that he does realize this is an "important issue" for Nancy Ruth, makes a tactical blunder in his next exchange with the dogged senator. Telling her that "I am not sure if this raises me up on a pedestal," he confessed that "one of my favourite groups within the veterans' community are the Nursing Sisters," adding that "every year since becoming minister, I have taken them to the Chateau Laurier for Valentine's Day." He went on to admit that "Many women are forgotten in the system. Generally, we hear about war heroes but the contribution by women is incredible. Those who worked in armaments, and any woman married to a soldier probably deserves a medal herself." Perhaps irritated by his clichéd portrait of women or by his continued side-stepping of her questions, Nancy Ruth again retorted, "So do the hookers who served them, sir. All the women do."[18] Her salty remark soon made the rounds of Parliament Hill and was reported a week later in the *Globe and Mail*, where she was quoted as saying, with a dash of understatement, that "she likes to remind ministers of the women who are marginalized in society."[19]

Only a few weeks later, Nancy Ruth took on a general in a meeting of the national security and defence committee. On June 2, 2008, Lieutenant-General W.J. Natynczyk, then vice-chief of the defence staff, appeared before the committee to discuss strategic planning in the Canadian forces, including the challenges they faced in recruiting and training qualified personnel. In response to his remarks, Nancy Ruth said, "Often, back in my hometown of Toronto, the forces have been down in the Rogers Centre putting on a big show with their guns and recruiting like heck. However, why not go to the pride parades in Toronto and Vancouver and other cities? I have been asked, as a member of the national security and defence committee, whether I believe that the forces remain as homophobic as forces around the world have been historically." She then went on to put her question: "Could you tell me why do you not recruit in the pride parades?" When the general assured her that the Canadian forces "welcomes diversity," she pushed back: "Do you recruit in that community?"[20] Unable to

Nancy Ruth in June 2005, with New Zealanders
Jennifer Rowan and Jools Joslin, whose marriage
she helped officiate, at the Women are Persons!
monument. Same-sex marriage became legal in
Ontario in 2003, and nationwide on July 20, 2005.

answer the question, Natynczyk ended by agreeing, at her insistence, that he would ask his chief of military personnel why this wasn't their practice. And years later, Nancy Ruth is proud to observe that the military now regularly recruits at Pride parades.[21]

Like Nancy Ruth's earlier comment on hookers, "this was an exchange that whistled around the Hill, certainly among the Senate staff."[22] It was also reported in a magazine article that fall: "Even in dry committee rooms, surrounded by her Conservative colleagues, Ruth doesn't think twice about outing herself as a feminist or a lesbian. Recently, she questioned a general on why the Canadian military doesn't regularly recruit at gay pride festivals. 'Nobody else would ask that,' she says."[23] Nancy Ruth was becoming known as an outspoken senator, pushing hard in her committees on the issues that mattered to her. Although gay rights were sometimes on her agenda, she explained in a 2007 interview that for the most part, "My first level of discrimination is as a woman, and I view the world through those eyes.... I am much more a women's rights activist than I am a queer activist." Women's rights, moreover, encompassed a broad range of concerns: "prevention of violence, fair trade, and poverty to name a few." In her words, "Those are all feminist issues."[24]

Those were the issues that would inform her work as a senator, where she always stood ready to apply a gender lens to any topic under discussion and in all the committees on which she served. The same day that she challenged Lieutenant-General Natynczyk about recruiting at pride parades, for example, she also pressed witness Lieutenant-General A.B. Leslie, chief of the land staff and later a Liberal MP, on training related to United Nations Security Council Resolution 1325. Adopted in October

2000, that resolution addresses the effect of war and conflict on women and girls, affirming the importance of engaging women in the prevention and resolution of conflict and stressing the need for gender training for all who are involved in peacekeeping operations.

Nancy Ruth began her exchange with Lieutenant-General Leslie by declaring, "One's perspective is a function of where one sits, and here I sit as a woman on this committee." With that opening volley she goes on to state, "My interest is in training, particularly with respect to the United Nations Security Council Resolution 1325, of which Canada was part of the drafting and accepting, on women, peace and security. It is of great concern to me that soldiers know about this before they go overseas.... Can you tell me a bit about how that feeds into your curriculum and what type of training soldiers get in that?"

Her question provoked the admission that Nancy Ruth almost certainly expected: "Senator, I am not aware—and I apologize for that—of any specific training that is based on United Nations Security Council Resolution 1325." When the lieutenant-general assured her that "soldiers are no longer defined by gender" and that "we have had female soldiers killed in combat," she made it clear that his comments were beside the point: "Resolution 1325 is about how soldiers go into a foreign country and treat civilians, particularly around issues of women, peace and security." Finally, she gave him his marching orders: "If you could find out if it is even mentioned in your curriculum, I would be most grateful," to which he responded, "Senator, I will do that."[25]

In another meeting of the veterans' affairs subcommittee, Nancy Ruth addressed a topic that she also framed within a feminist context. As a pacifist who made annual statements in Senate on National Conscientious Objection Day, she had long ties to the Voice of Women for Peace (VOW) and Conscience Canada, and held definite views about the impact of war on civilian women and children. When Bill C-287: An Act Regarding a National Peacekeepers' Day, was introduced, she spoke up forcefully. Although she supported the bill, in her opinion it focused disproportionately on the Canadian forces without paying adequate attention to the work of NGOs (non-governmental organizations), many of them staffed by women who worked tirelessly on the ground to secure conditions for a stable peace for civilian populations. As she argued, "Keeping the peace is what happens after the military pulls out and the NGOs are still dealing with the surviving children of war, raped women, etcetera. It is those people who try to set up justice systems and ensure access to them, who train the judges, who send the doctors, who train the police, etcetera, who need to be recognized."[26]

Although her proposal to add to the bill's wording an acknowledgement of "all Canadians who secure, make and attempt to keep the peace" was not accepted—in part so as not to delay its passage—the final version of the bill included an "observation" that "the purpose of National Peacekeepers' Day is to acknowledge the past, present and future efforts of Canadian peacekeepers and all Canadians who work for peace."[27] Such appended observations do not have legal force, but they can be used when a senator wants to make a specific point and they become part of the public record. Her "win" was perhaps a minor victory, but one that reflected her insistence throughout committee deliberations that her critical point not be lost.

Nancy Ruth's tenacity in applying the lens of gender was evident in all the Senate committees she served on.

Nancy Ruth's car outside the Parliament Buildings in Ottawa, sporting her licence plate, "SENATRIX," a gift from her Toronto staff in June, 2005.

On the social affairs, science, and technology committee, for example, during consideration of Bill C-277: An Act to Amend the Criminal Code (luring a child)—she observed that Internet luring is "arguably a gendered crime" because "on the whole we are talking about girls, and perpetrators that are usually men." She asked the committee witness, Normand Wong, counsel from the criminal law and policy branch of the department of justice, whether there were "other mechanisms in the justice system in place to deter other gendered crimes?" When he thanked her for the question she quickly added that "this gender neutral stuff is rubbish. We are talking about little girls and guys in this instance, as we often are in cases of rape." Although Mr. Wong admitted that the crime in question, Internet luring, does seem to be "a gender biased one," when Nancy Ruth pressed him further about tools in the justice system to combat gender-specific crimes, he countered that "we try to use completely neutral language to make sure we capture the criminal activity regardless of what gender perpetrates it."[28] He did not acknowledge her point—that neutrality masks the crime and therefore the remedy—and his response was characteristic of what she faced again and again in her campaign to make gender bias visible in Canada's legal system.

None of her campaigns was more fraught—or more passionately pursued—than the one to add "sex" to groups that the Criminal Code protected from hate crimes. She took on this cause, a long-standing campaign of the Canadian women's movement, when she became a senator and saw it through to become law over the years that she served—and it did take years. An inquiry into "the erosion of Freedom of Speech in our country," launched in the Senate in March 2010 by Senator Douglas Finley, former campaign director of the Conservative Party of Canada, provoked Nancy Ruth's first major speech on the topic. Senator Finley's inquiry was an example of the government's practice of "testing the waters" for a piece of legislation that they wished to introduce and was the backdrop to a proposal that eventually emerged as a Conservative MP's private members' bill in the House of Commons: to remove from the *Canadian Human Rights Act* (CHRA) section 13, the section that governed Internet hate speech. Nancy Ruth, while acknowledging the need to balance free expression with the protection of individuals and groups from hate crimes, argued forcefully against the proposal.

> I have a particular concern about the call for the removal of section 13 of the *Canadian Human Rights Act*. That section prohibits the repeated electronic transmission of messages that are likely to expose an individual or group of individuals to hatred or contempt based on a prohibited ground of discrimination. Under the CHRA, the prohibited grounds include race, national or ethnic origin, colour, religion, age, sex, sexual orientation, marital status, family status, disability or conviction for which a pardon has been granted.[29]

If section 13 were removed, she pointed out, "the only remaining prohibitions would be section 318 and section 319 of the Criminal Code of Canada"—and there is a "world of legal difference" between the provisions of the *Canadian Human Rights Act* and those of the Criminal Code. As she argued at the outset of her speech, "I disagree with the removal of section 13 of the *Canadian Human Rights Act*, especially since sections 318 and 319 of the

Criminal Code do not extend protection on the basis of sex and some other categories enumerated in section 13."[30] She ended her address to Senate with an impassioned plea:

> It is beyond ironic—it can have deadly consequences—that women and girls have been excluded from these protections because of the difficulty of distinguishing between everyday treatment and acts of hate. Do we want to break the direct and strong links in the chain connecting disregard and disrespect for women with violence against women? If so, then we must protect women and girls from hate crimes.
>
> Many Canadians are included under section 13 of the *Canadian Human Rights Act* hate speech provisions. Many Canadians are excluded from any protection under Criminal Code section 318 and section 319.
>
> While a study on how best to protect Canadians from hatred may be in order, I am opposed to proposals that have the immediate effect of putting more Canadians at risk of hate crimes with no recourse or remedy. Do remember that most of the groups who would be hurt by the loss of the *Canadian Human Rights Act* provision 13 are those who are under-represented in this Senate.[31]

Nancy Ruth made it clear that the prevention of violence against girls and women—a long-standing focus of her advocacy—was at the centre of her opposition to changes in the *Canadian Human Rights Act*. And the irony she alludes to is that sex, in her view, has been left out of the Criminal Code's past definition of hate crimes because of fears that the criminal justice system would be swamped by cases charging hate speech against women—the "everyday treatment" to which she refers and that women have had to endure through the ages. When, in the ensuing discussion, Senator Serge Joyal remarked on former but unsuccessful attempts to include sex in amendments to the Criminal Code, Nancy Ruth responded, "This phenomenon still exists in Canadian society, although perhaps not precisely in this or that chamber. If one works to protect women, one often loses a bill. Do not forget this, and I will not let the *Human Rights Act* go down without doing my part to protect it."[32]

She indeed fought valiantly to save section 13 of the *Human Rights Act*, but she also had to do battle on a separate but related front. On December 2, 2010, Canada's National Day of Remembrance and Action on Violence Against Women, she rose to inform her Senate colleagues that Bill C-389: An Act to Amend the *Canadian Human Rights Act* and the Criminal Code (gender identity and gender expression), introduced by NDP MP Randall Garrison in the House of Commons, was close to passage. The bill was intended to protect the rights of transgender people and, while Nancy Ruth agreed with the protection of those rights, she saw the failure to extend protection to other excluded groups as a serious injustice. As she observed that day, the bill "will expand human rights, transsexual rights, in Canada, but it will give transsexual women a right that other women in Canada do not have." She went on to exhort her Senate colleagues:

The Government of Canada should be using every means at its disposal to reduce exploitation and violence against women and girls in Canada.... Protection from hate propaganda and genocide is not a panacea;

it is a symbol, a statement of our values and another usable public measure in an ongoing effort to protect women from violence…. We must add "sex" to section 318(4) of the Criminal Code, so that all women are covered.[33]

The interplay of these bills to amend the *Canadian Human Rights Act* and the Criminal Code extended over the following three years. Despite Nancy Ruth's opposition, Bill C-304, calling for the removal of section 13 (Internet hate speech) of the *Canadian Human Rights Act*, ultimately passed both chambers and received royal assent in June 2013. Its movement through Parliament increased the urgency she felt to add sex as a grounds for protection in the Criminal Code. Yet her efforts to amend the "transgender rights" Criminal Code bill—which expired when Parliament was prorogued in March of 2011 but was reintroduced in the subsequent Parliament as C-279—were frustrated at every turn. She describes the complications she faced:

First of all I went to the NDP and asked them to make an amendment to the bill, and they refused to do it. I then went to the Liberals, who were then third party [in the House of Commons]. I went to Irwin Cotler, who had been minister of justice, Carolyn Bennett, who I knew personally [the MP from Toronto's St. Paul's riding, Bennett had been Nancy Ruth's family doctor], and the MP from BC who has the largest gay community, Hedy Fry, who had been minister of women [when Nancy Ruth received the Governor General's Persons Case Award in 1997], and asked them…to amend this bill.

In the end she "got nowhere" in her efforts to negotiate a resolution to what she felt strongly was not only an injustice to women and girls but a threat to their fundamental safety in Canadian society.[34]

On May 29, 2013, Nancy Ruth rose in the Senate chamber to say,

> Honourable senators, I speak in my pink shoes today in order to speak against Bill C-279, the Gender Identity Bill. I oppose this bill because proposed section 3 perpetuates a glaring gap. Women and girls in Canada are not protected from hate speech under the Criminal Code, and this bill does not rectify that when it could.... For 35 years, across numerous bills, Parliament has told the girls and women of Canada that, despite alarming rates of violence against girls and women, violence that typically includes hate speech, they are not worthy of protection.... This bill will privilege men who choose to become women over women who are born female. While I do not question the good intentions of the sponsor and the supporters of the bill, I simply do not understand how they could advance this bill without including all women. Passage of Bill C-279 will mean that only if a woman is born a man who later chooses to identify as a woman will she receive protection, but a woman born a woman will not receive the same protection.

She ended her remarks with these forceful words: "If we as Senators do not have the guts to stand up and include everyone in this country...then be damned all of us. It is now. It is now."[35]

Neither her pink shoes nor her eloquence carried the day in the Senate chamber. But behind the scenes she had been pursuing alternative routes, speaking to Prime Minister Harper and writing to him as early as December 2010, when the original Bill C-389 was under consideration. In a note handed to him in caucus and headed "Trans women to have more protection in CC 318.4 than other women if passed," she argued that the addition of new identified groups to the Criminal Code without the addition of all women "highlights the perversity of the exclusion of sex from protection."[36] Over the coming years she continued to raise the matter with the prime minister in caucus and in the end, she relates, "He didn't have any trouble with doing something about it."[37]

The prime minister's solution was to ensure that his government introduced, on November 20, 2013, government Bill C-13, an omnibus bill that included an expanded definition of "identifiable group" in the Criminal Code to add sex, age, and disability. In the months that followed it was unclear whether C-279 or C-13 would pass first and what effect their order of passage would have on their provisions. In the end, C-13 crossed the finish line first, receiving royal assent on December 9, 2014, and coming into force three months later. Because Bill C-279 had not passed the Senate when the general election of 2015 was called, it expired on the Senate order paper but was revived by the new Trudeau government as Bill C-16; it passed both chambers, received royal assent on June 19, 2017, and came into force immediately. The "gender identity and expression" provisions of C-16 were added to the Criminal Code's expanded definition of identifiable grounds—including sex—for which Nancy Ruth had so tirelessly fought. She looks back on the outcome with understandable pride: "It happened all right in the end. I consider it a big win."[38] When, in August 2019, the Ontario Court of Justice made the first conviction under this expanded version of the Criminal Code, handing magazine editor James Sears the maximum sentence of one year for promoting hate against women and Jews, she knew that the law she had helped put into place was indeed making a difference.[39]

Another vigorous campaign that Nancy Ruth waged throughout her time in the Senate was to see gender-based

Senator Nancy Ruth with Prime Minister Stephen Harper, at the breaking-ground ceremony for the pedestrian tunnel joining the Billy Bishop Airport on Toronto Islands to downtown Toronto, March 9, 2012.

analysis (GBA) applied to both policy-making and budgeting. As a member of the Senate standing committee on human rights, to which she was appointed shortly after she joined the Conservative caucus, she frequently challenged committee witnesses and library of Parliament clerks to "unpack" the relevance of gender to their testimony and briefing notes. When staff from Indian and Northern Affairs Canada (INAC) appeared before the human rights committee on June 5, 2006, for example, Nancy Ruth asked how their department met its GBA obligations in creating services to support Indigenous children. Assured by a senior staff member that "gender-based analysis is done on a daily basis," she continued to press for evidence: "Give me some examples, though. What difference does it make, if any?"[40] Her insistence on knowing both that a gender analysis was being applied and that its results were creating change would never waver.

Much of the work during her first term on the human rights committee focused on a major study of the rights and freedoms of children, and Nancy Ruth repeatedly questioned the invisibility of gender in the testimony submitted as part of the study. At one meeting, for example, she erupted with, "This is something that drives me crazy meeting after meeting, report after report where people refer to 'young people,' 'children,' 'youth population,' and there is no gender breakout.... My experience of life is that there are gender differences, girl children do learn differently, there are studies on the female brain." Later in the proceedings, a Child and Family Services staff member from Saskatchewan assured Nancy Ruth that "We collect data on both male and female children and we can provide that breakdown if you wish. Clearly, in the sexual exploitation area, the majority of children that come to our attention are female." In response, the senator urged her to make this information public: "it is time this stopped being an invisible statistic."[41]

Nancy Ruth's focus on applying a "gender lens" quickly expanded to an insistence that GBA be rigorously used throughout government and that its results be widely shared as a tool of transparency and accountability. She could point to a number of federal government commitments to GBA in support of her position, including the 1995 document *Setting the Stage for the Next Century: The Federal Plan for Gender Equality*, which called for the implementation of GBA throughout federal departments and agencies; and the *Agenda for Gender Equality* (2000), which urged accelerating GBA's implementation as a government-wide strategy. Yet everywhere she turned in her committee work, she found deficiencies in the understanding and use of GBA.

In her role as a member—and, for a period, vice-chair and steering committee member—of the Senate standing committee on national finance, the committee she had requested in her negotiations with Senator LeBreton, she was well placed to raise concerns about the impact of funding decisions on women and girls. When Minister Vic Toews, president of the treasury board, attended the committee on February 27, 2007, to talk about the government's expenditure management system, he was met with a barrage of questions from Nancy Ruth:

In my brief time here I have heard Minister Oda in her capacity as minister for the status of women say that women's concerns are in every department and there is analysis in every budgeting line of every department. I have been trying to figure out how or whether that really happens. How is an analysis of women's concerns conducted in departments and who measures the outcomes of that analysis? I do not get answers to my questions that are in any way satisfactory.

When Minister Toews asked, "Are you referring specifically to gender-based analysis?" she responded, "I want to know specifically who measures the impact of budget decisions for the poor, for women, for race issues, for those issues to which Canada theoretically has committed itself. It is the implementation part of it that is so difficult.... I want to know why that is, how to get at it, how to improve it and who will do it." Here she threw down the twin gauntlets of government accountability and social change to which she intended to devote her time in the Senate.

In answer to her questions the minister confessed that Nancy Ruth had identified "one of our biggest challenges" and that "there is a definite weakness in our overall system in that analysis." In what may have been an attempt to deflect her line of inquiry, he assured her that "We are always mindful of the gender issue in almost every decision that we make, such as the process of appointments of judges." Undeterred, she fired back, "I really want to know about the money, minister. It is about the money." During their subsequent exchange, he offered a lengthy description of the government's management, resources, and results structure, or MRRS, "which, when fully implemented, will provide government with a comprehensive picture of spending and performance by program. If a program has a gender-based outcome, the MRRS policy instructs departments to establish a target and a timeline to reach that target as well as indicators to inform program managers whether they are on track."

Nancy Ruth continued not only to press him but also to challenge him on his bureaucratic language: "Is there a way for me to find out when it is fully implemented and what these little bits in that paragraph you read actually mean?" Unrelenting, she added, "I want to know who is testing it; who is its evaluator; how do we know that it is being done; and whose criteria are being used to do it. It is a real struggle for me to find out how this is happening." Further attempts by Minister Toews and one of his senior staff members to provide examples of specific measures and results failed to satisfy Nancy Ruth, who told them, "I will provide an example. If a government makes recommendations for autism, they are effectively making recommendations for boy children and there is no comparative for girl children, be it on eating disorders or any other female-specific issue. That is the kind of thing that troubles me." She offered another example: "The Senate report on Sub-Saharan Africa does a micro-credit analysis but no gender analysis. Everyone knows that over 90 per cent of the returns of loans to women are better serviced than they are to men but there is no analysis in the report. Its absence scares me."

By this time, Nancy Ruth had gone far beyond any formulation of GBA that her government colleagues could address in simple terms. Her gender lens was all-pervasive, extending from budget decisions through health policy to foreign aid programs. And she was not content with being told that the "GBA box" on a Cabinet submission has been checked off. Earlier in their exchange, when she asked Minister Toews whether she could "see some of the internal documents that measure the impact of gender-based analysis," he replied, "We will see what we can provide for you in that respect." At the end of the meeting, however, when the committee chair reminded him that "You have undertaken to provide us with any analysis and testing of whatever programs are in place now," the minister realized the magnitude of what was being requested and answered more cautiously: "It may be quite an undertaking for every department to do that kind of analysis. I am not exactly sure what I can give you, but we can give you what treasury board does."[42]

Nancy Ruth would be satisfied with no less than an assurance that every department would do "that kind of analysis"—and she soon found her opportunity to move the campaign forward. She in fact helped create the opportunity by planting a seed with Sheila Fraser, the auditor general of Canada. As she recalls, her director of parliamentary affairs, Beth Atcheson, came up with the bold idea of asking the auditor general to do a GBA audit of several departments. Nancy Ruth had met Ms. Fraser, respected her highly, and the two of them shared a rapport. "So I saw her in the elevator one day and I asked her if she would be willing to do this. A twinkle in her eye, she laughed and said, 'Well, my staff won't be very happy changing plans midstream, but why not?'"[43] The auditor general's willing ear and her "why not" reply were just what Nancy Ruth needed to set her plan in motion.

There were, of course, steps that had to be taken to move the idea from "elevator pitch" to reality, and the first of these happened in the May 30, 2007, meeting of the national finance committee. Sheila Fraser was called as a committee witness that day, answering questions about the work of her office in conducting both financial and performance audits of government departments. On this day, rather than raising the topic of GBA herself, Nancy Ruth had asked Senator Grant Mitchell of Alberta to step in; Senator Mitchell referred to GBA as an "issue that Senator Nancy Ruth has raised at times here, and others of us are very interested in." In reply, Ms. Fraser commented that she and her staff were prepared for the discussion because—in what may have been a tip of her hat to their elevator conversation—she has "met Senator Nancy Ruth and suspected this question might come up."

Senator Mitchell then asked specifically whether the Auditor General's office would need to change its mandate in order to perform an audit on the use of GBA within government departments. Ms. Fraser's reply was clear and direct: "No, if there is a government policy and commitment, it would be within our mandate to ask how they are implementing that and if they know if they are being successful or not."[44] In answer to Nancy Ruth's question about whether a formal letter from an individual could catalyze such an audit, Ms. Fraser advised that a request from a committee would likely be taken more seriously, thus setting in motion the next steps in the campaign. Nancy Ruth soon learned that, among the steps required to trigger the audit, a request needed to be tabled in the House of Commons, which led her to work with the House's standing committee on the status of women. She had often attended the committee's meetings and knew several of its members, including those from her own caucus as well as members of the NDP opposition, in particular Irene Mathyssen from London/Fanshaw. For these colleagues, she recalls, "it was an exciting initiative."[45]

The auditor general did not appear before the status of women committee until almost a year later, however, and, in the meantime, Nancy Ruth continued to drive home the importance of GBA at every turn. At the November 20, 2007, meeting of the national finance committee, she pushed a senior assistant secretary of the treasury board to give examples of their GBA outcomes. When his answers did not satisfy her, she offered the example of wait times for medical treatment, where, she argued, there was

> significant and growing evidence that men and women are treated differently in many stages of health and in the health care system, including at least some of the five priority areas of radiation for cancer, hip and knee replacement, cataracts, cardiac bypass and diagnostic images.... How can we be assured that evidence-based benchmarks for medically accepted wait times address the needs of both men and women?

When she received the reply that "This is not something that has come through treasury board in terms of a federal program," she was unrelenting: "I will try another example." This time she raised the issue of the federally funded Canada Research Chairs Program, which had been under scrutiny because of "equity issues," and asked, "What has changed in both the awarding of the chairs and the evaluation of the programs that indicates that equity is being seriously addressed and that Canada's performance is more in line with the other OECD countries? Can you answer that question?" Once again, the response was, "I cannot."

Nancy Ruth made it clear that she believed the treasury board should be accountable for gender equity in its oversight of federal spending. "When a department makes a request for monies, you must figure out whether you will grant it or not and how it will be done, et cetera. Part of that analysis, surely, since Canada has this commitment to gender-based analysis, is to ensure that the department has done it." When her further attempts to elicit concrete examples of the treasury board's application of GBA did not yield an answer that satisfied her, she ended the exchange with an admonition: "Next time you come here, be prepared."[46]

Kevin Page, newly appointed as the first parliamentary budget office within the library of Parliament, was the next official to come under Nancy Ruth's fire. When he attended the national finance committee in the spring of 2008, she seized the chance to press her concerns further. In his opening remarks, Mr. Page referred to the library of Parliament's mission to provide "objective, non-partisan analysis and advice to Parliament," explaining that the specific mandate of his office included offering an "objective analysis" to Parliament of economic trends, the state of the country's finances, and government spending estimates. After his presentation, Nancy Ruth was quick to launch the committee's questions by challenging him on the basic concept of "objectivity," the assumption that "microeconomics is gender-blind and race-blind," arguing that traditional economic theory assumes that "market-based productive activities are preferred over other productive activities that are fundamental to the quality of our lives." She continued, "I am talking about such things as home care, child care, elder care, the environment, clean rivers, clean water.... For many equality-seeking groups, 'objective,' 'independent' and 'non-partisan' often means focused on the dominant norm or mainstream, and makes women's work not count."

Mr. Page had clearly been briefed to anticipate her line of questioning. He assured her that "progress has been made in terms of gender analysis in recent years" and added a tribute to her advocacy: "We can thank you, Senator, for much of that work and raising the level of attention to this issue.... Partly from the pressure from your office, much work has been done in recent years." If he hoped to sidestep her line of inquiry, however, he hoped in vain. She set aside his compliments—"It is not thanks to me; it is thanks to dozens of women who have gone before from all parties"—and questioned his assurances that he would have staff trained to carry out GBA. "To be frank, I am not very interested in the training that is given in government departments in gender-based analysis. It is not sufficient. It is not rigorous; it is not tested; and the impact is not evaluated." She had been told too many times that staff training would be the key to ensuring a vigorous and successful implementation of GBA within government and she clearly had no faith that it would make the needed difference.

As the meeting ended, after extensive questioning by committee members on the exact role of the parliamentary budget officer, Nancy Ruth called Kevin Page to account once more on the need to question his basic economic premises. "Mr. Page, I have listened to you twice and you have just said it again, that if gender-based analysis is a priority, then you would look into it. It is not that gender-based analysis is a priority; rather, it is that it is a fundamental aspect of an economic model. It is not something you do on an occasional bill; it is how you look at the world. I need to know that you understand that that is how I look at the world and that you will consider looking at it that way as well. It is not about priorities at all. It is about mindset."[47] Senator Grant Mitchell, who had supported Nancy Ruth's emphasis on the importance of gender to budget decisions in the committee meeting, sent her a note that evening telling her that she had been a "tour

For International Women's Day in 2016, a Senate publication, *SenCAPlus*, asked the members of the Standing Senate Committee on Human Rights to name a woman who had inspired them. Nancy Ruth said, "Rosemary Brown is important to me because she taught me that until all of us have made it [race and gender], none of us have made it."

de force" in their deliberations. "I am very proud of what you do on this issue of gender equality. You have opened my eyes to many things with your insights and determination."[48] Even though she remained frustrated by the lack of measurable progress, her steady and relentless questioning on GBA was having an impact on Parliament Hill.

Her behind-the-scenes work with other colleagues to bring the auditor general to the House of Commons status of women committee bore fruit on April 10, 2008, at a meeting that Nancy Ruth was invited to attend. There, in response to a question about what value the auditor general's department would bring "in doing a performance audit of gender-based analysis," Sheila Fraser answered, "We could look at whether government is actually doing gender-based analysis.... If a policy decision is made that doesn't take that analysis into account, we obviously can't comment on the policy itself, but we could look at the departments: Are they actually doing this analysis in their design of policies and programs?" After further discussion with committee members, Auditor General Fraser reminded them what needed to be done to move this initiative ahead. "When committees have a motion—and I know the chair [Yasmin Ratansi] is quite familiar with this from previous experience on other committees—asking us to do audits in certain areas, we certainly try to accede to those requests."

In her closing remarks, Ms. Fraser thanked the committee "for bringing a very interesting issue to our attention" and concluded, "I will certainly commit to looking at this and seeing what we can do. Perhaps we can get back to the chair and think about doing some sort of audit on how well government is actually doing in all this, which will provide you with some information across government."[49]

This is precisely the accountability that Nancy Ruth had been pushing for; here at last was a strategy to pull back the bureaucratic covers and reveal what lay underneath. Although, as a visitor to the committee, she didn't speak during the proceedings, we can imagine her jubilation at hearing these words.

At its meeting on April 17, 2008 — fittingly, Equality Day in Canada, which marks the day the equality provisions in the Charter of Rights and Freedoms came into effect—the status of women committee passed a motion, proposed by Irene Mathyssen and amended by Conservative MP Patricia Davidson, "that the Auditor General, taking into account all of the elements of Canada's framework for equality, including the Convention on the Elimination of all Forms of Discrimination Against Women [CEDAW] and Optional Protocol and the Canadian Charter of Rights and Freedoms, conduct an audit to review Canada's implementation of gender-based analysis using 'Setting the Stage for the Next Century: The Federal Guide for Gender Equality (1995)' as a guide, and review from the period of April 1, 2000 to March 31, 2008, and report the adoption of this motion to the House of Commons without delay."[50] The motion carried unanimously—and once again Nancy Ruth was in attendance for this milestone victory.

She in fact had input into the motion behind the scenes, suggesting to Conservative colleagues on the committee that Ms. Mathyssen's original motion, discussed in an earlier meeting on April 15, be amended to include the references to CEDAW and the Optional Protocol and to the Canadian Charter of Rights and Freedoms. She explained to them that "I think if the CPC [Conservative Party of Canada] move these additions to the NDP motion, strengthening the motion, it shows us as leaders,

Nancy Ruth at Café Luxe in Ottawa, 2005.

not followers."[51] She was prepared, as always, to seek alliances with like-minded women from other parties, but at the same time she never gave up working within her own party to engage colleagues in her mission for social change.

Following the committee's report of its motion in the House of Commons the next day, the auditor general's office, as promised, began its work. Their approach was to sample sixty-eight recent initiatives from seven federal government departments that were selected because their mandates had the potential to affect men and women differently. These departments—finance, justice, health, human resources and skills development, Indian and northern affairs, transport, and veterans' affairs—were assessed to determine whether and how they used GBA in their decision-making. In addition, the audit examined how three central agencies—the Treasury Board Secretariat, the Privy Council Office, and the department of finance—carried out their oversight responsibility to examine policy or spending proposals through the lens of GBA.[52] The auditor general's report, released in the spring of 2009, explained that the audit's objective was "to determine whether the selected departments can provide evidence that they are conducting, and the central agencies that they are reviewing, gender-based analyses to adequately support decision making on policy and program spending initiatives."[53]

The report's stark conclusion—that "gender impacts rarely influenced policy"—would have come as no surprise to Nancy Ruth.[54] Of the sixty-eight initiatives tested, only four had adequately integrated gender-based analysis into policy development.[55] Further, the audit found that the central agencies examined could not substantiate their claim that their analysts "had reviewed and challenged departments' consideration of gender impacts."[56] While the report acknowledged that the departments "are making efforts to improve their GBA practices," it also affirmed that "most are not applying GBA to identify gender impacts for use in the design of public policies, as the government undertook to do in 1995."[57] Its recommendations included a call for clear expectations and a plan of action, along with enhanced communication of requirements, greater documentation of results, and an ongoing assessment of outcomes.

Throughout the months and years that followed, Nancy Ruth continued to press for action on GBA, using the auditor general's report as a new weapon in her arsenal. In a September 2009 meeting of the Senate's human rights committee, for example, she reminded witnesses from the department of justice that "The Auditor General banged the Justice Department pretty hard for lack of a gender-based analysis, in her May 2009 report" and asked, "Tell me the story of how you conduct gender-based analysis. I have heard you say that victims of trafficking are mainly women and girls, but how do you look at the data; how do you measure it? How is the process of analysis carried out?"[58]

Seven years later and just a few months before the end of her term in the Senate, in another meeting of the human rights committee, she questioned John McCallum, minister of immigration, refugees, and citizenship, about Canada's recent intake of Syrian refugees:

> As I remember the initial announcement, it was Canada's intent to take the most vulnerable. Did the UNHCR [United Nations High Commissioner for Refugees] do any gender-based analysis, or GBA, when they selected the refugees, and have we done any as they came in? My next question is related to

the research you were planning to do. I know this will take years to accomplish, because you need hard data. How will your department use GBA in these evaluations? Finally, regarding the women's centres, does the language training incorporate any therapeutic things? Is there any discussion of women's health and, in particular, family planning?

When Minister McCallum replied, "We pretty well took the names the UNHCR gave us," Nancy Ruth continued to press her point, ending with, "For me, it's part of doing the gender-based analysis."[59]

Although her GBA advocacy did not have the transformative impact she hoped for, Nancy Ruth is confident that it has made a difference.[60] In a human rights committee meeting the fall before her retirement, the topic under discussion was "Gender-based analysis in the making of federal policy and legislation." The witnesses included representatives from the Privy Council Office, the Treasury Board of Canada Secretariat, and Status of Women Canada. Committee chair Senator Jim Munson opened the proceedings by underlining the seriousness of the topic under discussion and adding: "We want to thank Senator Nancy Ruth for giving us all the ideas on what's an extremely important issue before our country and this committee."[61] A couple of months after her retirement, on International Women's Day, the Honourable Peter Harder, government representative in Senate, stood in the chamber to "recognize former Senator Nancy Ruth, whose efforts have led to gender-based analysis becoming part of the criteria of government consideration."[62] GBA is clearly a central part of her legacy in the Senate. As a result of her relentless pursuit of answers, she made sure that future governments would think twice before ignoring the relevance of gender in decision-making.

The dogged senator was equally untiring in her insistence that UN Security Council Resolution 1325, on women, peace, and security, be adhered to by the Canadian government and its military forces. Shaila Anwar, deputy principal clerk for the Senate committees directorate, recalls that soon after Nancy Ruth became a member of the national security and defence committee, the committee's deliberations took a radical shift: "One could say that before her arrival, the committee might have had a bit of a reputation as being an old boys' club.... Suddenly we were discussing the participation of the Canadian forces in gay pride parades and UN Resolution 1325 and the promotion of women to officer-level positions in the Canadian military!"[63] Nancy Ruth had shown herself willing to question a general about whether soldiers being deployed overseas were trained in the requirements of Resolution 1325, as she did in a June 2008 meeting of the national security and defence committee, and she continued to raise the matter in discussions of military affairs within that committee.

She raised Resolution 1325 in Senate debates as well, on days that marked the anniversary of Resolution 1325— October 31, 2006, and on the same date in 2007. In 2006, she lamented "the ongoing violence in the Sudan, the Democratic Republic of the Congo and Afghanistan" as only "a few examples that demonstrate that the rights of girls and women continue to be violated in times of conflict and state fragility."[64] The following year she remarked, "Internationally, much remains to be done to operationalize Resolution 1325. Of the 60 million people worldwide who are displaced by conflicts and disasters, some 75 per cent, or 45 million, are women and children. Sexual violence is epidemic in [those] countries and regions, including those where Canada is involved.... Without basic human security, women and girls are unable to participate in debate, elections, or peace negotiations."[65]

While she pressed the topic of Resolution 1325 within the Senate chamber and on the national security and defence committee—including preparing a proposal for a special committee study on the subject—it was as a member of the human rights committee that Nancy Ruth was most able to escalate her crusade. Speaking as part of the Canadian Perspectives Lecture Series at the University of Toronto in January 2010, she told her audience that Resolution 1325 was one of the key campaigns she was working on in the Senate. In light of the disproportionate impact of war on women and girls, Resolution 1325 called for applying a gender lens to their needs during conflict, repatriation, reintegration, and post-conflict reconstruction. The intent of the resolution, she explained, was "to require the UN and its member states to consider and include women and girls in every decision made with respect to a conflict zone. Women and girls are to be key partners in matters that affect their lives and futures." The specific requirements that she enumerated for Resolution 1325 were "1. Protection of women and girls in respect for their rights, 2. Participation of women in peace processes, 3. Gender training for all involved in peacekeeping processes." And working with the chair and vice-chair of the human rights committee—both women, Senators Raynell Andreychuk and Mobina S.B. Jaffer—she had "advocated that this Committee undertake the first study of how Canada is implementing 1325."[66] The study would in fact be based on her earlier proposal to national security and defence that was never taken up by that committee.

Throughout the human rights committee's work on Resolution 1325, beginning with its meeting on September 14, 2009, Nancy Ruth took a leadership role in questioning witnesses; by the time the study was released in November 2010, she had been elected committee chair so her name, fittingly, appears on the title page along with that of deputy chair Senator Jaffer. Both Senator Jaffer and Senator Andreychuk, committee chair until March 2010, were active in shaping the study. Instead of being the outlier she often was on national security and defence, Nancy Ruth had colleagues on the human rights committee who shared her belief in the importance of the project. They also shared her determination to chart concrete and measurable results. At the conclusion of the September 14 meeting, Senator Andreychuk reminded committee members that their focus would be "what Senator Nancy Ruth provided for us a long time ago, something practical rather than theoretical."[67]

The committee met half a dozen times over the following months to hear testimony on the topic of Resolution 1325. When they questioned NGO witnesses, committee members heard over and over again of the need for a Canadian action plan on the implementation of Resolution 1325—that is, for "something practical rather than theoretical." Such a plan, they were told, had been started a few years earlier with a "brief civil society consultation" but had "disappeared into the ether." Representatives from the North-South Institute and from the Canadian Council for International Cooperation, when asked what they would like the committee to do with respect to Resolution 1325, agreed that applying pressure on the government to return to and complete the action plan would be of significant value. As one witness put it, "The biggest shortcoming is the national action plan, and the only way to move that forward is to put some political will behind it."[68]

Not surprisingly, government witnesses who followed the testimony of NGO leaders were pressed hard on the status of the missing action plan. Senator Jaffer, for example, put the question to a senior official from Foreign Affairs and International Trade Canada (DFAIT), who told her that he was "not certain I can provide an answer to that question at this time." When Senator Jaffer asked him more generally "what are we doing in Canada to raise awareness on Resolution 1325?" another official from the human rights policy division within DFAIT told her that they were looking at Resolution 1325 within the "bigger issues" of human rights but that, having been only one month on the job, he "did not have detailed project knowledge." Nancy Ruth, after this extended testimony, interjected with her usual bluntness that it was "like trying to catch an amoeba on what is happening in government around Resolution 1325."[69]

The need for a government action plan on the implementation of Resolution 1325 would be a recurring topic as committee deliberations continued. Another would be the need for specific and rigorous training of personnel on the principles of Resolution 1325 before they went on peace missions. Nancy Ruth raised this question during the September 2009 meeting and pressed to see actual training manuals from the department of national defence and DFAIT, while Senator Andreychuk underscored the committee's need to know if Canada's obligations under Resolution 1325 were being specifically addressed in training rather than indirectly alluded to under topics such as sexual harassment.[70] In the meeting of October 26, when questioning witnesses from the United Nations, Senator

Jaffer asked again for details about the training on 1325 that was being provided to UN peacekeeping forces—the number of modules being used, the length of training, and the way in which it was being tracked.[71] Their questions continued to highlight the committee's pragmatic focus and its insistence on accountability.

Underpinning their pragmatism, however, was a bold vision of women not just as participants but as leaders in peacekeeping throughout the world. Kate McInturff, a September 14 witness from the NGO Peacebuild, eloquently phrased the importance of 1325 as follows: "When women are at the table, women's needs and rights are on the table. There cannot be sustainable peace and development without addressing the needs of one-half of the population."[72] In the committee's final report, *Women, Peace and Security: Canada Moves Forward to Increase Women's Engagement*, twelve of the twenty-six recommendations for action focused on the need for women to be leaders and decision-makers in the peace process. Other recommendations, in keeping with the committee's areas of concern, emphasized the need to allocate adequate government resources, measure accountability, and ensure adequate training and education of personnel within the department of national defence, the Canadian forces, and the RCMP.[73]

To the human rights committee's surprise, *Building Peace and Security for All: Canada's Action Plan for the Implementation of United Nations Security Council Resolutions on Women, Peace and Security* was released in early October, just a few weeks before the committee's report, although it is quite possible this release was accelerated because of the light the committee had shone on the government's failure to complete its long-delayed action plan. This plan's release, however, triggered the need for some changes in the committee's final report. Instead of vigorously calling for a government action plan as originally intended, the report noted that during the committee's hearings it was clear that an action plan was needed but uncertain as to whether it would be forthcoming.[74] The committee was, the report affirmed, both encouraged by the government's action plan and "hopeful that the plan will serve to elevate the priority and propel the integration of women, peace and security concerns throughout Canada's foreign, development, defence, human rights and security sector policies and programming." At the same time, the report ended on a cautionary note: "As the Committee has stated expressly throughout this report, the actual implementation of the measures called for in the government's Action Plan is what counts."[75] Nancy Ruth and her colleagues wanted above all to see practical results, not empty bureaucratic promises.

In Ottawa and beyond, Nancy Ruth continued to advocate for the vital role of gender considerations in building lasting peace, including the importance of subsequent UN resolutions 1820 (condemning sexual violence as a weapon of war); 1888 (mandating that peacekeeping missions prevent and respond to sexual violence); and 1889 (aimed at increasing women's participation in peace processes). Under her leadership, the human rights committee followed up its study on Resolution 1325 with a short review of how the Canadian government could support the promotion and protection of women's rights in Afghanistan after its combat operations ended in 2011. The study, entitled *Training in Afghanistan: Include Women*, was reported out in December 2010, and its lead recommendation was that "the Government of Canada include the advancement of women's rights as one of its five priorities for Afghanistan post-2011, consistent with its obligations under United Nations Security Council Resolution 1325 on women, peace and security."[76] In 2011, when Nancy Ruth travelled to Ankara to speak on International Women's Day, she told her audience that Canada, like Turkey, was bound by the provisions of UN Security Council Resolution 1325, stressing that all UN members "must facilitate **women's full involvement in relevant decision-making. We must be at the peace table**" (emphasis in the original).[77] In her view, the work on women and peacebuilding that she carried out along with her Senate colleagues, in particular Mobina Jaffer, served as "the grain of sand in the oyster," an irritant that over time helped bring about constructive change.[78]

Nancy Ruth's resolute independence won the respect of her Senate colleagues, who, on her retirement, paid tribute to her for being courageous, outspoken, and a "force of nature."[79] Art Eggleton, who was appointed to the Senate by Paul Martin at the same time as Nancy Ruth and served with her on a number of committees, called her "a maverick right from the beginning," someone who "took her own stand on things and directions that had her values and her beliefs."[80] There were times, however, when her outspokenness sparked a negative outcry—picked up gleefully by the media—and those moments sometimes threatened to overshadow her substantive contributions as a senator. One such occasion occurred at a March 2009 meeting of the national finance committee. Witnesses from the Canadian Food Inspection Agency were there to discuss their budget for the upcoming year, but Nancy Ruth chose to ask them whether Canada was "seeing evidence of invasive species and other pests that are the result of climate change" since invasive species fell under the agency's mandate. When she was told that the agency was "paying close attention" to this matter, she veered in another unexpected direction: "In the summer community in which I live, the biggest pests and the cause of a great health hazard is Canada geese. Their waste product runs into waters in which people swim. These people come out of the water with swimmer's itch." She asked the agency witness, "Where in government could one ever get a policy passed to shoot some of the birds or feed them to the poor, which would be my preference especially in the city of Toronto. What can a citizen do about this bird?"[81] She was quickly assured—most likely with some relief on the part of the witness—that this matter was outside his agency's mandate and should be taken up with the Canadian Wildlife Service.

Her remarks made a splash in the Ottawa newspaper the following day under the headline "Let them eat geese, Senator says."[82] The exchange drew laughter from her Senate colleagues and quickly faded from the media, although Nancy Ruth learned more about Canada geese in twenty-four hours than she had ever imagined knowing, including "how often they pooped and how other cities like Seattle exterminated them."[83] But another Marie Antoinette-style pronouncement a few years later caused a much bigger stir. Michael Ferguson, the auditor general who had replaced Sheila Fraser on her retirement, launched an audit of senators' expense claims in the summer of 2013—an audit requested by Senator Marjory LeBreton, government leader in the Senate, in response to media reports about inappropriate Senate spending. On March 31, 2015, when the audit was near completion, Nancy Ruth was caught in a media scrum as she walked toward the foyer elevator of Centre Block in Parliament. With microphones in her face and cameras rolling, she managed to deflect questions about the audit for a couple of minutes—until she was drawn into making one of her characteristic off-the-cuff comments that she came to regret. Pressed on whether any of her own expense claims had been challenged, she gave one example: her claim for a per diem breakfast expense after having taken a business class flight on which breakfast was served. In her defence, she then made what became an infamous remark about the "awful" nature of airplane food: "If you want ice-cold Camembert with broken crackers, have it."

Her words were reported widely on Canadian television and in newspapers from coast to coast; in British and American media outlets; and in publications as diverse as *Maclean's* magazine, the United Food and Commercial Workers' union newsletter, and the food magazine *Gusto*. Some of the editorial cartoons were memorable. And an album by the Canadian Beaver Band included the song "Cold Camembert and Broken Crackers." John Oliver, host of the American late-night political satire show *Last Week Tonight*, featured the story as a cautionary tale with the punchline, "Let this be a lesson to all politicians: it is hard to elicit any kind of sympathy when you're uttering a sentence that includes the word 'camembert.'" And in the universe of social media, vastly expanded since the Canada goose episode, the story went viral with thousands of tweets and online posts. Most of the coverage was negative, focusing on the entitlement and privilege of the Senate elite, and many commentators jumped at the opportunity to criticize the Senate as an institution out of touch with ordinary people.[84]

What was Nancy Ruth's response to this firestorm

of publicity? At the Senate meeting before her retirement, when her colleagues lauded her accomplishments, Conservative Leader of the Opposition Claude Carignan said, "Let us not forget the cold camembert incident, where a very unhappy Senator Nancy Ruth came to see me during my tenure as Leader of the Government in the Senate to sincerely apologize for adding fuel to the fire and putting increased pressure on the Senate when it was already attracting a lot of criticism from the media."[85] A few months after her retirement she told a reporter that she regretted the comment. "It didn't push any issue at all. It was stupid."[86] In this instance, her maverick instincts, so often used to champion just and important causes, had turned against her. A moment of impatience with the media made her the whipping-girl of a scandal in which she played no real part. Other senators were ultimately investigated for and charged with expense violations, but for a time she became the face of the public outcry.

Experience had taught Nancy Ruth that "the press tends to cover the flamboyant" and neglect her substantive accomplishments. "Nobody asks me what I'm doing about trying to get women included in the Criminal Code of Canada under the hate sections or to [ensure compliance with] Canada's action plan on United Nations Security Council Resolution 1325."[87] Five years before the Senate expenses scandal she had also earned front-page coverage for a story that was actually her own, one that became known under the colourful banner, "Shut the Fuck Up" (STFU). On May 3, 2010, in advance of the upcoming G8 leaders' summit in Canada, Nancy Ruth hosted a meeting of about eighty representatives from the Association of Women's Rights in Development as well as other groups and politicians who focused on women's issues in international aid. Just a few days earlier, Harper's government had confirmed that abortion would not be funded as part of the child and maternal health plan that was to be the centrepiece of Canada's initiatives at the G8 summit.[88] The announcement generated concern among women's rights advocates, dominating their discussion at the meeting on Parliament Hill. At a key moment in the proceedings, an impatient Nancy Ruth told the assembled crowd, "We've got five weeks or whatever left until the G8 starts. Shut the f— up on this issue.... If you push it, there will be more backlash.... This is now a political football. This is not about women's health in this country."[89]

Reaction was swift. Her remarks were caught on tape by the *Toronto Star* and reported by some of the women at the meeting. As she recalls, Liberal MPs Carolyn Bennett and Anita Neville were quick to make political hay by sending out a press release that same afternoon "to sic the press right on me."[90] During question period in the House of Commons the following day, in an instance of the kind of partisan politics that Nancy Ruth abhorred—the scoring of points rather than the creation of good public policy—Liberal MP Bob Rae called her comments "part of the 'culture of intimidation and bullying' used by the Tory government to quiet their critics."[91] Although the *Toronto Star* article characterized Nancy Ruth's remarks as "intended more as friendly advice than a warning," it also quoted a strong rebuke from MP Anita Neville, the Liberal status of women critic, who had issued the press release shortly after the meeting:

Sending Conservative Senator Nancy Ruth to threaten and blackmail Canada's foreign aid community is the most extreme example yet of how this deceitful and intolerant prime minister operates.... Senator Ruth must apologize for her profane remarks, and Prime Minister Harper must cease his attempts to bully Canada's international development groups, who are only trying to help the world's poor and impoverished. This is truly appalling.[92]

On the evening of May 3, learning of the assault underway by the opposition party, Nancy Ruth worked to control the damage. Late that night, Joanna Kerr, then head of ActionAid International and chair of the Association for Women's Rights in Development, prepared a letter to Anita Neville in which she stressed Nancy Ruth's role in providing space to host the meeting and argued, "While we very much appreciate that you took the time to participate in the discussion, we disagree with your assertion that Prime Minister Stephen Harper used Conservative Senator Nancy Ruth to blackmail, bully and intimidate the international development community into toeing the Conservative line about abortion." She ended the letter by saying, "We believe that Senator Ruth's comments, while perhaps overly colourful, were made in good faith in the context of a challenging discussion on tactics moving forward. While we may not agree, we appreciate the opportunity to finally express dissent in an open and public forum and we owe thanks to Nancy Ruth for creating that space."[93] Dimitri Soudas, director of communications in the Prime Minister's Office, sent the following email to Nancy Ruth at 10:30 that night: "I've been in active politics for the last 17 years. I've never seen a group issue a press release providing a form of support to someone who told them to 'shut the fuck up.'"[94]

Looking back on the lead-up to the controversy,

Nancy Ruth argues that Harper had left no doubt from the outset as to his stand on the proposed 1.2 billion-dollar aid package for women and children. He "was consistent, consistent through all the ten years I sat in his caucus, to stop those who were trying to bring abortion to the table." She quotes him as saying in caucus, "Look. There are only two countries in sub-Saharan Africa in which it's legal to have abortion. We're not going to rock the African boat by doing this one, and it suits us, the Party." She understood that he would not yield on this point, so when those present at the meeting on Parliament Hill kept protesting that the aid package should be opposed because it did not include abortion, her reaction was equally unyielding. "Just don't spill the whole apple cart over it. You're not going to get it. Don't do it." She remains grateful to this day that Joanna Kerr, who was chairing the meeting, "understood what I was saying and why I was saying it."[95]

She had other supporters as well, including the prime minister, who responded to the outcry with equanimity. According to her account in a magazine article on the topic, "An inconvenient Ruth," when she ran into him a few days after the incident, "He put his arm around me and he said, 'I hear you had some press last week'...and that was the end of it." Conservative Senator Hugh Segal is cited in the same article as saying, "Any party that doesn't embrace somebody with that kind of passion and intensity is a small tent party that has no future."[96]

At the same time, there were many who took her to task, objecting more to her message than to her language. Soon after the incident she admitted, "I made a mistake.... I should never have said it. In any form of language. Groups need to talk when they need to talk."[97] Yet the spectre of women being silenced continued to hover

over the debate. Later that summer the Canadian Centre for Policy Alternatives, in its quarterly *CCPA Monitor*, included a supplement titled "Speaking truth to power," in which seventeen women from a range of NGO, academic, and political backgrounds argued that women should never shut up. Nancy Ruth was given the final pages in the supplement, a chance for her to explain both her remarks and her vision for advancing women's equality.[98] In late September, with interest in the topic still high in the feminist community, the CCPA published a monograph with a further seven essays added to the original material—and the same concluding essay by Nancy Ruth. Under the heading, "Why did I say, STFU?" she speaks to her change in "tactics" over five years in the Senate, where she had become "much more conscious of the need to build constructive relationships with parliamentarians, ministers, and civil servants, in order to obtain long-term objectives."[99] She had moved from "outside lobbyist" to "inside lobbyist" and had learned that her different position called for a different approach to advocacy.

After addressing the question of why she spoke so bluntly to her colleagues, Nancy Ruth asks in her essay, "What strategies will best advance the equality of women?" There she agrees with the other authors in the monograph: "History shows that advances in the struggle for women's equality have come in response to vocal demands and not to acquiescence or silence." In defence of her own position, however, she adds,

> We know "why" we seek change and "what" change we seek. The phrase "STFU" was made in the context of "how" we make change happen—or not happen…. There may be times when one needs to demonstrate

loudly on Parliament Hill, but there will be many other occasions when it is more expedient to work quietly behind the scenes with other like-minded people.... In the final analysis, our dreams, our proposals, become policy or law when they are adopted or advanced by government officials with the ability to exert significant influence in the system.[100]

Here is the crux of what she has learned in her years in government—the "long form" of her shorthand admonition to STFU.

Yet she does not end her essay on this note, but instead addresses a more profound question: "Will more women in Parliament really make a difference?" She had been badly bruised by the attacks on her from other women, including members of Parliament, and she says of Anita Neville,

> She has been an active participant in efforts to increase the representation of women in Canada's governing bodies. But the demands of keeping one's place in the party pecking order are so great that all of us succumb to it from time to time. The hurt or damage we may cause to others, even our friends and allies, is of little matter. Our allegiance is ultimately to the party, not to each other.

In her view, feminist solidarity can be no match for partisan politics under what she calls the current "patriarchal structure of Parliament, its party politics, and its power hierarchy."[101] She herself has reached out across party lines, financially supported women candidates from other parties, and worked to build alliances with other female politicians—and it has not been enough.

What then will be enough? Nancy Ruth turns to a "bold proposal" advanced by former Conservative prime minister Kim Campbell, in which "each party would run one female and one male candidate for each federal riding, and voters would vote for both a female and a male candidate."[102] The resulting gender parity, she believes, would overturn existing political traditions by radically changing party structures. In her view, only a solution as far-reaching as that could alter the power dynamics inherent in partisan politics and underpinned by a patriarchal world view.

Nancy Ruth concludes her essay with a plea to the feminist community. Under the current system of government, she argues, "To realize our cherished objectives, we need to cultivate and nurture broad-based coalitions of allies, both inside and outside government. We have to take advantage of those rare political openings with those rare political people. Good luck and *never* STFU!"[103] She may have been shaken by the charges that she tried to silence women for political purposes, but she is unwavering in her belief that she was justified in advising women to play "the long game" and stay focused on the big goals—and in the shorter term, to make smart choices that advance the cause rather than complicating it. Above all, she advances a vision in which those inside and outside government can act from a place of trust and good faith, claiming common ground on behalf of shared goals.

Although Nancy Ruth's reputation as a maverick was fed by occasional outspoken and sometimes outrageous remarks, she sees herself as having, for the most part, "toed the party line"—voting for bills even when she didn't like them, working within the system to effect change.[104] Such was the case when she advised her feminist colleagues to accept restrictions on abortion in the international aid package in order to ensure that the funds were delivered. Yet a few months earlier she had clashed violently with a member of her own government over a $750,000 annual cut to an ecumenical international aid agency, KAIROS. Jason Kenney, minister of citizenship and immigration, justified the cuts in the Conservative caucus by accusing KAIROS, which did aid work in Palestine, of being anti-Israel and antisemitic, claiming untruthfully that they were part of a boycott against Israel. Nancy Ruth recalls that "When Jason Kenney got up and used such inflammatory language against an NGO that I had known and supported for years...I was just beyond myself with his language.... I got up and said, 'Prime Minister, I find the minister's language inflammatory, unacceptable, inhuman, lying, deceitful.'"[105] The exchange was, of course, within the confines of caucus, so Nancy Ruth underscores that it was not a public criticism of her government. Yet she followed it with a public gesture that left no doubt as to where she stood. She had two valuable paintings with her in Ottawa—a Lawren Harris and an Emily Carr—that she immediately sold and gave the half-million-dollar proceeds to KAIROS as a show of her support.

While she spoke little about her gift at the time, journalist Jane Taber noted a few years later, just a few months before Nancy Ruth's retirement, that "the move was controversial, attracting negative publicity for the Harper government of which Nancy Ruth was a member." And Taber quotes Nancy Ruth as saying, "My mother gave me the paintings, and she would have approved of it.... I was just so annoyed with the government."[106] Her annoyance had indeed been compounded by an announcement seconds after Kenney's remarks, from Minister of Defence Peter MacKay, that the government was going to restore the gold braid on naval officers' uniforms—at a cost of four million dollars. "The juxtaposition of not helping the war torn poor and gold braid on officers' uniforms appalled me."[107]

If Nancy Ruth sees herself less as a maverick than as someone who tried to colour within the party lines, her fellow senators lauded her flashes of independence—perhaps especially, those senators who were members of an opposing party. Senator Joseph Day, for example, who was then leader of the Senate Liberals, praised her because, even after joining the Conservative caucus, "she did not abandon her personal convictions and, when appropriate, she voted against her own government…. Independence was and is more than just a word for Senator Nancy Ruth. As a self-described social activist, independence has always been a part of her very soul. The Senate was not about to change that."[108] Still, the Senate did take its toll on her spirit, leading her at times to think of quitting as the years passed by and she grew more disillusioned. "The only reason I didn't quit," she says, "was because I knew Harper would not appoint another feminist. So why would I give up that voice?"[109]

One of the last projects that Nancy Ruth took on as a senator was a campaign to amend Canada's Criminal Code to allow for medical assistance in dying. Debate on this topic had divided public opinion in Canada for many years, with discussion centring on high-profile cases such as that of Robert Latimer, who killed his profoundly disabled daughter in 1993 and was convicted of second-degree murder; and Sue Rodriguez, a woman with ALS who launched a Supreme Court challenge to the Criminal Code in 1992 but lost on a five-to-four decision. From time to time, bills on this topic had been introduced in Parliament—MP

Svend Robinson's Act to amend the Criminal Code (aiding suicide), for example, was introduced as Bill C-385 in late 1992 and again as Bill C-215 in 1994—but in each case the bill did not move forward and expired when a session or a Parliament ended. In June 2008, MP Francine Lalonde introduced Bill C-562: An Act to Amend the Criminal Code (right to die with dignity), but the bill died on the order paper with the dissolution of Parliament. When, in May 2009, Ms. Lalonde introduced Bill C-384, identical to her former bill, the bill finally went to a vote in April of the following year but was defeated 228 to 259. The subject was sensitive and contentious; few parliamentarians wanted to risk supporting medically assisted death.[110]

In March 2014, MP Steven Fletcher introduced in the House of Commons Bill C-581: An Act to Amend the Criminal Code (physician-assisted death), along with Bill C-582: An Act to establish the Canadian Commission on Physician-Assisted Death. Fletcher was a quadriplegic who had been in favour of assisted death for years, but he saw little chance of his private members' bills moving success-fully through the House. He and Nancy Ruth were friends, and Nancy Ruth recalls that he came to her in the fall of 2014 asking if she would introduce the bill in the Senate.[111] As Fletcher described his strategy to the press, he saw the initiative as a chance "for the Senate to shine, to demon-strate why the Senate is there." They would be "dealing with an issue that obviously most elected representatives do not want to deal with." Nancy Ruth was prepared to take up the crusade and, at the same press conference, she drew laughs when she speculated that "Senators are close enough to death to want to do this."[112]

On November 25, 2014, Nancy Ruth gave notice to her caucus that she was introducing a bill on assisted dying, telling them that "Parliament should follow the lead of Canadians on this issue."[113] She cited polls showing high percentages of public support for what was then being referred to as "physician-assisted death" (PAD). She also reminded her colleagues that a case currently before the Supreme Court, *Carter v. Canada*, might end in a decision that would legalize it. On December 2, Bill S-225 received its first reading on the floor of the Senate and, at its second reading on December 4, Nancy Ruth outlined the provisions of the bill and spoke passionately on its behalf, telling her colleagues, "It's been said that all politics is personal. The issue of end-of-life care, of having the right to manage pain and choose your exit, is as personal as it gets." And in her classic appeal for unity across party lines, she concluded, "What it isn't is partisan. Members of every party have publicly embraced the need for us to change our laws, and Canadians are already leading us there. We need to follow. Senators, please help me pass this bill."[114] Unfortunately, like Fletcher's bills in the House, Bill S-225 languished in the Senate, expiring when the federal election was called in August 2015.

In the meantime, however, the Supreme Court had brought down its decision on PAD in *Carter*, a decision that would at last force Parliament to take action. On February 6, 2015, the Court ruled that sections of the Criminal Code prohibiting PAD violated certain rights within the Canadian Charter of Rights and Freedoms. Suspending its ruling for one year, the Court called upon Parliament to "craft an appropriate remedy" within that timeframe. Although the federal government established an External Panel on Options for a Legislative Response to *Carter v. Canada* in July 2015, nothing substantive was accomplished before the Liberals won power in October.

The report of the expert panel was tabled in December 2015 and, in response to the looming deadline, the new government under Prime Minister Justin Trudeau ensured that Parliament quickly established a Special Joint Committee of the Senate and the House of Commons to review the report; to consult widely with experts and stakeholders; and to provide a final report with recommendations to Parliament by February 26, 2016.[115]

Not surprisingly, given her previous work on the topic, Nancy Ruth was one of the five members of Senate, along with ten members of the House of Commons, appointed to the joint committee. The Supreme Court had granted a four-month extension to its deadline for Parliament to pass appropriate legislation, but after the December recess, the joint committee had a scant five weeks between its first meeting on January 18, 2016, and the February deadline by which it was to table its report. It met intensively over that period and heard testimony from dozens of witnesses. The first concern raised by Nancy Ruth during joint committee deliberations was debated throughout passage of the ensuing bill: whether serious mental illness should be grounds for access to medical assistance in dying. She told a witness from the department of justice that her question was a "Charter question" and went on to say, "I spoke with a well-known constitutional lawyer who often appears before the Supreme Court and who mentally has issues. She said to me, 'How dare you design a law that would exclude us who have mental illness? If you do so, I'm in court.' What's your response to that?"[116] The witness admitted that such an exclusion could be challenged on section 15 of the Charter of Rights and Freedoms, the equality clause, but that it was one that would have to be settled in the courts.

In a subsequent meeting Nancy Ruth tackled another issue that would be equally contentious, the question of "advance consent" for a physician-assisted death of someone who was capable of making the decision at the time but might later lose capacity before the directive was carried out. She noted that Quebec, which had already passed a provincial law on physician-assisted dying, had not allowed for consent "prior to, say, getting dementia." The witness, a lawyer from Quebec, replied with what would remain a central objection for those opposed to advance consent: "How is it possible to know whether the person has changed his mind or not and if this truly reflects his or her wishes?"[117] Nancy Ruth continued to pursue the same matter in the joint committee's meeting the following day, asking a witness who had been a member of the External Panel on Options for a Legislative Response to *Carter v. Canada* about the panel's online questionnaire that had been answered by more than fifteen thousand Canadians. In that survey, she noted, "you asked Canadians whether they should be able to receive physician-assisted death based on an advance directive. Sixty-two percent of the balanced representative sample agreed or strongly agreed.... Am I correct that this scenario for an advance directive received the highest level of support of any that you proposed?"[118] The witness, after consulting with staff, confirmed the statistic but did not address the question of whether the scenario received the highest level of support before Nancy Ruth's allotted time for questions ran out.

In subsequent meetings, she continued to ask about mental illness as a condition that would qualify for physician-assisted death, as well as about the issue of equitable access to PAD for patients who were disadvantaged socially or economically or who live in rural communities—the latter a key concern in her advocacy for social justice.[119] On February 2, she brought up the critical issue of gender-based analysis with an academic witness who applies feminist theory to bioethics: "Could I ask you for a gender-based analysis of physician-assisted death? Are there particular matters in physician-assisted death relating to women, or men, of which this committee should take particular notice or that we should address in our recommendations?" The witness agreed that the question was germane and responded, "We're certainly aware that the population is aging, and women tend to live longer than men and tend to live poorer than men in terms of their resources. Some women who are at that age now are from generations that were trained and socialized to not think highly of themselves, to defer, and things like that."[120] When the bill for physician-assisted death—or Medical Assistance in Dying (MAID), as it came to be called—was debated in the spring of that year, Nancy Ruth pressed hard for answers about gender-based analysis.

The joint committee met its ambitious timeline and tabled its report, *Medical Assistance in Dying: A Patient-Centred Approach*, on February 25, 2016. Among its recommendations were three that Nancy Ruth strongly supported but that would prove to be contentious as the bill progressed through the House of Commons: to include psychological suffering as possible grounds for MAID; to allow for advance requests for MAID; and to revisit in three years the question of allowing "mature minors" to request MAID.[121] When Bill C-14: An Act to Amend the Criminal Code and to make related amendments to other Acts (medical assistance in dying), was introduced by the government in the House of Commons on April 14, 2016, it did not include these three key recommendations. The bill was passed by the House on May 31, 2016, and received its first reading in the Senate the same day.[122] On the following afternoon, when the Senate met to consider the bill, their meeting was attended by Minister of Justice and Attorney General Jody Wilson-Raybould and Minister of Health Jane Philpott. The ministers faced extensive questions, including those from Senator James Cowan, who had served with Nancy Ruth on the joint committee and who pressed the ministers as to why the government had rejected that committee's recommendations.[123]

When Nancy Ruth's turn for questions came, she began by asking the minister of health "What GBA was done in your ministry on this bill, and what did it come up with? What did it say?" Minister Philpott replied that she was not aware of the details—an answer Nancy Ruth had become accustomed to over the years—but agreed that "You are absolutely right that this is something where there may be different vulnerabilities according to people's gender." Nancy Ruth went on to press her point, stating her belief that "if GBA were done on this issue, it would lead to the necessity of advance consent." Women, she argued, lived longer, were more likely to be caregivers, and many ended up "stuck in some institution in front of the television, eating pap, and they are dependent on the effect of systemic disadvantage, be it in wages, pensions, or other issues in which women suffer in this country." Some of these women, in her view, would wish to avail themselves of advance consent, choosing medical assistance in dying to be granted at a later date, after they had become incapacitated and unable to request such assistance. Yet Bill C-14 did not allow for such a request to be honoured. "Madam Justice Lynn Smith [a former chair of the Women's Legal Education and Action Fund], of the trial division in the

Carter decision," she argued, "called medically assisted dying this ultimately personal and fundamental choice. Bill C-14 falls short of this standard because Bill C-14's overarching failure is that it does not trust us—it does not trust Canadians—to make the best choices for ourselves."[124]

On June 15 the Senate passed the bill with amendments and returned it to the House, whose members accepted some but not all the amendments and returned the bill to the Senate. The Senate ended by voting in favour of the bill on June 17, and it received royal assent on the same day.[125] Nancy Ruth recounts that "Our conclusions [of the Joint Committee] were not accepted.... [T]hey removed a number of the good recommendations we had made.... One is prior consent, for adults. The other is do we allow those with mental health histories to ask for assisted death? And the third thing is minors."[126]

The final bill did in fact include a clause that required "an independent review of issues relating to MAID for mature minors, advance requests for MAID, and requests for MAID where mental illness is the sole underlying condition," along with a "requirement that the report of any such review be laid before each House of Parliament within two years of the start of the review."[127] This mandated review was subsequently assigned to the Council of Canadian Academies, and Nancy Ruth continued after her retirement to lobby for gender-based analysis to be incorporated into the review. On January 19, 2017, she wrote to the Council telling them that their attention to GBA offered "an opportunity to correct a critical deficiency in the development of, and debate on" Bill C-14.[128] In her final year in the Senate, she had helped secure a victory on behalf of legislation that supported medical assistance in dying, yet in her view the legislation was "deficient" and the victory only a partial one. Looking back in the fall of 2019, she observed that "To this date, nothing has really happened with that report and the lobby group Dying with Dignity continues to lobby for changes. There has been no bill, and it is not an election issue."[129] At the time of writing, Parliament is considering a bill that will change the criteria for access to medical assistance in dying—to allow it whether a person's death is naturally foreseeable or not—and some other modest changes to safeguards and to final consent. The federal government has not yet indicated how it will undertake the 5-year review required in the original legislation, nor has it yet indicated how it will proceed on the outstanding issues of advance requests, mental illness and mature minors.

Another campaign that was incomplete when she left the Senate but was ultimately a resounding success came from Nancy Ruth's initiative to make the words of Canada's national anthem gender neutral. "O Canada" had only been officially adopted by Parliament as the country's national anthem in 1980. A joint committee of the House and Senate had been first tasked with studying the question of a national anthem in 1967, issued its report in 1968, and then—nothing. By 1980, given the length of time that the project had languished, parliamentarians agreed that passage of Bill C-36, creating the national anthem act, should be expedited. On June 27, Francis Fox, secretary of state and minister of communications, introduced the bill acknowledging that "a number of members on both sides of the House have expressed concern over some of the wording of the version recommended unanimously by the 1968 joint committee." In particular, he cited a desire to see "the words 'sons' and 'native land' replaced...to better reflect the reality of Canada." He believed, he said, that "all members are sympathetic to these concerns" and ended by assuring the members that "in the course of the next session the government would be more than willing to see the subject matter of a private member's bill on this question."[130]

The House of Commons passed Bill C-36 on the day it was introduced and it then moved immediately to the Senate, where Senator Raymond Perrault, leader of the government, was clearly eager that the bill should be passed without amendment. He recapped the history of the anthem and the length of time it had been in use without official endorsement: "One hundred years have gone by since Sir Adolphe-Basile Routhier wrote the French words for 'O Canada' and Calixa Lavallée set them so admirably to music. Similarly, it is almost 80 years since Judge Robert Stanley Weir wrote the words that were to become the most popular English version of 'O Canada'.... We are being asked to give official recognition to the choice which our fellow Canadians made with their hearts long ago." In the discussion that followed, while a number of senators acknowledged the importance of at last taking action rather than getting bogged down in debate over amendments, at the same time they stressed the imperative need for future changes to the English lyrics — they are not a translation of the French lyrics, which are gender neutral and have never been changed. Senator Florence Bird, for example, who had chaired the Royal Commission on the Status of Women more than ten years earlier, argued that "'true patriot love' should be commanded in all of us, and not just in the sons of this country, because I assure you, honourable senators, I am nobody's son." Senator Perrault, echoing the words spoken in the House of Commons, assured his fellow senators "that in the course of the next session the government will be more than willing to have considered proposals for word changes which may come forward in the form of a private members' bills. Such bills in both houses will be welcomed."[131]

Like the House, the Senate voted that same day to pass Bill C-36 and it was proclaimed as the *National Anthem Act* on Canada Day, July 1, 1980. Any thought of amending the act, however, was soon eclipsed by the government's move to patriate the constitution, which began in earnest in the fall of 1980. It was not until June 1984 that the first private members' bill to replace "thy sons" with "of us" was introduced in the House of Commons—without success—by Conservative MP Howard Crosby. Over the next eighteen years, eight more private members' bills proposing gender-neutral language were introduced, by MPs from the PC, Liberal, NDP, and CPC parties. The only proposals that proceeded past a perfunctory first reading and received any form of discussion or debate were Bills S-39 and S-3, introduced by Liberal senator Vivienne Poy in 2002 and 2003.[132]

In a press release issued by Senator Poy during the Senate's consideration of Bill S-39: An Act to Amend the National Anthem Act to Include All Canadians, she brought forward "an amazing discovery" that proved useful to Nancy Ruth in her own efforts to change the anthem. Because of the publicity about her bill, Senator Poy announced, an individual had come forward with the 1908 text of Judge Weir's lyrics, which predated the 1914 copyrighted version. In the earlier version, rather than "all thy sons command" Weir had written "thou dost in us command." Here was an argument to counter the claim that the anthem's "original intent" should not be altered. Senator Poy is quoted in the release as saying, "While I never agreed with that line of reasoning, the fact that the original wording was inclusive of both men and women should assuage concerned Canadians: clearly, we are honouring the spirit of Weir's anthem."[133]

While Senator Poy used Weir's 1908 version to argue that a gender-inclusive anthem had existed in the past and should now be reclaimed, her bill recommended contemporary language rather than Weir's archaic "thou dost." Her proposal was for a simple shift from "thy sons" to "of us." When she spoke to the bill at second reading in the Senate, she cited letters of support from women and men across the country and gave examples of work being done in churches and in the media to adopt gender-inclusive language. She also underscored the massive social changes that had taken place over the past century, including women's gaining the vote; their steady advance within professions; and the protection of their rights in the Charter of Rights and Freedoms. She ended her presentation with a stirring appeal: "Let us take one more step in the right direction, honourable senators. Let us join the leading nations of the world. I would ask that you support this amendment in the name of fairness, historic tradition, and because it is the right thing to do for all Canadians."[134]

Senator Poy's advocacy did not prevail and Bill S-39 died on the order paper when Parliament was prorogued in September 2002. She fared better when she reintroduced the bill as S-3 in the next session of Parliament a month later; this second bill reached the standing committee on social affairs, science, and technology, where it received the unanimous support of the committee but died during third reading when Parliament was prorogued in November 2003.[135] Though she did not abandon her dream of seeing the anthem changed, this was the last bill that Senator Poy introduced on the topic. In the coming years, she handed the torch to Nancy Ruth, who proved to be a determined and able champion of the cause.

In January 2008, in advance of the government's tabling its 2008 budget, Nancy Ruth wrote to the prime minister urging him to develop an "Action Plan for Advancing Women's Equality" that would outline "concrete measures for the next phase of our strategy to ensure that policies and programs enhance women's equality in this country."[136] When the budget plan tabled in the House of Commons the following month did include a commitment to the government's "development of an Action Plan that will advance the equality of women across Canada," Nancy Ruth was ready to seize the opening.[137] That summer, she took to the annual national caucus meeting a list of four actions that the government could undertake on behalf of Canadian women. Three of them she grouped under "making life better for Canadians and their families"—the improvement of maternal and parental leave benefits; the expansion of the National Child Benefit; and the launch of a national strategy on family violence. The fourth, which she designated as an initiative "in our tradition of nation-building," was aimed at the national anthem. In her words, "In 2010, Canada will mark the 40th anniversary of the Royal Commission on the Status of Women. **It is time to include us in the National Anthem—all 'of us'**" (emphasis in the original).[138]

She had now entered the fray. Over the following year she continued to dig into the topic, asking Beth Atcheson and summer student Kat Chuba to prepare a history of the English national anthem. She walked the resulting paper into the national caucus on February 25, 2009, along with a cover note with information on women in the armed forces who had been killed in combat.[139] She continued her work over the following months and in the fall sent a letter to James Moore, the minister of Canadian heritage and official languages, and Helena Guergis, the minister of state for the status of women, urging them "to announce legislation to amend our National Anthem, *O Canada*, to remove the dated reference to 'sons' and to return to the original, inclusive English words."[140] By this point, she had decided that her efforts would stand a better chance if she shifted from changing the language ("all of us") to restoring the earlier gender-neutral words of Weir's anthem: "thou dost in us command." Prime Minister Harper was also given a copy of this letter and on that Christmas Eve he wrote to thank her for her proposal, adding his expression of appreciation for her "efforts to ensure full equality between women and men in Canada."[141]

On January 13, 2010, a few weeks before the opening of a new session of Parliament, the prime minister wrote to his caucus inviting them to give some input into his upcoming throne speech. Nancy Ruth was ready and eager to take up the invitation. She responded in less than a week, sending him six recommendations. The fifth was for him to follow through on his 2008 commitment to develop an action plan to advance the equality of women; the last urged him to return to "the original 1908 English words" of the national anthem.[142] While the speech from the throne made no mention of a national action plan on women, to Nancy Ruth's astonishment it did include this reference to the national anthem: "Our government will also ask Parliament to examine the original gender-neutral English wording of the national anthem."[143] Nancy Ruth had "no idea this was coming" and as the prime minister walked out of the Senate chamber past her front row desk, she leaned forward to thank him.[144]

Vivienne Poy was one of the first to congratulate Nancy Ruth; she sent her an email within a couple of hours that read: "You must have done something right and something great in order to have the National Anthem mentioned in the Throne speech. I want to congratulate you for all that you have done."[145] Yet the elation was short-lived. As Nancy Ruth explained, because she had had "no warning" from the prime minister that he would take this step, there had been no opportunity to "drum up support in advance."[146] Opposition to the proposal, on the other hand, was quick and ferocious. There was an overwhelming protest from Legion branches to the prime minister. Also, to begin with, there was apparently little support for the initiative in Harper's Conservative caucus; one reporter claimed that an inside poll of the caucus found most of them opposed any change to the anthem, adding that, "It's rare to find so many

The Honourable Nancy Ruth and the Honourable Vivienne Poy celebrate the change to "all of us" in the English national anthem at a party at the home of Senator Donna Dasko, Toronto, February 4, 2018.

senior members of the government candidly opposing an initiative or admitting local voters are infuriated by his move."[147] Nancy Ruth also points to "the distorted CBC reporting" that followed the throne speech as one cause for the proposal's demise.[148] Within two days, the government announced that it would not proceed with plans to revisit the anthem, "citing an outpouring of opposition from Canadians."[149]

Nancy Ruth was disappointed but undeterred. On March 11, she stood in the Senate to say, "Honourable senators: O Canada! I could not possibly stand by this week without saying a word or two, so here we go." Taking pride in Harper's gesture—despite his subsequent reversal—she thanked the prime minister "for supporting gender-inclusive language in the Speech from the Throne." She thanked as well "anyone else who wants to see a gender-inclusive anthem." But, addressing those who opposed such a change, she added, "I have a couple of words. The next time honourable senators sing the anthem in caucus, try singing 'in all our daughters command.' See how that feels until the Easter Break."[150] She was signalling that the fight was not over; she would find other ways to ensure that her colleagues understood how the anthem felt to Canadians who are excluded by its language.

Years later, when pressed about Harper's speedy retreat from the anthem initiative, Nancy Ruth continued to defend him for being willing to take such a risk. Even if he backed down, she exclaimed, "He did it!... He did it!" In her view, "it wasn't managed well on the communications end" and he "wasn't going to take the political risk to do it again."[151] By 2013, with the small Toronto team that consisted of her executive assistant, Martha Grantham; her partner, Elizabeth Riddell-Dixon; and Beth Atcheson, director of parliamentary affairs, she had begun to consider hiring a public relations firm and putting her financial resources into a campaign that would build broad awareness and support. Early that year she tried her hand with the prime minister once again, writing to ask whether he would change the *National Anthem Act* if she were to "create a groundswell of support for it."[152] The response was swift and not encouraging: a staff member in the Prime Minister's Office (PMO) wrote back to say that "in our view, a consensus of caucus would be required before we would consider re-opening this issue" and advised her to "work through the caucus system prior to PMO."[153] She knew then, without a doubt, that the prime minister would expend no further political capital on her initiative. She would have to find other ways to move this campaign forward and she would be resolute in doing so.

In the fall of 2013, she and her team launched, at her foundation's expense, a public education campaign designed to encourage Canadians to tell their MPs that they supported changing the anthem. Jennifer Shah, who, along with Leah Richardson, worked on the project as part of the firm of Fleishman-Hillard that Nancy Ruth had hired, wrote on October 3 that "We've had more than 1,300 stories so far in traditional media. We've seen a lot of regional coverage begin and we've also gone international with the BBC picking up the story. Social media chatter continues with more than 2,400 Twitter mentions, totaling 13 million impressions. Video views are almost at 10,000."[154] Dozens of prominent figures came out in support during the following weeks, including Margaret Atwood, Sheila Fraser, and Sally Armstrong as well as a number of politicians, such as former prime minister Kim Campbell, former Progressive Conservative leader of the government

The founders, along with Nancy Ruth, of the campaign
for a gender-inclusive English national anthem. Clockwise
from top left: the Right Honourable Kim Campbell;
Margaret Atwood; Sally Goddard (nicholagoddard.com);
and the Honourable Vivienne Poy.

in Senate Lowell Murray, Senator Hugh Segal, former minister of defence and foreign affairs Bill Graham, MP Carolyn Bennett, and, of course Vivienne Poy. Even Nancy Ruth's brother Hal lent his voice, writing, "I support your initiative to make our national anthem gender neutral."[155]

Yet despite the attention the Restore our Anthem campaign generated, Nancy Ruth soon conceded that there was "almost NO traction here in Ottawa."[156] She had a draft private members' bill in hand that fall but questioned whether she could muster the support needed to make its introduction in the Senate worthwhile. Just at that point, however, she made a connection that would prove to be as fortuitous as her elevator encounter with Sheila Fraser. In early December she ran into Liberal MP Mauril Bélanger in the parliamentary dining room, and the two of them set out on a path that would lead to a gender-inclusive anthem, though the journey took twists and turns that neither could have foreseen.

As Nancy Ruth describes that fateful encounter with Bélanger, he told her that "he had been successful in the draw for the Order of Precedence of Private Members Business" and therefore "could introduce a Private Members Bill that had a chance of passing the House of Commons." He knew about her leadership in the campaign to make the English national anthem gender inclusive, and he was considering putting forward a bill to that end. Would she share her knowledge with him? Would she support his bill? She found the proposal appealing "in very practical political terms," reasoning that

spirits were up as an election (and Canada's 150th birthday) came closer, and a bill from the elected Commons would have momentum coming to the Senate. The party leaders (Harper, Trudeau and Mulcair) had put themselves on the sidelines and left the playing field open. Canadian media coverage and citizen support had grown appreciably in the fall of 2013 as a result of the Restore our Anthem campaign.

Mauril Bélanger, she concluded, "was being the best of politicians—he could move on something he valued for the country at a time when the conditions aligned for success."[157]

Nancy Ruth not only supported Bélanger's initiative but continued to pursue her media campaign, shifting from a focus on restoring the 1908 words to a bold invitation to "sing all of us"—a suggestion driven by Devlin Multimedia, whose principal, Cath Devlin, had worked with Nancy Ruth on *CoolWomen* and was a former director of the National Action Committee on the Status of Women. Over time, the campaign's website, www.singallofus.ca, amassed videos of Canadians across the country singing the gender-neutral anthem. And in June 2014, she saw all the parliamentarians off for their summer recess with a package of "sing all of us" cards and buttons, along with a letter that urged them to promote the initiative with their constituents, family, and friends. If they went to the website, her letter told them, they would find "some really endearing videos of crossing guards etc. singing and Church organists playing.... [M]any voices singing for All Of Us."[158]

On September 22, 2014, Mauril Bélanger introduced in the House of Commons Bill C-624: An Act to Amend the National Anthem Act (gender), which proposed a single change in the anthem's wording, from "thy sons" to "of us." The bill met with staunch opposition from the

Conservatives, who argued that reaction to the prime minister's 2010 throne speech made it clear that Canadians did not support such a change.[159] On April 29, 2015, Bill C-624 was defeated on second reading by a vote of 144–127, in line with the Conservative majority.[160] It now seemed likely that there would have to be a change in government before the bill could succeed.

That change came just a few months later, when Justin Trudeau's Liberals won a majority government on October 19, 2015. Bélanger had been widely favoured as the next speaker of the house, but he withdrew his name from consideration on November 30, 2015, announcing that he had been diagnosed with ALS. On January 27, 2016, when Parliament returned after the holiday break to begin work in earnest, he introduced Bill C-210 (identical to the previous C-624) in the House of Commons. Thereafter, as a private members' bill, C-210 moved through the House in prescribed stages with voting at fixed points. By the time of its second reading on May 6, 2016, Bélanger's declining condition required him to use text-to-speech software to move that the bill be read the second time and referred to committee. In his remarks he urged his colleagues in the House to support a change that would reflect the country's current reality: "Canada is all of us, not some of us." He went on to chronicle the progress made in women's status over the past century—the federal right to vote in 1918, the first female MP in 1921, the Persons Case in 1929, the first female senator in 1930, the first female Canadian soldier to die in combat in 2006. Citing the results of a 2015 national poll, he argued that "Canadians are now ready for an inclusive national anthem" intended to show that "all of us, regardless of our gender or our origins, contribute to our unique country."[161]

The Toronto "O Canada" team for the
English national anthem campaign, L to R:
Martha Grantham, Beth Atcheson,
Elizabeth Riddell-Dixon, and Nancy Ruth.

Within a month, Bill C-210 was reported back to the House from committee without amendments. On June 10, because a member must be present to move his or her bill to third reading, Bélanger was brought by ambulance to the House. Once again, using text-to-speech software, he moved that the bill be read a third time and passed. The voice vote, however, was not unanimous, so in response to a call for a recorded vote, final passage was deferred to June 15.[162] On that day, with Bélanger once again present, the House voted 225–74 in favour of the bill—and ended by singing the gender-inclusive version of the anthem.[163] Mauril Bélanger, with the support of colleagues who both believed in his cause and deeply admired his courage, had won a race against impending death to see his bill through the House of Commons. The bill had its first reading in the Senate on that same day, but Bélanger did not live to see it proclaimed into law; he died two months later. Fittingly, the outpouring of tributes at his funeral included singing "O Canada" with "all of us."

Nancy Ruth had of course been chosen by Bélanger as sponsor of C-210 in the Senate; the torch was once again in her hands. The bill received second reading in the Senate on June 21, 2016, where she rose to remind senators that when the English national anthem was given official status by Parliament in 1980, a promise had been made that "thy sons" would be reconsidered at a later time. Now, thirty-six years after that promise, she drily told them that "this is the later time." She assured the Senate that "Canadians are ready and waiting for this change" and in her closing remarks stated, "We strive to be an open, diverse and inclusive community. Bill C-210, by changing two small words, makes a large statement about the importance of these values." In the ensuing debate, several Senators spoke

Nancy Ruth with her
"O Canada" tablets.
Up with "All of Us,"
down with "All Thy Sons."

in favour of the bill, including Ratna Omidvar, who had recently been appointed to Senate as an independent under Prime Minister Trudeau's new selection system, which was moving to non-partisan, merit-based appointments. Senator Omidvar told her colleagues, "I support this bill whole-heartedly, and I would like to congratulate and commend Senator Nancy Ruth for championing this for God knows how many years. It is time to bring this home."[164]

Despite this initial support, any hopes for the bill's speedy passage through the Senate were soon dashed. After debate was adjourned on June 21, it did not resume until October 27, 2016—and time was growing short for Nancy Ruth. Her mandatory retirement would take place on her seventy-fifth birthday, January 6, 2017. The bill was debated again on November 1, 2, 15, and December 1, and it was at last referred to the Senate standing committee on social affairs, science, and technology on December 6. The committee referred the bill to the Senate with no amendments on December 15, the last day before the holiday recess, and at that time a motion was approved to read the bill for the third time at the next sitting of Senate— which would occur after Nancy Ruth's retirement date had come and gone. As she left the Senate for the final time, her dream of a gender-inclusive "O Canada" remained a dream deferred.[165]

Frances Lankin, another independent senator appointed in March 2016 by Prime Minister Trudeau, was Nancy Ruth's choice to take over sponsorship of C-210. Senator Lankin readily embraced the project, although she could not have known that debate on the bill's third reading would be extended through twenty of the days that Senate sat during 2017, stretching from March 7 to December 12.[166] On May 18 the first amendment to the bill was proposed, by Conservative Senator Donald Plett, who moved that the words "in all of" should be replaced by "thou dost in."[167]

When the bill was next debated on May 30, Senator Lankin informed the Senate that she had checked the rules of the House and the Senate and had learned that "the effect of Senator Plett's amendment would be to kill the bill." If the bill were to be amended, it would have to go back to the House where, she explained, "Sadly, with the passing of MP Bélanger, the sponsor is no longer a member of the House of Commons and, therefore, a new sponsor would have to be found. Under the rules, that would require unanimous consent. It has become clear that unanimous consent would not be given. At least 70 voted against this bill in the first place." She went on to state frankly that she has spoken with a number of members who "have been quite honest and forthright that the intent is to delay this bill until after prorogation and to see it die."[168]

The gloves were off and the issue of tactics now out in the open. The Plett amendment was defeated on June 8, but the following months saw multiple amendments and sub-amendments introduced to a bill that had only a single clause. It had clearly become a floor fight, with senators opposed to the bill relying on the tradition that a final vote would not be called on a bill until every member's desire to debate it had been satisfied. By December, Senator Lankin sought a way to end this stalemate and found it in a little-used strategy called a "disposition of bill motion," along with another rarely used motion on "the previous question." If these two motions are carried, then debate on a bill is curtailed and the vote can be called. She gave notice of her disposition of bill motion on the Senate order paper and notice paper of December 4, 2017, to be considered

Senator Frances Lankin, the Honourable
Nancy Ruth, and Senator Chantal Petitclerc
singing "O Canada" in the Senate foyer
immediately after passage of the bill to change
the words to "all of us," January 31, 2018.

at the meeting of January 30, 2018, immediately after the holiday recess.[169]

At that sitting, when Senator Lankin's motion was put on the table, Senator Chantal Petitclerc, who sat next to Senator Lankin and was thus in the speaker's direct line of sight, was recognized by Speaker George Furey and immediately moved "the previous question"; her motion if passed would trigger a vote on the disposition motion without debate. Senator Donald Plett argued that he should have been recognized before Senator Petitclerc, which would have allowed for debate, but the speaker stood by his decision. A voice vote appeared to carry in favour of Senator Petitclerc's motion, but once again there was a call for a recorded vote to take place the following day. Protests that the proceedings had not been fair erupted on both January 30 and 31—from members opposed to Bill C-210. But the speaker, while acknowledging the disappointment of some senators, remained steadfast. On January 31, the recorded vote on Senator Petitclerc's motion was 41–5, with two abstentions—a clear sign that most of those opposed to the bill, including all the Conservative senators—had by then walked out. Senator Lankin's motion for disposition of the bill then carried on a voice vote, which meant that Bill C-210 could be put to the vote immediately. After the outstanding amendments were voted on and defeated, Bill C-210 was moved and carried by voice vote. Through a complex set of manoeuvres, those supporting the bill had at long last prevailed. Canadians would now have an inclusive national anthem.[170]

Having been alerted to the expected outcome, Nancy Ruth, Elizabeth Riddell-Dixon, and Beth Atcheson flew from Toronto to Ottawa on the afternoon of January 31. As Atcheson recalls,

We arrived in the swirl of a snowstorm. While inching our way to the Hill in a taxi, it occurred to us that we could listen to what was happening in the chamber via the audio feed on SenVu. We tuned in just as the recorded vote on Petitclerc's motion on the previous question was being taken. To us, the chamber was very quiet given the history of "all of us" and we eventually twigged to the walkout. After that, the votes moved very quickly and we finally arrived in the lobby of the Senate chamber just as Senators were leaving, just in time for NR [Nancy Ruth] to join the press scrum and for hugs all around. A swirl indeed.[171]

But for Nancy Ruth, her jubilation at the outcome was shadowed by regret over how long the process had taken and how little support she had received from her Conservative colleagues. Elizabeth Riddell-Dixon notes that "it was hard for her coming out of the Senate. I think she felt very frustrated because 'O Canada' hadn't passed before she left."[172] Her former Senate colleague Art Eggleton agrees:

I think it was very disappointing for all of us, and I'm sure very disappointing for her, that her retirement from the Senate came before the vote could be completed…. Not to let it come to a vote on the "O Canada" bill before she retired I think was particularly an unkind cut…. [T]he reason it took a long time was because of the other members of her caucus. They were on the other side of the issue. Most of them or a few of them that weren't necessarily on the other side just didn't want to stand out or take on the caucus position with respect to the "O Canada" change.[173]

In Nancy Ruth's words, "The 'O Canada' thing is just this bad taste for me—I mean, it's nowhere near as important to me as the gender-based analysis by the Auditor General…because it was such a disheartening and deceitful trip." She recalls the afternoon she went to the senators' gallery in the House of Commons wearing her "Sing all of Us" T-shirt to hear the debate on third reading of Bill C-210. She was the only person in the gallery, positioned above the Conservative seats, and she would "stand up and whoop and holler" at key points in the debate. "When Mauril, with his ALS, couldn't talk anymore, he'd put his thumb up. You know, 'Yes,' 'OK' type thing. So he put his thumb up and I went and put my thumb up. Then as I turned to leave the chamber, because I had to go back to my chamber, I turned it down over the Conservatives." One of her Conservative colleagues, Michael Chong, saw her action and as a consequence she had her "knuckles rapped very badly": "You don't dis your colleagues in public…. You do not break caucus loyalty." She had made a conscious decision when she joined the Conservative caucus to abide by party discipline and for the most part she believes that she carried through on that decision: "There's no point going to Parliament unless you are willing to submit, if you want to be part of a party caucus."[174] Yet there were clearly times when her political agenda coupled with her independent spirit made such submission a struggle.

In a talk she gave less than a year after she was appointed to the Senate, when she was being honoured by WXN Ottawa as one of Canada's "most powerful women," Nancy Ruth described the proudest moment of her life to date as the first day I walked up to Parliament Hill, up to the Peace Tower, as a Senator—in the footsteps of my grandfather, my father, the Famous Five who fought for women in the Senate (and for whom my grandfather acted), all of the women who have sought legal and policy change over the years, all of the women who have served there, all of the women who have challenged and lost, all of the women who will be a force for change in the future.[175]

Thirteen years later, looking back on her service as a senator, she tells a different story: "It's not the proudest or happiest time in my life.... I think of the Charter days, the early eighties, to be that. Those are the days I enjoyed most."[176] Yet without doubt, during her years as a senator, she was one of those women whose lives she held up as a talisman as she looked forward to her Senate career: a woman who challenged—sometimes winning, sometimes losing—and a woman who became "a force for change in the future."

The tributes paid to Nancy Ruth by her Senate colleagues on her retirement had to be curtailed for lack of time, even when there remained, according to the speaker, "a long list of senators who wish to join." Her colleagues were consistent in their praise for her unstinting activism on behalf of social justice, her leadership on women's and minority rights, and her fearless advocacy on behalf of the causes she championed. They also cited specific accomplishments: her work on gender-based analysis; UNSCR 1325; the Afghan women's study; medical assistance in dying; and changing the national anthem. And, in contrast to Nancy Ruth's more muted assessment of her years in the Senate, a number of senators made strong claims about her legacy. Frances Lankin remarked on "the difference she has made in our country, in our lives and beyond." Linda Frum said that "she will serve as an example and a role model for generations of feminists and poverty activists yet to come." Salma Ataullahjan lamented that "When you go, my friend, this place will be losing a thoughtful and dedicated advocate that will not be easily replaced. You never lacked the courage to speak your mind." James Cowan concurred in lauding her courage—"If ever there was a senator unafraid to speak her mind, that senator is Nancy Ruth"—and then added, "Throughout her life, Nancy Ruth has been an activist, a feminist, a crusader, a reformer and a philanthropist. She has never been content to be a spectator. She has left her mark on every cause and every organization or institution with which she has been associated—and that includes the Senate of Canada."[177]

Nancy Ruth's friends and colleagues who stayed close to her during her Senate years share this belief in the difference her work as a senator has made. Beth Atcheson, who headed up her staff throughout her term, says of Nancy Ruth's advocacy on gender-based analysis that "ninety percent of where we are today is [because of] her doggedness."[178] Eleanor Moore thinks that "her presence there allowed some of the feminists who are there now to actually say yes [to their appointment]. To actually say yes because you might not have said yes before."[179] Tuan Nguyen, reflecting on his conversations with Nancy Ruth, says that "Sometimes she thought her time in Senate was a waste of time…. But I beg to differ, because I think she has paved stepping-stones for the future generation."[180] Pat Hacker, commenting on Nancy Ruth's time in the Senate, agrees that "everywhere she has gone she has left a trail of open doors for other women to walk through," adding,

"Nancy Ruth will be remembered because she dared."[181] Dottie Graham remarks in a similar vein that "She empowered other women because she was able to be bold and brash."[182] And Denise Arsenault, summing up what for many was a hallmark of Nancy Ruth's contribution to the Senate, says "She brought a voice that wasn't there" and the addition of that voice "was a gift to women."[183]

In November 2017, Nancy Ruth was awarded the Senate 150th Anniversary Medal commemorating the first time that senators came to Ottawa to sit in Parliament, on November 6, 1867. She wrote to Art Eggleton that "The Senate was not the kindest 12 years of my life, so the medal is doubly sweet."[184] In an interview a month later she worried that "I think I became an embittered old bitch and not a very nice person because of the Senate."[185] Martha Grantham, her long-time executive assistant, believes that being in the Senate was difficult for Nancy Ruth because "she felt quite alone there a lot of the time." In Martha's view, Nancy Ruth was set apart both by her "feminist agenda" and by the fact that "she is a strongly voiced woman with many opinions" who "can get annoyed when things don't go the way they should."[186]

Yet in the years that have followed her retirement, Nancy Ruth has shown more willingness to acknowledge the value of her work. In a May 2019 interview, for example, she commented that her "endless questioning over the years," in particular about gender and gender-based analysis, "moved the markers for sure." She also noted that during her last year, when Prime Minister Trudeau significantly increased the number of women appointed to Senate and those new senators started arriving, she offered them some "undercover training," stressing, for example, that they needed to ensure that "every bill must be tabled with a GBA analysis of it so it's transparent and clear."[187] Senator Ratna Omidvar attests to this influence, saying at Nancy Ruth's seventy-fifth birthday party that, when she was a rookie in the Senate, Nancy Ruth helped her with "information, advice, and guidance of things sublime, political and practical." She ended her remarks by telling Nancy Ruth, "I believe I will be a more effective senator because of you and will carry on the fight to achieve true gender equity."[188] It is clear that before she left, the veteran feminist senator was busy passing along to the women who came after her the knowledge they would need to make their voices heard in the Senate, to make a difference for women as she had.

The role of a contrarian, however, is not an easy one. The qualities for which Nancy Ruth is known—the courage to be a lone voice, the willingness to challenge authority and orthodoxy—made her a force in the Senate, but they also served to isolate her, especially when she didn't have a large feminist community around her. Yet she was willing to pay that price in her quest for women's equality and social justice. A woman always in search of a vocation—jeweller, Charter activist, minister, clown, philanthropist—Nancy Ruth found yet another calling when she was appointed to the Senate and she left her indelible mark on that Canadian institution.

Footnotes for this chapter can be found online at:
http://secondstorypress.ca/resources

Nancy Ruth and Elizabeth Riddell-Dixon
at a family wedding in 2008.

Chapter 12

ROADMARKERS

Unless we print our own history, there is no history.
It doesn't exist unless it's printed or filmed or recorded.
—Nancy Ruth[1]

If Nancy Ruth didn't exist, the Canadian
Women's Movement would have had to invent her.
—Shari Graydon[2]

IN REMARKS she made on International Women's Day 2009, Nancy Ruth urged her audience to learn "the stories of the women who came before us" because those stories "provide roadmarkers—go here, dead end, steep curve. Most importantly, they make it clear that our cause is legitimate, that we are not alone, and that we can succeed."[3] Her own life's journey has had its share of steep curves—academic struggles, family conflicts, and her search for a meaningful profession. Some of the turns she took may look like dead ends—she never completed her senior matriculation, never became a skilled jewellery designer, failed to achieve an enduring vocation within the church. Yet in each case, her aspirations shaped the woman she became. Her Covenant College diploma and MA from Whitworth College are a testament to what she could accomplish when she at last found academic programs that suited her learning style and ignited her mind. Her training as a jeweller was an outlet for her creativity and afforded meaningful work during the year she lived with Trudy van Asperen in Holland. And her application to be commissioned as a diaconal minister was part of a spiritual quest she has never abandoned, though the established church was not capacious enough to give her a professional home.

Nancy Ruth's story does indeed assure us that women can succeed. While she came from a privileged background, she was a stuttering, obese child with learning disabilities, one who felt she could never meet her father's expectations or compete with her brothers' accomplishments. Her mother nurtured and supported her, but Mary Jackman was also an "odd person out" in the family dynamics and it was not until Nancy Ruth encountered feminism at the age of twenty-six that she could fully understand and cherish her mother's gifts. As a teenager she dreamed of fulfillment through a conventional marriage, but her growing recognition that she was a lesbian placed her outside social norms of the time. Though she believed she could make a difference as an elected politician, she failed to win political office. She had to climb barriers, ford streams, overcome crippling self-doubt to make her way in the world. Significantly, when she did gain her foothold, she devoted substantial energy to helping ensure that future generations of girls would not have to struggle in the same way she had. Her support for The Linden School, her founding of the women's history site

CoolWomen, and her role in establishing the Canadian Women's Foundation were all aimed at giving girls the faith in their potential that had eluded her throughout her youth.

We read biographies in part to learn what lessons a life has to teach us. Women's stories—absent from the record for so much of human history—can tell other women, in Nancy Ruth's words, that we are not alone and that our cause is legitimate. The quest for community is central to her story. In speech after speech she has extolled the need to find like-minded allies in any campaign for social change. When she returned to Toronto in 1978, she found those allies in the feminist movement. Her work on the Ad Hoc Committee, the Charter of Rights Coalition, and the Women's Legal Education and Action Fund (LEAF) was done shoulder to shoulder with other women who shared her vision of justice for women. Her friend Janet Somerville describes Nancy Ruth as a person "who by temperament was a misfit in her social circle" but who ended by helping "forge a new kind of community and belonging, primarily through the women's movement."[4]

Nancy Ruth's conviction that the causes she fought for were legitimate flourished in that communal environment. Someone who had often felt like a misfit began to understand that many of the barriers she faced affected not just herself but all girls and women. In remarks she made when she was named one of the WXN "Canada's Most Powerful 100 Women" in 2006, she identified learning to become "productive after a pretty rocky start" as one of her two most satisfying career accomplishments. The second was her discovery, after her legal battles with the United Church over being removed from its ministerial rolls, that there was a "critical connection" between her own experience and that of other women. The injustice done to her

> happened to me as an individual, but variations of it were happening to women in all kinds of situations and they had little practical recourse—even if they had the resources (and most don't), the law was not on their side. I saw the systemic problems for women and girls. The personal is indeed political. We all have the personal—are we prepared to make it "political," to be a change-maker?[5]

Her conversion to the role of change-maker is a critical "roadmarker" in Nancy Ruth's story, one that signals for us to "go here," this is not a dead end, this is a way forward to a purposeful life. Many of her friends and colleagues, when asked to reflect on her legacy, cite the force of her commitment to social change, particularly on behalf of women. Feminist theologian Ruth Evans observes that "she certainly had the determination to make things happen and was willing to stick out her neck and give leadership" within the women's movement.[6] Martha Grantham, who has been her executive assistant for more than twenty-five years, says that Nancy Ruth's biggest accomplishment has been "making people aware that women are a huge part of history. That women are capable of anything. That 'feminist' is not a bad word."[7] James Cowan, who served alongside Nancy Ruth in the Senate for twelve years, calls her "formidable" in terms of her advocacy on behalf of social justice issues.[8] And feminist legal scholar Catharine A. MacKinnon remarks that "she's been herself on a rather large canvas. Resisting limitations on her left, right, and centre...she's made a major difference for women in her own time."[9]

On January 6, 2017—Nancy Ruth's seventy-fifth birthday and the official date of her retirement from the Senate—close to two hundred people gathered at Nancy Ruth's Auditorium in the Toronto Young Women's Christian Association (YWCA) to celebrate their friend. Fifty-four years had passed since she went to bed with a cold and sore throat after a day skiing in Lech, Austria, writing forlornly in her diary that she "tossed & turned w/ my nose dripping until the end of my 21st birthday." In those intervening years, her youthful longing to "be something" took her down paths she could scarcely have imagined. Her work as an activist and feminist philanthropist garnered awards that included the YWCA Woman of Distinction, the Order of Canada, the Government of Ontario Human Rights Award, the Governor General's Award in Commemoration of the Persons Case, recognition as one of Canada's 100 Most Powerful Women, and four honorary doctorates. Her appointment to the Canadian Senate when she was sixty-three, almost "normal retirement age," at last gave her access to the legislative realm where she could advocate—as she had done as one of LEAF's founders—for equality for women under the law. Her friends were there at the YWCA not only to feast, dance, and have a good time—always expected at one of Nancy Ruth's parties—but to pay tribute to her accomplishments at the end of an illustrious public career.

The Honourable Elizabeth Dowdeswell, lieutenant governor of Ontario, brought greetings to the assembled guests, and Julie Nesrallah, mezzo-soprano and CBC radio host, led them in singing "O Canada"—fittingly, in the gender-neutral version that had not yet been passed into law by the Canadian Senate. There were toasts from her friend and colleague Beth Atcheson; Go Home Bay neighbours Richard Bingham and Tuan Nguyen; Diane Goudie and Eleanor Moore of The Linden School; and Pat Hacker and Marie Frye, sister activists in the feminist movement. In the evening's keynote speech, constitutional lawyer and long-time friend Mary Eberts reflected on what makes Nancy Ruth "such a compelling figure," telling the guests,

> Nancy has a big heart, and she does not hesitate to show it. The courage that lets her do that is not courage born of wealth or any amount of privilege. It is the courage of a big heart and big spirit that want to connect with people, and bring what is good in her and what is good in others together. It is the courage to live a bold life.[10]

In other letters and notes sent to Nancy Ruth for the occasion, Margaret McCain, philanthropist and former lieutenant governor of New Brunswick, wrote that she had "made a difference in the lives of countless women in our country, in a multitude of ways,"[11] while feminist lawyer and author Linda Silver Dranoff observed, "Nancy has been at the heart of every issue affecting women over the years of the second-wave women's movement in Canada.... Women in Canada owe Nancy Ruth an enormous debt of gratitude for her long-standing devotion and commitment to the wellbeing of other women."[12]

These remarks affirm what the story of her life tells us, that Nancy Ruth's legacy has been secured, that her "courage to live a bold life" has indeed had an impact. At the same time, in an interview at the end of 2017 she was quick to lament the "things that we tried to change, like equal pay for work of equal value"—all the "stuff that still hasn't been done."[13] In the years since her retirement from the

Senate, she has continued to engage with the "unfinished business" that matters to her—the "Sing All of Us" campaign, for example, that helped bring about Senate's final approval for a revised national anthem in January 2018, and the still-hoped-for revision of the medical assistance in dying law to include advance consent.

She has also been seeking to rebuild the network of friends that languished during her time in Ottawa. Relationships remain a central part of her life, including her long-standing partnership with Elizabeth Riddell-Dixon. In the fall of 2019, she travelled to Ghana to visit her old friend from Covenant College, Comfort (Baifie) Osei-Tutu. Her house in Rosedale has once again become a hub of activity and her summers spent with Elizabeth at Go Home Bay are filled with visitors to their cottage. Her friends sometimes comment on her brusque nature—Martha Grantham observes that "a lot of people have told me they have felt intimidated by her" because she can be "an overpowering person."[14] And yet, as childhood friend Mary Martin says, behind the brusqueness is "a real loving personality that we get to be the beneficiary of."[15] Catharine A. MacKinnon sees in Nancy Ruth someone who has survived by "living large," refusing to make herself "small and nice and ingratiating" and demonstrating that "there are ways of living with integrity that don't rely on caving in."[16]

If Nancy Ruth shows little patience for "making nice," she nevertheless places a high value on kindness, remarking that one of the lessons she has learned in life is that being kind is more important than her youthful dream of "being something."[17] Years earlier, Mary Jackman had wished for her daughter to learn to combine "the strength and fearlessness" of her father with her mother's "thoughtfulness and gentleness." Kindness may not always come easily as

Nancy Ruth struggles with the physical effects of aging and of now being legally blind, yet she is determined to cultivate a gentler part of her nature. And she is equally determined to keep living as fearlessly as she can. After a weekend together talking about all she is still driven to do, we race her motorboat at full throttle across Go Home Bay, Nancy Ruth navigating for me by shapes, shadows, and the memory of how things were.

The last words in this story belong to Nancy Ruth:

> Dad told me that women can do anything. Mom showed me that women can endure anything. They taught me to make the world a better place. I hope my story encourages you to do so too, even in old age.
>
> I have much for which to be thankful. I was born into a family of privilege which opened many doors and facilitated creating and sustaining feminist organizations and other social justice movements and groups. In these endeavours, I have met many amazing and dedicated people who have greatly enriched my life. They have my heartfelt thanks!
>
> Looking back on my life, I think my greatest strength is networking—bringing people together to advance a common cause. At 79, I am still working on being kinder and more patient!
>
> Making the world a better place is a lifelong quest. I am currently supporting Dying with Dignity in its efforts to get legislation passed to allow advanced consent in Medical Assistance in Dying. I want to know that my request as a competent person for Medical Assistance in Dying will be honoured if there comes a time when I can no longer make medical decisions for

myself. I want this right for myself but I also want all Canadians to have this option.

Each of us has a responsibility to make the world a better place. I hope my story encourages you to continue to work for positive change, both here in Canada and in other parts of the globe.

Footnotes for this chapter can be found online at:
http://secondstorypress.ca/resources

NOTES

Abbreviations used in the notes

NAMES
NR   Nancy Ruth

BOOKS
LDHRJ   *The Letters and his Diaries of Henry R. Jackman*, the Honourable Henry N.R. Jackman, ed., Toronto: Harmony Printing Ltd, 2003–2008.

UNPUBLISHED MATERIAL
CA   Written correspondence with the author

IA   Interview with the author

NR diary   Nancy Ruth's diaries

MANUSCRIPT COLLECTIONS AND REPOSITORIES
NRP   Nancy Ruth's papers

LIST OF PEOPLE INTERVIEWED

Denise Arsenault
Elizabeth (Beth) Atcheson
William Berinati
Richard Bingham
Barbara Bouck
The Honourable James Cowan
Mary Eberts
The Honourable Art Eggleton
Ruth Evans
Marie Frye
Dorothy (Dottie) Graham
Madeleine Gilchrist
Diane Goudie
Martha Grantham
Pat Hacker
Marian Hebb
Catharine A. MacKinnon
The Very Reverend Bruce McLeod
Mary Martin
Eleanor Moore
The Honourable Nancy Ruth
Tuan Nguyen
Elaine Peacock
Elizabeth Riddell-Dixon
Virginia (Ginny) Dobson Shrivastava
Janet Somerville

ACKNOWLEDGEMENTS

In Nancy Ruth's words, "When you have friends and allies beside you, it makes the journey a lot more enjoyable." I'm indebted to all who walked alongside me and made the writing of this book a joyful experience. The accomplished authors and friends in my writing group—Binnie Brennan, Carol Bruneau, and Lorri Neilsen Glenn—told me from the get-go that I could do it and never let my confidence flag. Other dear friends generously offered their time to read and comment on drafts: Beth Church, Janice Drakich, Barbie Goldbloom Hughes, and Joanne Steadman, along with my beloved sister Linda Lumpkin Mallory and brother Mike Lumpkin.

Without Beth Atcheson I could never have done justice to Nancy Ruth's years in the Senate. Besides having been Nancy Ruth's Director of Parliamentary Affairs during those years, Beth is a scrupulous researcher and record-keeper. She provided invaluable documentation, expert guidance, and a full measure of patience and kindness.

Nancy Ruth herself threw open her treasure-filled basement, letting me rummage through decades of speeches, diaries, private correspondence, photographs, and ephemera. On all my visits, she and her partner Elizabeth Riddell-Dixon graciously hosted me, entertained me, fed me—and kept out of my way except when I needed them. I'm deeply grateful to them both.

My thanks also to Martha Grantham, Nancy Ruth's long-time executive assistant, who worked diligently behind the scenes on critical tasks like securing permissions. Alexia Major-Aulenback and Andrea Winn, graduates of my beloved Mount Saint Vincent University, provided first-rate support as copyeditors; both do their alma mater proud.

Many of Nancy Ruth's friends and colleagues—whose names are listed under my sources—agreed to interviews, sharing their rich insights into her character and achievements. I'm thankful for all that they contributed to my portrait of this complex woman.

Amelia K. Smith did a superb job of transcribing the interviews for this book. Amelia was introduced to me over the internet by Evelyn C. White, who encouraged me to take on this project and whose own fine biography of Alice Walker served as an inspiration. Amelia transcribed Evelyn's interviews for the Walker biography and currently lives in Paris with her teenaged daughter Olga. After spending a magical afternoon in Paris with Amelia and Olga, my husband and I feel fortunate to count them as friends.

My husband Bill Blackburn supported me, cheered me on, bore with me throughout this journey, and read every word of the manuscript. My gratitude to him is unbounded.

Finally, to the staff of Second Story Press and the members of the Feminist History Society, I extend my warm thanks for their belief in the value of this book; for their professional expertise in bringing it into being; and for their unflagging commitment to telling the many stories of feminism in Canada.

INDEX

feminism, 416, 422, 425; and
Restore our Anthem campaign,
398–399, *404*; work on *CoolWomen*,
318
Greece, NR's travels/work in, 68,
69, 115
Greene, Nancy, 17
Group of Seven, *28*, 31

H

Hacker, Pat: feminist work of, 167,
168, 175; friendship with NR, 266,
306; on NR's Georgian Bay cottage,
279, 283; on NR's philanthropy, 319
Hackett, Barbara, *177*
Hadfield, J.A., 60
Hall, Barbara, 11, *234*
Hall, Heather, 211
Harder, Peter, 365
Harper, Stephen: conservative
politics of, 330–331, 383; reversal
of anthem decision, 398, 399,
402; stance on abortion, 376, 377,
378; support for national anthem
change in Speech from the Throne,
396–398; support for NR, 348, *349*
Harris, Mike, 237, 244, *245*, 246,
264
Hebb, Marian, 59
Hebrew Union College, 109–110
Hebrew University of Jerusalem,
109–110
Herizons (magazine), 104–105
Hockin, Kay, 127
Hogarth Press, 24, 255
Horan, Margaret, 297
Hošek, Chaviva, 166, 168, *306*
Hubble, the Rev. Gwenyth: as
Baptist minister, 84, 107, 139;
friendship with NR, 85–87, 120,
125–126; illness and death, 106, 124,
125–127; as teacher of Bible studies,
85–87, *86*, 90, 117, 126–127

I

India: NR's travels in, *80*, 81;
political turmoil in, 75, 78
Indigenous peoples of Canada, 165,
321, 350
Indonesia: NR's work in, 73–81, *76*,
77, 98, 249; political turmoil in, 75, 78
Institute of Child Study (University
of Toronto), 26, 33
International Institute of Concern
for Public Health, 11, 231
International Women's Day, 365,
372, 419
Internet: *CoolWomen* website, 310,
312, 314–315, 317–319; hate speech
on, 343, 346; luring, as gendered
crime, 342
Iqaluit, Nunavut, NR's travels in,
278
Isaacs, the Rev. Dr. Marie, 107, *138*,
139–140, 142
Israel: conflict with Palestine, 382;
NR's travels in, 106, 108–115, *111*

J

Jackman, Deone (Griffith), 92–93
Jackman, Duncan (NR's nephew),
92, 94, 119
Jackman, Edward John (NR's
brother): childhood of, 21, *22*,
25, 251; and division of family
estate, 95–96, 155, 157, 256–258; as
Dominican priest, 23, 92–93, 95,
256, *328*; education of, 23, 30, 255;
relationship with NR, *151*
Jackman, Frederic Langford (Eric)
(NR's brother): childhood of, 21, *22*;
and division of family estate, 95–96,
119, 155–157, 256–258; education of,
23; at family gatherings, 150, *151*, 152;
marriage and children of, 92–93;
on mother's influence, 271; political
career of, 45
Jackman, Henry (NR's nephew),
92–93, 119
Jackman, Henry Newton (Hal)
(NR's brother): childhood of, 21,

22, 23, 24, 40; and division of family
estate, 155–157, 256–258; education
of, 21, 60, 255; as head of family's
financial empire, 93, 94–96, 112, 119,
155–157, 211; marriage and children
of, 92–93; political career of, 45, 67,
216–217; relationship with NR, 119,
151, 209, 211, 244, 401
Jackman, Henry Rutherford (Harry)
(NR's father): as abusive spouse,
25–26, 271, 273, 274, 290; business
career, 19, 92–94, 116; and concerns
over NR's future, 67–68, 72, 92, 94,
106, 116–117, 128; conflicts with NR,
33, 40, 46, 51–52, 90, 92, 252–253;
conflicts with sons, 92, 96, 119;
division of estate, 92, 94–97, 119,
155–157; at family gatherings, 150, *151*,
152; and financial support for NR,
65, 83, 87, 90, 106; illness and death,
152–153; marital troubles of, 23–24,
33, 153–155, 252–253, 264; in NR's
childhood, *22, 24*, 33, 46; personal
history of, *16*, 17, 19; political career
of, 17, 212, 214, 216, 330; preference
for sons/male heirs, 92–94, 211, 212;
pride and respect for NR, 79, 81,
90, 94, 101, 120, 129, 152; running
male-dominated household, 23,
25–26, 99–100, 211, 212, 253, 267,
290; and support for NR's career,
135, 137, 152; values of, 15, 23–24, 103,
153, 267–268; virtues of, 153, 155; at
West Wind Island cottage, *28*, 31
Jackman, Maruja (Duncan), 92,
109–110, 119
Jackman, Mary Coyne Rowell
(NR's mother): abuse suffered in
marriage, 25–26, 271, 273, 274, 290;
art collection of, 20, 23–24, *28*, 31,
44, 57, 254–255; awarded YWCA
"Woman of Distinction," 212, *215*;
charitable donations to feminist
organizations, 256, 259, 262, 273,
294, 297, 301; charitable donations
to Victoria College, 24, 251, 255,
258; conflicts with NR, 39–42,

252–253; deepening relationship
with NR, 52, 87, 90, 253, 254, *263*,
264; and division of family estate,
256–258, 264; education of, 20,
101, 254–255, 258, 260–262, 273;
at family gatherings, 150, *151*, 152;
family history of, 19–21, 24, *43*, 52;
film biography of, 268–271, 273;
honorary doctorate, 260–262, *260*;
illness and death, 248, 260, 262,
263, 264–266, 273; international
social work, 68, 79; legacy of, 250,
264, 267–271, 273, 309–310, 319;
literature collection of, 24, 57, 251,
255–256, 273; love of fashion, *54*, 64,
67, 250, *250*, 265; marital troubles
of, 23–24, 153–155, 252–253, 264;
as Methodist, 19–21, 52, 181, 190;
in NR's childhood, *14, 22*; NR's
childhood contempt for, 15, 25–26,
40–42, 252–253, 268; shielding
NR from father, 23–26, 249–250,
252–253, 264, 420; support for NR's
education, 249, 252, 254; support for
NR's political career, 231, 237; travels
of, 20–21, 135–136, 140; values of,
15, 19–21, 23–24, 52, 249, 259–262,
267–268; WCC connection, 68, 249;
at West Wind Island cottage, *28, 29*,
31, 249, *272*; work for Metropolitan
United Church, 23, *182*, 183, 190,
259–261, 273; work for SCM, 23, 101
Jackman, Nancy Ruth *see* Nancy
Ruth
Jackman, Tara (NR's niece), 92–93
Jackman, Tom (NR's nephew),
92–93
Jackman, Victoria (NR's niece), 92,
119
Jackman Foundation: division of
assets, 256–258, 294; donations
given by, 26, 135, 160, 289–290,
297; establishment of, 95; Harry
Jackman's estate bequeathed to, 155,
160; meetings of, 96, 256
Jackson, A.Y. (Alec), *29*, 31, 251
Jaffer, Mobina S.B., 367–370, 372

Sriharan, Geetha, *296*
St. Andrew-St. Patrick riding, 225–226, 230–231, 235, 264
St. Anton, Austria, 63, *64*, 65
St. Clement's School, 303–305
St. George-St. David riding, 225, 236–238, 240–241, 244, 246–247
Stewart, Elizabeth, 301
Strashun, Olga, *280*
Student Christian Movement (SCM): Mary Jackman's work with, 20, 24, 82; NR's work with, 97, 103, 117; Trudy's work with, 90, 101, 103
Supreme Court of Canada, 174, 187
Syria, refugees of, 364–365

T

Taber, Jane, 382
Tanner, Susan, *176*
Tel Aviv, Israel, 108–115
Thompson, Greg, 334–336, 338
Toews, Vic, 351–354
Toronto Foundation, 262
Toronto Star (newspaper): on CFW, 298, 299, 301; on LEAF gala for NR, 209; on NR's political career, 218, *245*; on STFU controversy, 376
Tory, John, 233
transgender rights *see also* LGBTQ rights, 345–348
Trudeau, Justin: appointment of women to Senate, 408, 416; and Criminal Code, 348, 386; and national anthem change, 402, 403, 406
Trudeau, Pierre: and Charter of Rights and Freedoms, 163; and LGBTQ rights, 103; patriarchy of Constitution, 161, 168
Turkey, NR's travels in, 115
Turku (Finland), World Student Christian Federation conference (1968), 90, 97–100, 107, 139

U

United Church of Canada, The (UCC) *see also* Metropolitan United Church; feminist movement within, 198, 199–200; few roles for women in, 82–83, 99, 139, 143, 199–200; formation of, 181; NR as organizational development consultant for, 142; NR rejected by, 186–189, 202–203, 421–422; NR's desire to serve in, 82, 135–136; NR's work at Naramata Centre, 129–140, *133*, 186, 211; patriarchy within, 194, 197, 198–199; NR's upbringing in, 73; theological college of, 127–128
United Nations Conference on Women, 325
United Nations High Commissioner for Refugees (UNHCR), 364–365
United Nations Security Council Resolution 1325, 338–339, 366–372, 370–371, 375, 414
University of Grenoble, 62
University of New Brunswick, 47, 48
University of Toronto (U of T): Mary Jackman's education at, 20, 101, 254–255, 258, 260–262; Nell Langford Rowell's education at, 19, 254–255
University of Utrecht, 101, 120
USSR, NR's travels in, 56, *56*

V

van Asperen, Marit, 108
van Asperen, Trudy (Geertruida Maartje): break-up with NR, 123; career successes of, 107, 114, 120, 123; correspondence with NR, 105, 107–108, 110, 112–113, 119; friendship with NR, 105, 121–122, 124; illness and death, 124; life with NR in Holland, 120–121, 122–123, 420; marriage of, 113, 123–124; meeting NR, 90, 100, *102*; relationship with NR, 100–105, 108, 113–115, 116, *118*, 279; relationships

PHOTO CREDITS

Page 8: Courtesy of Nancy Ruth, photo by Pamela Harris

Page 10: (top and bottom) Courtesy of Nancy Ruth, photos by Pamela Harris

Page 13: Courtesy of Nancy Ruth, photo by Pamela Harris

Page 14: Courtesy of Nancy Ruth

Page 16: Courtesy of Nancy Ruth, photo by Meyers Studios (Canada) Ltd.

Page 18: Courtesy of Nancy Ruth

Page 22: Courtesy of Nancy Ruth

Page 24: Courtesy of Nancy Ruth

Page 27: Courtesy of Nancy Ruth

Page 28: Courtesy of Nancy Ruth

Page 29: (all photos) Courtesy of Nancy Ruth

Page 32: (both photos) Courtesy of Nancy Ruth

Page 36: Courtesy of Nancy Ruth, photo by M. Russell Reid Studio

Page 43: Courtesy of Nancy Ruth

Page 54: Courtesy of Nancy Ruth, photo by Randolph Macdonald

Page 56: Courtesy of Nancy Ruth

Page 64: (top and bottom) Courtesy of Nancy Ruth

Page 69: Courtesy of Nancy Ruth

Page 70: Courtesy of Nancy Ruth, photo by Rawood Ltd.

Page 71: Courtesy of Nancy Ruth, photo by Portman Press Bureau Ltd.

Page 76: (top and bottom) Courtesy of Nancy Ruth

Page 77: (top and bottom) Courtesy of Nancy Ruth

Page 80: Courtesy of Nancy Ruth

Page 86: Courtesy of Nancy Ruth

Pages 88–89: Courtesy of Nancy Ruth, photo by Panda Associates Photography and Art Services (reference no. 65835-3)

Page 91: Courtesy of Nancy Ruth, photo by Ballard & Jarrett

Page 100: Sir Edmund Wyly Grier (1939), The Law Society of Ontario Art Collection, FA75

Page 102: Courtesy of Nancy Ruth

Page 111: Courtesy of Nancy Ruth

Page 118: Courtesy of Nancy Ruth

Page 133: Courtesy of Nancy Ruth

Page 134: Courtesy of Nancy Ruth

Page 138: Courtesy of Nancy Ruth

Page 146: Courtesy of Nancy Ruth

Page 148: Courtesy of Nancy Ruth

Page 151: Courtesy of Nancy Ruth

Page 158: Courtesy of Nancy Ruth, photo by Ron Bull

Page 160: Courtesy of Nancy Ruth

Page 168: Courtesy of Nancy Ruth

Pages 176–177: Courtesy of Nancy Ruth

Page 180: Courtesy of Rafy

Page 182: Courtesy of Nancy Ruth

Page 191: Courtesy of estate of Johnnie Eisen

Page 210: Courtesy of Nancy Ruth

Page 213: Courtesy of Nancy Ruth

Page 215: YWCA of Metropolitan Toronto

Page 222: Courtesy of Nancy Ruth

Page 224: Courtesy of the E.P. Taylor Library and Archives, Art Gallery of Ontario

Page 227: Courtesy of Nancy Ruth, photo by Pamela Harris

Pages 228–229: Courtesy of Nancy Ruth, photo by Pamela Harris

Page 232: Courtesy of Nancy Ruth

Page 234: Courtesy of Nancy Ruth

Page 237: Courtesy of Nancy Ruth

Page 239: Originally published in the *Toronto Sun*, a division of Postmedia Network Inc.

Pages 242–243: Campaign literature courtesy of Nancy Ruth, photos courtesy of Rafy and Pamela Harris

Page 245: Courtesy of Aislin

Page 250: Courtesy of Nancy Ruth

Page 260: Courtesy of Nancy Ruth

Page 263: Courtesy of Nancy Ruth

Page 272: Courtesy of Nancy Ruth

Page 276: Courtesy of Nancy Ruth

Page 278: Courtesy of Elizabeth Riddell-Dixon

Page 280: Courtesy of Nancy Ruth

Page 282: Courtesy of Nancy Ruth

Page 284: Courtesy of Nancy Ruth

Page 285: Courtesy of Nancy Ruth

Page 287: Courtesy of Nancy Ruth

Page 292: Courtesy of Mitchel Raphael

Page 296: Courtesy of Nancy Ruth

Page 300: Courtesy of Nancy Ruth

Page 306: Cpl Monique Fortin, Rideau Hall © OSGG, 1997

Page 311: BDS Studios Inc., Gary Beechey

Page 316: Nancy's Very Own Foundation, illustration by Martha Newbigging

Page 320: Office of the Lieutenant Governor of Ontario. John Smee Photography

Page 324: Sgt Michel Roy, Rideau Hall © OSGG, 1995

Page 328: Senate of Canada, photo by Michael Bedford

Pages 332–333: Courtesy of Mitchel Raphael

Page 337: Courtesy of Nancy Ruth

Page 341: Courtesy of Nancy Ruth

Page 349: Courtesy of the Right Honourable Stephen Harper

Page 359: Senate of Canada

Page 362: Courtesy of Nancy Ruth

Page 397: Courtesy of Neville Poy

Page 400: (clockwise from top left) Courtesy of the Right Honourable Kim Campbell; Courtesy of Margaret Atwood, photo by Luis Mora; Courtesy of the Honourable Vivienne Poy, photo by Neville Poy; Courtesy of Sally Goddard

Pages 404–405: Courtesy of Nancy Ruth

Page 407: Courtesy of Mitchel Raphael

Page 410: Courtesy of Senator Chantal Petitclerc

Page 419: Courtesy of Nancy Ruth

Page 428: Courtesy of Nancy Ruth

Cover: Originally published in the *Toronto Sun*, a division of Postmedia Network Inc.

ABOUT THE AUTHOR

Shari Tucker

DR. RAMONA LUMPKIN joined Mount Saint Vincent University as President and Vice-Chancellor in 2010. She retired from her position on June 30, 2017, and was named President Emerita in recognition of her contributions to the University. Her previous roles included Principal of Huron University College and Vice-President Academic and Provost of Royal Roads University. Dr. Lumpkin began her university career in Kentucky where, for 13 years, she held a variety of positions in higher education that included institutional planning, continuing education, faculty development, and university teaching. She holds a PhD in English

Literature from the University of Kentucky and is a former Fulbright Scholar to England.

Throughout her career, Dr. Lumpkin has been actively engaged in advocacy on behalf of women's issues, in promoting the role of women in higher education, and in enhancing access to education for Indigenous learners.

In 2014, Dr. Lumpkin was appointed as a Member of the Order of Canada in recognition of her leadership in post-secondary education, her promotion of community-based learning initiatives, and her support for the advancement of women. In October of 2017, she received the Governor General's Persons Case Award for her advocacy on behalf of women's rights.

THE FEMINIST HISTORY SOCIETY SERIES

The Feminist History Society is committed to creating a lasting record of the women's movement in Canada and Québec for the fifty years between 1960 and the year of the Society's founding, 2010. Feminism has a history that predates the 1960s and continues long after 2010.

The energy that women brought to their quest for equality in these decades is beyond dispute, and it is that energy that we capture in this series. Our movement is not over and new campaigns are upon us. But the FHS series presents an opportunity to take stock of the wide-ranging campaigns for equality that occurred in Canada between 1960 and 2010. There was much transformative social, economic, civil, political, and cultural change.

We maintain an open call for submissions (https://secondstorypress.ca/submissions/) across a full range of approaches to the period, including autobiographies, biographies, edited collections, pictorial histories, plays and novels. There will be many different authors as all individuals and organizations that were participants in the movement are encouraged to contribute. We make every effort to be inclusive of gender, race, class, geography, culture, dis/ability, language, sexual identity, and age.

Beth Atcheson, Constance Backhouse, Lorraine Greaves, Diana Majury, and Beth Symes form the working collective of the Feminist History Society. Margie Wolfe, Publisher, Second Story Feminist Press Inc. and her talented team of women, are presenting the Series.

https://secondstorypress.ca/
feminist-history-society-series/